# Praise for
# *The Social Media Survival Guide*

"*The Social Media Survival Guide* is the most authoritative, comprehensive, and technically accurate guide I have ever seen to social networking—bar none."
—Bob Bly, "America's Top Copywriter" and author of over 70 classic marketing books

"Deltina Hay's book is your ally. Her plain talk, plentiful visuals, and step-by-step instructions walk you through the essentials of using the most popular social media tools. Whatever your objective, Hay's hands-on guide shows you how to find the right people and deliver the message in the quickest way possible."
—From the Introduction by **Paul Gillin,** Author of *The New Influencers* and *Secrets of Social Media Marketing*

"Social media offers incredible potential for growing a business or reputation online. But using social media can be an incredible time suck if you don't know what you're doing. Deltina's book will help you make the best use of social media. Read it. Put it into practice."
—**John Kremer,** Author of *1001 Ways to Market Your Book*

"Deltina Hay's *Social Media Survival Guide* can help anyone—from the newbie Twitterer to the seasoned code monkey—maneuver the Social Web like a Jedi master. Read this book and join the revolution!"
—**J.D. Lasica,** Founder, Socialmedia.biz

"A very practical and hands-on book for both the techie as well as the not-so-techie. If you are looking for a results-oriented read on what you need to be doing to optimize your web presence for Web 2.0, you have found your book. Needless to say a highly recommended read!"
—**Neil Schaffer,** Author of *Understanding, Leveraging & Maximizing LinkedIn*

"This book will not only help you survive, it will help you thrive in the Web 2.0 world. If you are new to social media, this survival guide will undoubtedly save you time and anguish. And if you are an advanced Web 2.0 user, it will help you flesh out a solid strategy to harness your own social media power."
—**Sue Rostvold**, Founder of Verysupercool Web 2.0 consulting and coaching

# The Social Media Survival Guide:
*Strategies, Tactics, and Tools for Succeeding in the Social Web*

## by Deltina Hay

**Fresno, California**

# Notice of Copyright

Published by Quill Driver Books,
an imprint of Linden Publishing.
2006 S. Mary, Fresno, California, 93721
559-233-6633 / 800-345-4447
QuillDriverBooks.com

Edited by Ric Williams; Cover design by Jason Hranicky; Interior layout by Deltina Hay and Jason Hranicky

ISBN: 978-1884995-70-5. Printed in the USA on acid-free paper. Second printing

Library of Congress Cataloging-in-Publication Data:

Hay, Deltina.

The social media survival guide : strategies, tactics, and tools for succeeding in the social web / by Deltina Hay. -- 2nd ed.

    p. cm.

Previously published under title: A survival guide to social media and Web 2.0 optimization.

Includes index.

ISBN 978-1-884995-70-5 (pbk. : alk. paper)

1. Web 2.0. 2. Web site development. 3. Online social networks. I. Title.

TK5105.88817.H39 2011

006.7'54--dc22

        2010044071

# Notice of Liability

The author and publisher have made every effort to ensure the accuracy of the information herein. However, the information contained in this book is sold without warranty, either express or implied. Neither the author or Linden Publishing, nor its dealers or distributors will be held liable for any damages to be caused either directly or indirectly by the instructions contained in this book, or by the software or hardware products described herein.

*For my Mother,*

*without whose continued support all would be lost...*

# Changes from the First Edition

## A Note to Text Book Purchasers

Though released under another name and with a different publisher, this text is the second edition of *A Survival Guide to Social Media and Web 2.0 Optimization* by Deltina Hay, ISBN 978-0-9817443-8-4.

Changes to the second edition are substantial, and it is highly recommended that this book be used in place of the previous edition.

## General Changes Throughout Entire Book

Demonstrations of social media tools have been updated to reflect their present versions and features, and many tools have been added. The chapter numbers, names, and general topics, however, remain the same.

## Major Changes and Additions by Chapter

- Chapter 1: "Creating Your Social Media Strategy"
  - › Includes an additional section reporting the findings of a recommended social media tools survey
  - › Additional strategies added
- Chapter 4: "Building a WordPress Powered Website"
  - › Examples now based on WordPress 3.0, the latest major version
  - › Advanced feature examples added
- Chapter 6: "Social Networking & Micro-Blogging"
  - › Expanded Facebook section
  - › MySpace section removed
  - › Substantially expanded Twitter section
  - › Discussion of the future of social networking
- Chapter 8: "Media Communities"
  - › A major section on "Document Sharing Sites" added, including demonstrations and strategies
- Chapter 9: "Widgets & Badges"
  - › Many new examples and tools added
  - › Major section on using social widgets to personalize Websites

- Chapter 11: "More Social Tools"
  - › Many tools from the first edition have moved to other chapters
  - › Additional tools added such as geo-tagging and collaborative tools
- Chapter 12: "Pulling It All Together"
  - › Substantial additions to this chapter, including many new tools
  - › Major section on "Mapping Your Own Integration Plan" added
- Chapter 13: "Looking to the Future"
  - › Discussions of Web 3.0 added, including the Semantic Web, structured data, linked open data, and cloud computing
  - › Optimizing for the Mobile Web is also discussed
- Chapter 14: "Measuring Your Success"
  - › Now includes a substantial section on "Search Optimization"
  - › New analytics tools and tactics added
- Appendix C: "Building Your Own Widget"
  - › A simplified example is used
  - › Methods and tools have been updated
- Appendix D: "Preparing Your Content for the Semantic Web"
  - › This appendix replaces the previous "WordPress 2.7" appendix
  - › Provides examples and explanations of how to prepare Website content for semantic search engines

# Acknowledgments

## Thanks

Thanks to Dalton Publishing's authors and fans for the use of images, videos, screen shots, and galleries.

Special thanks to Chavah Aima, Cynthia Baker, Kimberlie Dykeman, and Les McGehee for volunteering their social media strategies as examples. Thanks to Neil Kahn and Tamar Wallace for their contributions to the first edition, to Lisette Sutherland for her help on this second edition, and a special thanks to Jason Hranicky for his hard work and patience on both editions.

Thank you to the following companies for use of their social media newsrooms and news releases as examples:

© Fathom SEO 2009. All Rights Reserved. Screen shots used by permission.
© SHIFT Communications, LLC 2009. All rights reserved. Screen shots used by permission.
© Accolades Public Relations 2009. All rights reserved. Screen shots used by permission.
© Les McGehee 2009. All rights reserved. Screen shots used by permission.
© Kimberlie Dykeman 2009. Pure Soapbox is a registered trademark of Kimberlie Dykeman. Screen shots used by permission.
© Owen Egerton 2009. All rights reserved. Screen shots used by permission.

Thanks go to Kent Sorsky and Steve Mettee of Quill Driver Books for their confidence and willingness to bring the book to a larger audience, and to Paul Gillin for his generous foreword.

And even though he now knows more about "this stuff" than he ever cared to, this is a better book thanks to my editor Ric Williams' dogged persistence to keep my writing understandable and in the present tense. I also thank him for his friendship and steadfast encouragement, despite my occasional whining.

## Permissions Granted

The author would like to thank the following companies for permission to use their screen shots. The following are trademark holders of the listed services' logos, graphics, designs, page headers, button icons, scripts, and other services. All rights are reserved and used by permission:

The author would like to thank the following organizations for permission to use their logos:

StumbleUpon, Blinklist, Faves, Mixx, Reddit, Podnova, Newsgator, Netvibes, Odeo, PageFlakes, Juice Receiver, FireAnt, Doppler, Nimiq, Winpodder, Ziepod, Typepad, Bebo, LiveJournal, Vox

# Trademark Notice

Rather than indicating every occurrence of a trademarked name as such (except as requested), this book uses the names only in an editorial fashion and to the benefit of the trademark owner with no intention of infringement of the trademark.

# Notice of Liability

The author and publisher have made every effort to ensure the accuracy of the information herein. However, the information contained in this book is sold without warranty, either express or implied. Neither the author or Quill Driver Press, nor its dealers or distributors will be held liable for any damages to be caused either directly or indirectly by the instructions contained in this book, or by the software or hardware products described herein.

# Table of Contents

Change from the First Edition.............................. 7

Acknowledgments.......................................... 9

Foreword by Paul Gillin.................................. 19

Introduction............................................ 21

*About this Book*
*A Brief Primer Before You Continue*
*Who Should Read This Book*
*How to Use This Book*

1. Creating Your Social Media Strategy...................29

*Important First Decisions Regarding Websites, Blogs, and*
 *RSS Feeds*
*Mapping Your Strategy*
*Advice from the Power Users*
*Sample Strategies*

2. Preparation ......................................... 47

*Key Terms or "Tags"*
*Important First Decisions Regarding Your Social Media Profiles*
*Optimizing File Names*
*Preparing Your Multimedia Items*
*Gathering Content for Blog Posts*

3. RSS Feeds & Blogs.................................... 53

*RSS Feeds*
 *The Feed Reader*
 *The Feed*
 *Options for Creating an RSS Feed*
 *Planning Your Feed*
*Blogs*
 *Options for Starting Your Blog*
 *Main Elements of a WordPress Blog Post*
 *Planning Your Blog*

*Optimizing and Promoting Your Blog and RSS Feed*
   *Your Feed or Blog Content*
   *Search Engine Optimization (SEO)*
   *FeedBurner*
   *RSS Feed and Blog Directories*
   *An Optimization Plan for Your Blog or RSS Feed*

## 4. Building a WordPress Powered Website ............... 97

*Using WordPress as a CMS*
*Diversity of WordPress Sites*
*The Anatomy of a WordPress Site*
*Installing WordPress as a CMS*
*A Brief Look at the WordPress Dashboard*
*Important Initial Settings*
*Planning Your Site*
*Themes*
*Plugins*
*Creating Your Navigation Menu*
*Setting Up Your Sidebars*
*Building Your Pages*
*Posting Blog Entries*

## 5. Podcasting, Vidcasting, & Webcasting .................129

*What Will Your Podcast Be About?*
*Publishing Options for Your Podcast*
*Creating and Uploading Podcast Episodes*
*Publishing Your Podcast*
*Optimizing Your Podcast*
*Webcasting*

## 6. Social Networking & Micro-Blogging ...................145

*Facebook*
   *The Facebook Home Page*
   *The Facebook Profile*
   *Facebook Groups*
   *Facebook Pages*
   *Promoting and Analytics*
   *Facebook and Privacy*
*LinkedIn*
*Twitter*

*Setting Up Your Account*
*Finding People*
*Posting Updates or Tweets*
*Twitter Lists*
*Promoting Your Account*
*External Tools*
*Other Social Networking Tools*
*Social Bookmarking and Media Communities*
*Niche Social Networking Sites*
*Social-Networking-Like Tools*
*Creating Your Own Social Network*
*The Future of Social Networking*
*A Social Networking Strategy*

## 7. Social Bookmarking & Crowd-Sourcing ..............193

*Social Bookmarking*
*Social Bookmarking in Action*
*Using Social Bookmarking Sites*
*A Social Bookmarking Strategy*
*Purpose-Built Delicious Pages*
*Crowd-Sourcing*
*Crowd-Sourcing in Action*
*Using Crowd-Sourced News Sites*
*A Crowd-Sourcing Strategy*
*Preparation and Tracking Your Progress*
*A Note on Making Your Content Sharable*

## 8. Media Communities.............................................211

*Image Sharing Sites*
*Image Sharing in Action*
*Using Image Sharing Sites*
*Image Sharing Strategy*
*Video Sharing Sites*
*Using Video Sharing Sites*
*Video Sharing Strategy*
*Document Sharing Sites*
*Document Sharing in Action*
*Using Document Sharing Sites*
*Document Sharing Strategy*
*Searching and Search Engine Placement*
*Connecting with Others*

## 9. Widgets & Badges..................................247

*Highlighting Your Social Web Presence*
*Sharing and Syndicating Your Content*
*Making Your Site More Interactive*
*Personalizing Your Site for Visitors*
*Promoting Products and Making Money*
*Using Widgets in WordPress*
*Placing Widgets in Other Websites*
*Widget Communities and Directories*
*Creating Your Own Widgets*
*Working Widgets into Your Strategy*

## 10. Social Media Newsrooms......................287

*What Is a Social Media Newsroom?*
*Do You Need a Social Media Newsroom?*
*Building Your Social Media Newsroom*
*Populating the Newsroom*
*Social Media News Releases*
*Social Media Newsroom Examples*

## 11. More Social Tools...........................311

*Social Calendars and Event Tools*
*Geo-Tagging or Location Tools*
*Hybrid Social Tools*
*Social Pages*
*Collaborative Technologies*

## 12. Pulling It All Together.............................323

*Integration Methods*
*Integration Tools*
   *Distributed Social Networking*
   *Streamlining Tools*
*Optimizing Your Website*
*Streamlining Your Social Web Presence*
*Mapping Your Own Integration Plan*

## 13. Looking to the Future...........................353

*Web 3.0*
*The Semantic Web*

*Cloud Computing*
*The Mobile Web*
*Keeping Your Eye on the Social Media Pie*

## 14. Measuring Your Success...................367

*Know Your Goals*
   *A Qualitative Framework*
   *A Quanitative Framework*
*Search Optimization*
*Tracking Tactics*
*Tools to Help You Measure*
*Social Analytics Services*
*Come to Your Own Conclusions*

## 15. Conclusion...................387

## Appendix A: Installing WordPress...................391

## Appendix B: Creating Your Own RSS Feed...................403

## Appendix C: Building Your Own Widget...................419

## Appendix D: Preparing for the Semantic Web...................437

## Index...................445

# Foreword

Social media is the great equalizer. It gives voice to millions of people who, until just a few years ago, were shut out of the media equation. Armed with their blogs, podcasts, video galleries, photo streams, and Twitter accounts, individuals and businesses of all sizes now can reach a global audience.

This changes the rules in so many ways. A person with a remarkable story to tell or skill to share can find an audience of like-minded enthusiasts and create a knowledge sharing community almost overnight. When all the pieces come together, one person can share a message with millions of others worldwide.

But social media is less about millions than it is about thousands, hundreds, and even a few dozen people committed to a revolution in democratized communication. And they can make this world-changing move happen because the global village of the Internet is really a collection of millions of small villages where people who were once separated by barriers of time and distance now can meet around a great virtual campfire.

The growth and impact of social media over the last five years has been nothing less than stunning, and it is transforming the institutions that have defined our world. In 2009, people spent six billion minutes on Facebook, downloaded one billion YouTube videos and logged over 1.4 million blog entries *every* day. The iPhone became the first mobile phone to be used more for data than for voice. The Internet became the second most popular news medium behind television. Wikipedia posted its three millionth article. People conducted 131 billion searches in the month of December.

Meanwhile, U.S. newsroom employment fell to a 25-year low and magazine newsstand sales dropped 63 percent from their 2001 peaks. *Reader's Digest* declared bankruptcy and NBC was bought by a cable company. Indeed, these are amazing times.

Mainstream media's influence is rapidly being replaced by connections between small groups of highly engaged individuals. This will transform nearly every institution in our society. It will alter the way we make decisions, redefine the way we conduct business, and expand and enrich our personal connections. Social media is changing nearly everything about the way we live.

## Not About the Tools

The tools of social media can be captivating, addictive, and ultimately baffling. The range of options is overwhelming, and the urge to master so many channels can easily leave newcomers feeling that they're running in place and getting nowhere.

But tools are the least important factor for success. Choosing a tool first and then figuring out what to do with it is like buying a hammer and then looking for nails to pound. Tools are the last choice you need to make. The more important decision is to understand your personal or business objectives and then select the tools that will get you there the quickest.

This is where Deltina Hay's book is your ally. Her plain talk, plentiful visuals, and step-by-step instructions walk you through the essentials of using the most popular social media tools. You aren't a dummy to Hay; you're a grown-up who wants to bypass the long learning curve and quickly start moving toward an objective. Maybe that's promoting your business. Maybe it's reaching out to people who share an interest. Or maybe you just have something important to say and want other people to hear it.

Content is king, but having great content is only part of the equation. Success in social media involves packaging material in a compelling manner, reaching out to others who share your interests, building link networks, optimizing contacts, and cementing new relationships. We instinctively know how to do this in real life, but the means by which relationships are formed and nurtured in the link-driven online culture require some adaptation. Hay understands how these dynamics work and she explains what you need to know while also tipping you off to cool online tools that save you time and amplify your voice.

Whatever your objective, Hay's hands-on guide shows you how to find the right people and deliver the message in the quickest way possible. In this second edition, she tackles the growing opportunities to use social media tools in concert with each other to enhance the impact of your message. This is exciting stuff. People are learning that by leveraging tools in combination, they can multiply their potential audience and get others talking about them.

So what are you waiting for? It's time to head on down the social media path. Let Deltina Hay be your tour guide.

*Paul Gillin*
*Framingham, MA*
*February 2010*

# Introduction

## About this Book

It is no secret that the future of the Internet is the Social Web, and that the future is very much this very instant. Millions[1] of people and businesses are interacting and collaborating on social networking sites, media communities, social bookmarking sites, wikis, and micro-blogging sites, as well as sharing information via millions of RSS feeds and blogs. They are doing it right now, 24/7, and you and your business want to be a part of this extraordinarily powerful movement with as professional and efficient a presence as possible while optimizing your business potential and keeping your expenses to a minimum.

Success in today's Internet absolutely depends on your entire Web presence, not just on search engine optimization (SEO). Spreading your net as wide as possible by improving your presence in the Social Web helps you reach millions of potential clients or readers that you may not have reached otherwise. You cannot afford to bet that a customer will somehow stumble upon your Website on page 100 in a Google search. Learn and implement the Social Web tools described in this book and you will be surprised at how easily you can access potentially millions of new customers who might otherwise be unreachable. And, yes, a residual benefit of using these tools is improved placement on that proverbial Google search results page.

So, what is this social media and Web 2.0 optimization that helps you maximize your Internet presence? It can be summed up with three general terms: interactivity, sharing, and collaboration. Focusing on these three general areas, both at the level of your own Website and in the areas of the Social Web most suited to your book or business—areas we will help you identify—will greatly enhance your chances for success in this open-ended world of Internet opportunity.

---

[1]http://www.web-strategist.com/blog/2009/01/11/a-collection-of-soical-network-stats-for-2009/

Happily, building a strong presence in the Social Web does not have to break the bank or your back. With careful planning and preparation, you can build an impressive presence that you can maintain with little effort. The trick is to know what makes sense for your particular business or product, and only incorporate the tools that fit those goals. By planning ahead, you can also implement tools that will enhance each other and ultimately work together to help improve your presence and reduce your workload.

Research has shown that users of the Social Web actually want and encourage businesses and professionals to interact with them on their turf.[2] Of course you have to keep in mind that succeeding in the Social Web requires an authentic message. If you are going out there as a business or are promoting a product, just be up-front about it. Always read a site's submission guidelines and/or terms of use before proceeding. Some sites have no problem with having their service used to promote business, others have strict policies against it. There is a place for everyone in this new Internet arena if you simply present yourself authentically.

There are many books out there that discuss the theory of the Social Web and how to market within it. This is not one of them. This is also not a book about blogging, nor is it a book about how to get a zillion friends on your favorite social networking site. Blogging and social networking are only a small part of an optimized Social Web presence.

As a social media pioneer, the author has seen many tools come and go over the past few years. Her goal is to help you build a solid foundation in the Social Web using the tools of Web 2.0 that have weathered the social media storm. Once that foundation is in place, you will be equipped to integrate or utilize whatever new tools emerge next on the social media horizon.

*The Social Media Survival Guide* shows you *how* to use strategies and tactics and the tools of Web 2.0 to build a successful Web presence. This book offers you the nuts and bolts of the Social Web through hands-on, real-world examples. You will be pleasantly surprised at how easy most of it is!

So push up your sleeves and let's get Social....

---

[2]http://www.readwriteweb.com/archives/majority_of_social_media_users_want_businesses_attention.php

# A Brief Primer Before You Continue

In this section we discuss a few concepts and terms that you should have a general idea about before you delve into the body of the book. Though most of these items are defined in their respective sections, they are concepts that are used throughout the entire book.

## RSS Feeds

RSS stands for Really Simple Syndication. An RSS feed is a file containing information that allows you to syndicate (share) that information across the Internet. Think of a feed as a subscription to individual packets of information. Imagine that instead of getting your local paper delivered to your door each day, every story within the paper was delivered to your desktop. This is what happens when you subscribe to a news site's RSS feed.

## Widgets and Badges

Widgets are snippets of HTML, JavaScript, or Flash code, usually displayed graphically, that can be used to syndicate content (RSS feeds, for example) or to add interactive features that users can drop onto their own blogs or Websites. Widgets are often customizable by the user and typically offer ways for users to pull information from the widget's originating site, while badges are graphical links composed of an image and a link only.

Many widgets are no more than glorified links rendered by graphics, while others are mini-applications that pull their functionality from other sites that visitors can use right on your own Website. Two examples that you have probably already encountered are the Google ads and Amazon products frequently featured on Websites or blogs that, when you click on them, take you to the respective site or product.

## Content Management System (CMS)

By definition, a CMS is an application that is used to create, edit, manage, and publish content in an organized way. Web applications like WordPress, Joomla!, and Drupal do this by storing information in a database, and using scripting languages like PHP to access the information and place it on a Website.

CMSs are the perfect way to create a Website that is social media and Web 2.0 optimized because they have built-in RSS feed and widget technology.

## WordPress

Though WordPress began as a blogging platform, it has evolved into a very user-friendly CMS. We demonstrate the use of WordPress to power a Website throughout the book.

## Placing Code

Much of the Social Web is about sharing information. Many times this means pulling information from outside sources onto your own Website or blog. This is typically accomplished by copying some kind of programming or scripting code like HTML, Javascript, or Flash from another site and "placing" (or copying) it on your own site.

We first discuss placing code when we show you how to pull others' RSS feeds onto your site in Chapter 3. Throughout the rest of the book, the concept is discussed as we show you how to promote your presence in the Social Web, and especially when we discuss widgets and badges.

If you are using a CMS to power your site, placing code is a function that is built into the CMS infrastructure, so the process is relatively painless.

If you are placing the code on a traditional Website, however, only you will know where and how to place the code within your own HTML. Regardless of how you created your Website, whether with Dreamweaver, Site Builder, or just within a text file, your end result (as long as you did not use a scripting language to build it) will consist of a series of HTML files. The code you copy from the widget source is placed directly inside your HTML code using whatever method you typically use to edit your HTML code.

If you use a developer to maintain your Website for you, it is probably best for you to copy the code you want placed on your Website and send it to the developer. Tell them where you want the widget or application to appear on your site.

# Search Engine Optimization (SEO) Jargon

## Metadata

As we mention in the "Interchangeable Terms" section on page 27, key terms, tags, and keywords are used interchangeably throughout the book. Keywords or key terms are the terms that help search engine robots properly categorize your Website in the search engines. Think of them as the words or terms someone would enter in a Google search to find your site. In social applications and tools, "tags" are the equivalent of key terms.

It is also important that you know what we mean by "Meta Keywords" and "Metadata" in general. Generically, the term "metadata" means information about information. Metadata, as it is used in Websites, is information about the information contained on a Website. This information helps search engine robots better categorize a Website. A Website's page rank in a search engine like Google is greatly affected by how well the site's metadata actually matches the information contained in the body of the Website.

The metadata of a Website is defined in the header of the Website's HTML. There are three main sections of metadata: Title, Description, and Keywords. The title should only be around 75 characters, while the description will be more like 160 characters. The meta keywords are separated by commas, and should not exceed 20 terms, though most search engines only look at the first 10. It is important to repeat a Website's keywords within its meta title and meta description as well.

**IMPORTANT:** Using consistent key terms throughout your entire traditional and Social Web presence is essential to your overall success in both the Social Web and in how you and your Website are ranked in traditional search engines! We discuss how to use key terms effectively throughout the entire book.

## Landing Pages

A landing page is the page on a Website that a specific link returns to. So, if you place an ad or post a blog comment somewhere on the Internet and include a link within that information, the landing page for that link is the page on your Website where the user ends up ("lands") after they click on the link. It is common practice to create specific landing pages for tracking ads and other campaigns since page traffic is easily measured.

# Who Should Read this Book

This is a book for the do-it-yourselfer: the resourceful business owner, the motivated author, the innovative publisher, the head of your company's IT or marketing department, as well as the student of marketing, media, PR, Web development, or Internet studies.

Anyone who wants to succeed in today's Internet can benefit from reading this book, even if you have already started building a Social Web presence.

The first edition of this book is already being used in many college and university courses covering the subjects of Social/New Media, PR, Marketing, Advertising, English Communications, and SEO.

# How to Use this Book

If you want the full benefit of this book, start at the beginning. Read the "Creating Your Social Media Strategy" chapter and complete the worksheet for your own strategy. This will save you time overall, since planning your strategy will bring to light which social media tools will work best for your own business or product.

Then, move straight on to the "Preparation" chapter. Following the guidelines there will save you much time in implementing your plan. Pretty much every subsequent chapter in the book will refer back to this chapter.

From here, you can use your strategy as a guide to the chapters on tools that will benefit your presence the most.

Conclude with the "Pulling It All Together" and "Measuring Your Success" chapters. The former will help you integrate many of the tools you choose to implement, and the latter will show you ways to see what part of your strategy is working best for you. The "Looking to the Future" chapter will help you determine what tools you should consider for your long-term social media plans.

## Chapter Autonomy

This book is written so that each chapter can be a stand-alone guide to its topic. You can skip around all you wish, but it is recommended that you read the chapters "Creating Your Social Media Strategy" and "Preparation" first.

## Resource CD

The resource CD contains linkable resources and suggestions for further reading organized by chapter. The CD also contains fillable forms and worksheets to be used in your entire Social Media Strategy. You will notice references to the sheets and forms throughout the book. Each chapter concludes with a section that outlines what can be found on the CD for that chapter.

Replacement CDs can be purchased from the publisher.

## Appendices

There are four appendices ("Installing WordPress," "Creating Your Own RSS Feed," "Building Your Own Widget," and "Preparing Your Content for the Semantic Web") that were pulled from the regular flow of the book because of their complexity. They are all straightforward guides to their respective topics, but may be a bit advanced for some readers.

## Conventions

**Footnotes:** Traditional footnote references are used for standard footnotes, and bracketed footnotes are used for references to URLs.

**Navigation:** Navigation on a site or within an application is depicted as "First Level Menu Item/Second Level Menu Item/Third Level Menu Item" and so forth.

## Interchangeable Terms

**Key Terms:** The terms "Key Term," "Keyword," and "Tag" are used interchangeably throughout the text.

**Widgets:** The terms "Widget," "Badge," and "Gadget" are used interchangeably throughout the text.

**WordPress:** The terms "WordPress admin panel," "WordPress backend," and "WordPress dashboard" are used interchangeably throughout the text.

## Online Support

The author has a companion Facebook page to the book.[3] Please visit this page if you have any questions about *The Social Media Survival Guide* or want to connect with other readers. The author also posts updated information about the book's content to this page.

## Platforms Discussed in the Book

We discuss many different software and online platforms throughout this book. It is important for you to note that these platforms are constantly changing. However, we have tried to give you a general idea of the capabilities of each one, so that even if the look and feel of a platform changes, you will still have an understanding of its functionality.

Even though we may demonstrate only one platform for a given topic, please be aware that there are many other choices available. For instance, we discuss WordPress a lot as a blogging platform and content management system, but you could just as easily use Blogger, Typepad, Joomla!, or Drupal. Our demonstration methods are not meant to be preferential; they are meant to offer the reader the best overall approach to a successful experience in the Social Web.

---

[3]    http://www.facebook.com/pages/Deltina-Hay-A-Survival-Guide-to-Social-Media-and-Web-20-Optimization/45443682193

# 1 Creating Your Social Media Strategy

There are three general concepts to keep in mind when planning a strategy for optimizing your presence in the Social Web: interactivity, sharing, and collaboration. Interactivity can come in the form of writing blog posts, commenting on others' posts, or participating in social networking communities. Sharing can be as easy as uploading images and video clips onto media communities. Collaboration can be achieved by contributing to social bookmarking sites or wikis.

It is important to understand the difference between optimizing your presence in the Social Web versus optimizing your Website *for* the Social Web. Optimizing your presence in the Social Web does not necessitate having a Website. Many of the tools you want to use are hosted on other social Websites or platforms like social networking, social bookmarking, or crowd-sourcing sites. If you do have a Website in place, include optimizing it for the Social Web in your strategy.

It is easy to get overwhelmed with all of the new social media and Web 2.0 tools and technologies that pop up on the Internet on an almost daily basis. But a carefully planned and executed strategy can alleviate your stress and ensure your successful transition into the Social Web.

# Mapping Your Strategy

The first step in a successful strategy is to decide which tools make sense for you or your business to implement. Just because a tool exists, doesn't mean it is right for your needs. Choose tools that best fit your *current* content, not content you plan to create later. This is key to creating a manageable strategy out of the gate—you can add to it later if you choose.

Most social media tools fall into certain fairly broad categories. Here are some general areas to consider for your strategy, and the chapters in this book in which they are discussed:

- RSS Feeds/Blogging (Chapter 3, Chapter 4)
- Podcasting/Video Blogging (Chapter 5)
- Social Networking (Chapter 6)
- Micro-Blogging (Chapter 6)
- Geo-Tagging (Chapter 6, Chapter 11)
- Lifestreaming/Social Pages (Chapter 11, Chapter 12)
- Social Bookmarking (Chapter 7)
- Crowd-Sourcing (Chapter 7)
- Image Sharing (Chapter 8)
- Video Sharing (Chapter 8)
- Document/Slide Sharing (Chapter 8)
- Social Calendar/Event Sites (Chapter 11)
- Wikis (Chapter 11)
- Virtual Worlds (Chapter 11)
- Social Media News Release/Newsroom (Chapter 10)
- Custom Applications/Widgets (Chapter 9)
- Custom Social Network (Chapter 6)
- Mobile Site (Chapter 13)
- Mobile Application (Chapter 13)
- Distributed Social Networking (Chapter 12)
- Linked/Structured Data (Chapter 13)
- RDF/FOAF File (Chapter 13)

# Advice from the Power Users

In May 2010, we launched a survey to ask social media consultants and strategists, media and marketing professionals, public relations professionals, and managers which tools they would recommend within specific industries.

Figure 1.1 shows the classification of the 213 reliable responses we received. Figure 1.2 gives us an idea of how long each of our participants have considered themselves social media professionals.

## Figures 1.1 and 1.2. Survey Respondent Classification

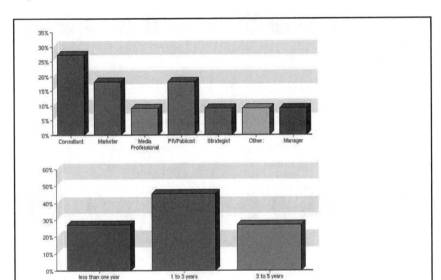

The following pages show the results of how highly our participants would recommend specific social media tools for each corresponding industry type listed.

| Tactics & Tools | RSS Feeds | Blogging | Podcasting | Video Blogging | Social Networking | Micro-Blogging |
|---|---|---|---|---|---|---|
| Arts and Entertainment | 😎 | 😎 | 😎 | 😎 | 😎 | 😎 |
| Business Services | 😎 | 😎 | 😎 | 😎 | 😎 | 😎 |
| Consumer Goods/Services | 😎 | 😎 | 🙂 | 🙂 | 😎 | 😎 |
| Creative Professionals | 😎 | 😎 | 😎 | 😎 | 😎 | 😎 |
| Education and Training | 😎 | 😎 | 😎 | 😎 | 😎 | 😎 |
| Entrepreneurs | 😎 | 😎 | 🙂 | 😎 | 😎 | 😎 |
| Government Agency | 😎 | 😎 | 🙂 | 😎 | 🙂 | 😎 |
| Marketing/Advertising | 😎 | 😎 | 🙂 | 😎 | 😎 | 😎 |
| News and Media | 😎 | 😎 | 🙂 | 😎 | 😎 | 😎 |
| Non-Profit | 😎 | 🙂 | 🙂 | 😎 | 😎 | 😎 |
| Public Relations | 😎 | 😎 | 😎 | 😎 | 😎 | 😎 |
| Publishing | 😎 | 😎 | 😎 | 🙂 | 😎 | 😎 |
| Small Business | 😎 | 😎 | 😎 | 😎 | 😎 | 😎 |

😎 = Highly Recommend   🙂 = Might Recommend    = Would Not Recommend

| Tactics & Tools | Geo-Tagging | Lifestreaming/ Social Pages | Social Bookmarking | Crowd-Sourcing | Image Sharing | Video Sharing |
| --- | --- | --- | --- | --- | --- | --- |
| Arts and Entertainment | ◉ | ◉ | ◉ | ◉ | ◉ | ◉ |
| Business Services | ◉ | ◉ | ◉ | ◉ | ◉ | ◉ |
| Consumer Goods/Services | ◉ | ◉ | ◉ | ◉ | ◉ | ◉ |
| Creative Professionals | ◉ | ◉ | ◉ | ◉ | ◉ | ◉ |
| Education and Training | ◉ | ◉ | ◉ | ◉ | ◉ | ◉ |
| Entrepreneurs | ◉ | ◉ | ◉ | ◉ | ◉ | ◉ |
| Government Agency | ◉ | ◉ | ◉ | ◉ | ◉ | ◉ |
| Marketing/Advertising | ◉ | ◉ | ◉ | ◉ | ◉ | ◉ |
| News and Media | ◉ | ◉ | ◉ | ◉ | ◉ | ◉ |
| Non-Profit | ◉ | ◉ | ◉ | ◉ | ◉ | ◉ |
| Public Relations | ◉ | ◉ | ◉ | ◉ | ◉ | ◉ |
| Publishing | ◉ | ◉ | ◉ | ◉ | ◉ | ◉ |
| Small Business | ◉ | ◉ | ◉ | ◉ | ◉ | ◉ |

| Tactics & Tools | Document/Slide Sharing | Social Calendar/Event Sites | Wikis | Virtual Worlds | Social Media News Release | Custom Applications/Widgets |
|---|---|---|---|---|---|---|
| Arts and Entertainment | ● | ● | ● | ● | ● | ● |
| Business Services | ● | ● | ● | ● | ● | ● |
| Consumer Goods/Services | ● | ● | ● | ● | ● | ● |
| Creative Professionals | ● | ● | ● | ● | ● | ● |
| Education and Training | ● | ● | ● | ● | ● | ● |
| Entrepreneurs | ● | ● | ● | ● | ● | ● |
| Government Agency | ● | ● | ● | ● | ● | ● |
| Marketing/Advertising | ● | ● | ● | ● | ● | ● |
| News and Media | ● | ● | ● | ● | ● | ● |
| Non-Profit | ● | ● | ● | ● | ● | ● |
| Public Relations | ● | ● | ● | ● | ● | ● |
| Publishing | ● | ● | ● | ● | ● | ● |
| Small Business | ● | ● | ● | ● | ● | ● |

| Tactics & Tools | Custom Social Network | Mobile Site | Mobile Application | Distributed Social Networking | Linked/ Structured Data | RDF/FOAF File |
|---|---|---|---|---|---|---|
| Arts and Entertainment | 🙂 | 🙂 | 🙂 | 🙂 | 🙂 | 🙂 |
| Business Services | 🙂 | 🙂 | 🙂 | 🙂 | 🙂 | 🙂 |
| Consumer Goods/Services | 🙂 | 🙂 | 🙂 | 🙂 | 🙂 | 🙂 |
| Creative Professionals | 🙂 | 🙂 | 🙂 | 🙂 | 🙂 | 🙂 |
| Education and Training | 🙂 | 🙂 | 🙂 | 🙂 | 🙂 | 🙂 |
| Entrepreneurs | 🙂 | 🙂 | 🙂 | 🙂 | 🙂 | 🙂 |
| Government Agency | 🙂 | 🙂 | 🙂 | 🙂 | 🙂 | 🙂 |
| Marketing/Advertising | 🙂 | 🙂 | 🙂 | 🙂 | 🙂 | 🙂 |
| News and Media | 🙂 | 🙂 | 🙂 | 🙂 | 🙂 | 🙂 |
| Non-Profit | 🙂 | 🙂 | 🙂 | 🙂 | 🙂 | 🙂 |
| Public Relations | 🙂 | 🙂 | 🙂 | 🙂 | 🙂 | 🙂 |
| Publishing | 🙂 | 🙂 | 🙂 | 🙂 | 🙂 | 🙂 |
| Small Business | 🙂 | 🙂 | 🙂 | 🙂 | 🙂 | 🙂 |

Of particular interest is how some of the tools are recommended "across the board": blogs, social networks, micro-blogs, image sharing, and video sharing in particular.

This confirms what can be considered a realistic and manageable starting strategy. If you don't know where to begin, have limited resources, or are just too overwhelmed to even think about any of it, here is a good strategy to get you going:

- Start a blog using WordPress.com
- Create an account in Facebook
- Create a page on Facebook
- Create an account in LinkedIn
- Get a Twitter account
- Get an account with Flickr
- Get a YouTube account

Once you have a strong presence in these areas and are comfortable using the tools, you can start adding more tools to enhance your presence.

We also asked our survey participants to give some advice (in 100 words or less) to those just starting out with social media. The following are selected quotes:

*Don't think of this as a set of tools or pipes you use to deliver content to consumers. It's a whole new ballgame, so start a conversation with some of your most dedicated fans.* —JD Lasica, founder of Socialmedia.biz and Socialbrite.org

*Start with Facebook to generate a basic "Online Presence." Connect with organizations of similar motivations. Access competitor websites to gain insight into what tools and/or services are already in place, implement services that competitors utilize and grow additional tools, incentives, services, and promotions which are not being used and adopt for use. Encourage constant feedback from services/products and respond to user comments within 48 hours.* —Sabrina Morris, founder of SMediaMarketOrg, firm and consultancy.

*As a creative professional, none of the available tools can be ignored. The ability to drive business online is at an all time high. Social media has been a game changer—we know what and how our competitors are approaching*

*new deals and the pressure is on.* —Kelley Burrus, CLINK Events / VP of Corporate Events + Destination Management Programs

*Each organization is different and must take into account its individual audience(s) and products. Additionally, the organization must factor in the resources they are able to commit to each tool. Having a bevy of social media profiles doesn't do an organization any good if they don't have the staff on hand to monitor and maintain them. Try to stay away from "shiny object" syndrome and stick with the basics if you're a small shop.... There are a lot of options out there, but having a presence on all of them isn't going to improve your results if they're stale.* —Jennifer Milikien, Director of Public Relations at RCCO in San Antonio, TX

*I see a lot of businesses overextending themselves by using too many social media tools. Pick three or four: YouTube, Facebook, Twitter and FourSquare, for example. Integrate them, and focus your energy instead of having a small presence across the board.* —Kimberly A. Kitchen, Social Media Strategist, Boundless Flight, Boundlessflight.com

# Sample Strategies

The following pages outline various social media strategies based on the case studies that are featured throughout the book. Keep in mind that these strategy profiles present people or companies with an already-mature social media presence, and therefore may include terms and tools you haven't heard of before (but don't worry, you'll get there!).

You can use the strategy worksheet on the resource CD to create your own customized strategy. There is a lot of redundancy in these plans, so if you are looking for a strategy for a specific type of business, focus on the one that makes the most sense for you. The sample strategies are:

- Service Business/Consultancy
- Author/Media Personality
- Publisher/Product Business
- Entrepreneur/Performer/Small Business Owner
- Public Relations Firm
- Author/Speaker/Trainer/Consultant
- Spiritual Alchemist/Yogini

| Tactics & Tools | Service Business/Consultant www.SocialMediaPower.com |
|---|---|
| Strategic Needs and Goals | This Web 2.0 firm specializes in resources for small business. The need for an impressive social media presence is obvious, but they also test many tools before recommending them to clients. |
| Website and RSS Optimization | Their Website is entirely powered by WordPress, so their RSS feed is their blog. Their feed is submitted to and optimized on FeedBurner. Their site is easy to share and subscribe to. |
| Blogging Podcasting Video Blogging | Many of their posts are instructional so they tend to be quite long. They offset by offering "Social Media Tips of the Day," which also keeps the blog dynamic. They also post podcasts. |
| Social Networking Micro-Blogging Geo-Tagging | They maintain a Facebook profile and a Facebook page, with additional profiles in LinkedIn and Twitter. Their updates to these communities focus on information, resources, and tips. |
| Social Bookmarking Crowd Sourcing Blog Commenting | They contribute to social bookmarking and crowd-sourcing sites, trying to bookmark sites, articles, and blog posts regularly. They comment on social media blog posts they find interesting. |
| Image Sharing Video Sharing Document Sharing | Since most of their content is written, they post documents, presentations, and Webinar slides to document sharing sites. They also maintain a YouTube account. |
| Social Calendars Event Sites | They offer Webinars regularly, so they have an account with Eventbrite, which they integrate easily with their WordPress site and their social networking accounts. |
| Collaborative Tools (Wikis, E-learning, Virtual Worlds) | They utilize GoToWebinar for their Webinar offerings. |
| Social Media Newsrooms News Releases | Their PR firm releases their news using PR Web's social media optimized news releases. |
| Lifestreaming Social Pages Other Tools | They maintain a "Lens" on Squidoo for each main topic they write about. They also have a FriendFeed account. |
| Custom Applications/Widgets Custom Social Networks | They have a Facebook application that is built using Widgetbox. They also create their own free WordPress themes that help get their name into the Social Web. |
| Mobile Site Mobile Application | They use a WordPress plugin that serves up their Website as a mobile friendly site. Their CEO also has her own mobile site. |
| Distributed Social Networking Linked/Structured Data | They use a WordPress plugin to help structure their data, and also maintain an RDF file (a resource description framework file for structuring data for the semantic web). |

| Tactics & Tools | Author/Media Personality www.PureSoapbox.com |
|---|---|
| **Strategic Needs and Goals** | An author and motivational speaker whose brand is perfect for the Social Web, her goal is to promote her brand and book, as well as position herself as a tech-savvy media personality. She maintains two sites to this end. |
| **Website and RSS Optimization** | Both of her sites do a good job of making it easy for others to share or comment on her content. She also displays badges and widgets from other social sites where she has a presence such as Facebook and LinkedIn. |
| **Blogging** <br> **Podcasting** <br> **Video Blogging** | She blogs about her events and accolades on her personal blog, while limiting her brand blog entries to her signature vignettes. She also submits to sites that solicit guest bloggers, and spotlights one of her vignettes in each submission. |
| **Social Networking** <br> **Micro-Blogging** <br> **Geo-Tagging** | She maintains a presence in several social networking and micro-blogging sites, including Facebook, LinkedIn, and Twitter, posting her vignettes to these sites for promotion. She maintains a Facebook page for her brand. |
| **Social Bookmarking** <br> **Crowd Sourcing** <br> **Blog Commenting** | -- |
| **Image Sharing** <br> **Video Sharing** <br> **Document Sharing** | She has accounts in image and video communities. As a media personality and interviewer, promoting herself through these outlets is imperative. She integrates these accounts with her other social accounts. |
| **Social Calendars** <br> **Event Sites** | She uses Upcoming.org to input her events, and offers a feed to them via a widget on her WordPress site. |
| **Collaborative Tools** | -- |
| **Social Media** <br> **Newsrooms** <br> **News Releases** | Since she has quite a bit of media coverage, she has a social media newsroom that is maintained as a courtesy of her publisher. |
| **Lifestreaming** <br> **Social Pages** <br> **Other Tools** | Her blogs and on-camera updates also plug into Blogger, Gindie, and Naymz sites. A Squidoo Lens is in her immediate plan. |
| **Custom Applications/Widgets** <br> **Custom Social Networks** | She maintains a "blidget" from Widgetbox that also serves as a Facebook and Bebo application, and another Widgetbox widget that highlights her YouTube videos. |
| **Mobile Site** <br> **Mobile Application** | -- |
| **Distributed Social Networking** <br> **Linked/Structured Data** | -- |

| Tactics & Tools | Publishing/Product Business www.DaltonPublishing.com |
|---|---|
| Strategic Needs and Goals | As a publisher, their primary goal is to sell books. The goal of their social media strategy is to get the word out about their authors and their books, with the intention of generating sales. |
| Website and RSS Optimization | Their WordPress site is organized like a traditional site, with bookstore and media pages for each book, but it is easy for them to integrate badges and widgets throughout the entire site. |
| Blogging Podcasting Video Blogging | Most of their posts are announcements about author accomplishments or events. They also blog about industry news and events as well as social media tips for other publishers. |
| Social Networking Micro-Blogging Geo-Tagging | They have a presence in Facebook, MySpace, Twitter, GoodReads, and Shelfari, where they announce events and author kudos. They also maintain a Facebook page and a Facebook group. |
| Social Bookmarking Crowd Sourcing Blog Commenting | They contribute regularly to several social bookmarking and crowd-sourcing sites. They bookmark info on their authors, so they create purpose-built pages for news releases. |
| Image Sharing Video Sharing Document Sharing | They upload event and author photos, book covers, etc. to Flickr, and add author's videos to their YouTube playlists. Document communities offer them a way to share selected book chapters. |
| Social Calendars Event Sites | They post their author events on Upcoming.org, and add events to their Facebook, Twitter, and other accounts for extra exposure. |
| Collaborative Tools (Wikis, E-learning, Virtual Worlds) | -- |
| Social Media Newsrooms News Releases | They create and maintain social media newsrooms for each of their authors, who tend to acquire a lot of media coverage. They also use the PR Web service for optimized releases. |
| Lifestreaming Social Pages Other Tools | -- |
| Custom Applications/Widgets Custom Social Networks | They maintain a custom social network for their authors and fans at Ning.com. They also create custom widgets for the books that can benefit from them. |
| Mobile Site Mobile Application | This is in their immediate future. |
| Distributed Social Networking Linked/Structured Data | They structure their contact and product content for semantic browsers using microformats. |

| Tactics & Tools | Entrepreneur/Performer/Small Business Owner www.LesMcGehee.com |
| --- | --- |
| Strategic Needs and Goals | His goals are to promote his speaking and comedy events and get the word out about his books and upcoming events. He also has two comedy franchises, and maintains social accounts for them as well. |
| Website and RSS Optimization | His main site is a WordPress site, so his blog is his RSS feed. He also maintains a social media portal for his comedy franchise. The portals pull in and highlight all of the social accounts for the franchises. |
| Blogging<br>Podcasting<br>Video Blogging | He does not have much time to blog, so he has found an alternative: He populates his home page with the newsletter he sends out to his mailing list. Though this is not an optimal solution, it keeps his site from sitting stagnant for too long. |
| Social Networking<br>Micro-Blogging<br>Geo-Tagging | He has a healthy presence in several social networking and micro-blogging communities, including Facebook, LinkedIn, MySpace, and Twitter. He maintains a Facebook page for both of his franchises. He is adding geo-tagging tools for his café soon. |
| Social Bookmarking<br>Crowd Sourcing<br>Blog Commenting | -- |
| Image Sharing<br>Video Sharing<br>Document Sharing | He has accounts with Flickr and YouTube, and imports images and video onto his site using widgets and badges. He especially relies on video to get his message out and promotes them in his social networking accounts and other social sites. |
| Social Calendars<br>Event Sites | He uses Upcoming.org to input his events, and offers a feed to them via a widget on his site. He also adds his events to his Facebook profile and pages to get them extra exposure. |
| Collaborative Tools<br>(Wikis, E-learning,<br>Virtual Worlds) | -- |
| Social Media<br>Newsrooms<br>News Releases | Since he has a fair amount of media coverage, he also maintains a social media newsroom. |
| Lifestreaming<br>Social Pages<br>Other Tools | -- |
| Custom Applications/Widgets<br>Custom Social Networks | -- |
| Mobile Site<br>Mobile Application | -- |
| Distributed Social Networking<br>Linked/Structured Data | -- |

| Tactics & Tools | Public Relations Firm www.AccoladesPR.com |
|---|---|
| **Strategic Needs and Goals** | As a PR firm, their goals lie in their need to market themselves and their clients. To that end, their goals are to position themselves as a strong force in "PR 2.0" and promote their clients through social media outlets. |
| **Website and RSS Optimization** | Their WordPress site maintains the feel of a traditional site. They maintain several feeds for client news, PR news, etc. They make it easy for visitors to bookmark their site and they link to their social networking profiles in their sidebar. |
| **Blogging** **Podcasting** **Video Blogging** | They do not blog as regularly as they would like, but they offer dynamic content in their social media newsrooms. When they do blog, though, their posts address issues within their industry, especially as it applies to social media and PR. |
| **Social Networking** **Micro-Blogging** **Geo-Tagging** | They maintain active profiles and pages in Facebook, MySpace, LinkedIn, and Twitter. They integrate their social networking accounts with their blog and other social accounts. |
| **Social Bookmarking** **Crowd Sourcing** **Blog Commenting** | They contribute regularly to several social bookmaking and crowd-sourcing sites. They bookmark their clients' news items and create purpose-built pages to include in news releases. |
| **Image Sharing** **Video Sharing** **Document Sharing** | They have accounts in Flickr and YouTube. They integrate the firm's photos and their clients' images and videos into their Website, as well as into their social media newsrooms and releases. |
| **Social Calendars** **Event Sites** | They use Upcoming.org and Eventbrite to promote client events, and they also promote events on social networking sites. |
| **Collaborative Tools** **(Wikis, E-learning, Virtual Worlds)** | They contribute to and manage a wiki for PR 2.0 professionals. |
| **Social Media** **Newsrooms** **News Releases** | In addition to maintaining their own newsroom, they maintain newsrooms for their clients as well. They also take full advantage of social media optimized news releases for their clients. |
| **Lifestreaming** **Social Pages** **Other Tools** | They use social ROI tools like Radian6 and JitterJam to help their clients manage their online reputation and to help manage their clients' presence on the Social Web. |
| **Custom Applications/Widgets** **Custom Social Networks** | -- |
| **Mobile Site** **Mobile Application** | -- |
| **Distributed Social Networking** **Linked/Structured Data** | -- |

| Tactics & Tools | Author/Speaker/Trainer/Consultant www.Deltina.com |
|---|---|
| Strategic Needs and Goals | Her goals are to establish herself as a thought leader; get exposure for her workshops, Webinars, and books; and to promote her businesses. |
| Website and RSS Optimization | She uses WordPress to power her site, but relies on a FriendFeed widget as her home page. She has so much activity in the Social Web, this widget is an ideal way to pull it all into one location. |
| Blogging Podcasting Video Blogging | She maintains two blogs. Her personal blog offsets her more technical blog with photographs and poetry. Her other blog talks about the tools and technologies she features in trainings. |
| Social Networking Micro-Blogging Geo-Tagging | She maintains a Facebook, LinkedIn, and Twitter account for herself, and a Facebook page for her book. She offsets her promotional posts with nature photography. |
| Social Bookmarking Crowd Sourcing Blog Commenting | She bookmarks interesting resources in her field and uses them as purpose-built pages. She uses the tool Intense Debate to manage her blog commenting. |
| Image Sharing Video Sharing Document Sharing | She has a Flickr account for her photography, and a Youtube account for her training videos. She gets good exposure on document sharing sites where she posts presentations. |
| Social Calendars Event Sites | She uses Eventbrite to promote her workshops and Webinars. |
| Collaborative Tools (Wikis, E-learning, Virtual Worlds) | She teaches online classes for a university, and uses the tool Dimdim to teach the classes. She also uses GoToMeeting for her Webinars, and is a contributor to Examiner.com. |
| Social Media Newsrooms News Releases | Her press releases are created with PR Web, which means they are social media and search engine optimized. |
| Lifestreaming Social Pages Other Tools | She uses FriendFeed to pull her entire Social Web presence into one place. She maintains a Squidoo lens on the topics in her book, and has a Posterous account. |
| Custom Applications/Widgets Custom Social Networks | She uses a custom widget from Widgetbox to promote her RSS feeds. |
| Mobile Site Mobile Application | She has a mobile site that is built using a Widgetbox mobile site tool. |
| Distributed Social Networking Linked/Structured Data | She structures her Website contact and other relevant content using microformats, and maintains an RDF file. |

| Tactics & Tools | Spiritual Alchemist/Yogini<br>www.ChavahAima.PlumbSocial.com |
| --- | --- |
| **Strategic Needs and Goals** | As a spiritual alchemist and yogini, her desire is to activate and empower the divine being that lies within, as well as promote her inspirational books, CDs, workshops, and retreats. |
| **Website and RSS Optimization** | In addition to her main Website, she maintains a social media portal that hosts her blog, integrates her presence in the Social Web, and optimizes her content. She also sells her products from this site. |
| **Blogging**<br>**Podcasting**<br>**Video Blogging** | Her blog posts are very consistent. She regularly offers inspirational messages, current news in her field, tips on how her readers can find enlightenment, and tips for eating well. |
| **Social Networking**<br>**Micro-Blogging**<br>**Geo-Tagging** | She maintains a presence on Facebook, LinkedIn, Twitter, Gaia, and Care2. Her message is also clear in these sites: to offer enlightenment and to promote her products and retreats. |
| **Social Bookmarking**<br>**Crowd Sourcing**<br>**Blog Commenting** | She comments on blogs of particular interest in her field. |
| **Image Sharing**<br>**Video Sharing**<br>**Document Sharing** | Imagery is an important part of her message, so she maintains Flickr and YouTube accounts. She then creates image and video galleries on her site by integrating Flickr and YouTube. |
| **Social Calendars**<br>**Event Sites** | She uses Eventbrite to promote her retreats on her site, and within Facebook and LinkedIn. |
| **Collaborative Tools**<br>**(Wikis, E-learning,**<br>**Virtual Worlds)** | -- |
| **Social Media**<br>**Newsrooms**<br>**News Releases** | -- |
| **Lifestreaming**<br>**Social Pages**<br>**Other Tools** | She maintains a Squidoo lens. She also sends out a newsletter using Constant Contact, and so has a widget on her site to promote it. |
| **Custom Applications/Widgets**<br>**Custom Social Networks** | -- |
| **Mobile Site**<br>**Mobile Application** | Her social portal hosting service uses WordPress plugins to help her site display better on mobile devices |
| **Distributed Social Networking**<br>**Linked/Structured Data** | Her social portal hosting service uses microformats to structure her contact and product content as well as RDF files. |

A successful social media strategy involves identifying and understanding the tools best suited to help you accomplish your goals, and the rest of this book is dedicated to helping you gain that understanding. Every organization is different, and so are their objectives. Only you are going to know which tools will best benefit you, your organization, or your client. Learn the tools well, and trust your own judgment.

# Important First Decisions Regarding Websites, Blogs, and RSS Feeds

Before you get into the nuts-and-bolts of your social media strategy, there is an up-front decision you must make regarding the one bit of technology *essential* to your Social Web success: an RSS feed. This subject is discussed in great detail in Chapter 3: "RSS Feeds & Blogs," but for now, in brief, you have two choices to consider:

- Start a blog which has built-in RSS feed technology, or
- Create your own RSS feed using an XML file.

Creating a blog is by far the easiest solution to this, and you do not need to become a "blogger" to take advantage of the technology.

If you choose to create a blog to accommodate your RSS feed, you then need to decide whether you will create the blog external from your site (on WordPress.com, Blogger.com, or Typepad.com, for example) or host it on your own Website.

Finally, if you choose to host the blog yourself, does it make sense to completely replace your existing Website (or build a new one) using WordPress as a Content Management System (CMS), or another CMS like Joomla! or Drupal? This latter choice is an optimal solution, since using a CMS as a platform for your Website means that you get a built-in RSS feed and the ability to integrate widgets and other social media tools with little effort. See Chapter 4: "Building a WordPress Powered Website."

If you are not in a position to rebuild your existing Website or start a new one using WordPress, the recommended solution is to create a blog in a directory on your own server or hosting account. Many hosting sites offer one-click installations of WordPress toward this end, allowing easy installation on your Website. (Free blog hosting services like WordPress.com, Blogger.com, and Typepad.com tend to restrict many plugins and other advantageous features you may want to implement.)

Another option is to create a separate site to use as a "social media portal." This site would serve as a place to highlight your presence in the Social Web. This can work well for businesses who already have a Website that is not convenient to change.

Here is a list of possible scenarios based on the options above:

- Keep your existing Website in place, and:
    › Create your own RSS feed
    › Create a blog external to your site
    › Host a blog in a directory on your site
    › Create a social media portal
- Rebuild your Website or create a new one using WordPress as a CMS, or another CMS.

## This Chapter on the Resource CD

- Further Reading
- Linkable Resources
- Fillable Forms:
    › Social Web Strategy Worksheet

# 2 Preparation

Now that you've selected your social media strategy, the next step is to prepare the content you will need to implement it. Try to resist the urge to just "wing it." Now is the time to think carefully about how you will present yourself to others. Proper preparation of your descriptions, biographies, and other blurbs will greatly increase your exposure in the Social Web.

There is a fillable preparation worksheet on the resource CD that covers and helpful organizes the following information, as well.

## Key Terms or "Tags"

You are probably familiar with key terms or "keywords" since they are used in search engine optimization. Keywords are the terms that help search engine robots properly categorize your Website in the search engines. Think of them as the words or terms someone would enter in a Google search to find your site.

In social media applications and tools, "tags" are the equivalent of key terms and keywords. You want to generate a good list of one-, two-, and three-word tags that will help define your presence in the Social Web. You will use these tags often as you implement your strategy.

Start by making a list of at least 20 tags. Choose tags that are not too generic, the same way you would choose good key terms for your website. For instance, the tag "fiction" is too generic. Using tags like "young adult fiction" or "ontological fiction" will get you better results. Be sure and include the name of your business, book titles, authors, and business principals in your tag list as well.

There are a number of useful tools for finding good keywords.[1] Refer to the resource CD for more options.

# Important First Decisions Regarding Your Social Media Profiles

## Before setting up your profiles, you need to decide two things:

1. What "entity" will you be representing in the Social Web? If you are an author, this will be your book; if you are a business owner, this will be your business. If you are a publisher or an author who intends on writing more than one book, you may want to think this through. For instance, if you are a publisher, you may decide to create a presence for your press as well as for each of your titles. Whereas if you are an author with several books, you may want to make your name/pseudonym or the name of your book series your entity as opposed to just the name of one of your books.

2. Which person within your organization will be representing you in the Social Web? You cannot always use your business or book name as the account holder of social sites. You will need to populate many of the profiles for an actual person. If you are an author, this is a given; but if you are a business, you will want to choose someone within your organization who has the time to contribute to these sites on occasion. This person should also feel comfortable disclosing a certain amount of personal information about themselves.

Once you have decided on your entity and your representative, gather the following information. Be sure to use one or more of your best tags in every description and biography.

---

[1] http://www.google.com/sktool/

# Information for Entity:

- Name of entity
- Tag line
- Short description
  - › 50 to 60 words
  - › Use at least two of your best tags
- Long description
  - › 175 to 200 words
  - › Use at least three of your best tags
- Website URL
- Year entity was founded
- Mission statement
- Product list with short descriptions (if applicable)
- Gender and birth date (These fields are required to register in some social sites, and since the age of your book or business would not make sense, use something else that has meaning for you.)
- Logo or book cover art

# Information for Representative:

- Name of representative
- Brief biography
  - › 100 words
  - › Use two of your best tags
- Gender
- Birth date (This does not need to be public.)
- The following information is optional in most sites, however, it will make your representative more likely to find contacts in social networking sites:
  - › Hometown
  - › Activities
  - › Interests
    - Music
    - TV

- Movies
- Books
  › Favorite quotes
  › Favorite people/heroes
  › Education
    - College/university
    - Class year
    - Concentration
  › Work
    - Employer
    - Position
    - Description
    - City/town
- Photo to use for social networking profiles

# Your Existing Social Presence

Compose a list, along with user names and links to your profile pages, of the places where you already have a presence in the Social Web. Many of the new accounts you create will allow you to provide links to your other social sites, and you want to take advantage of this.

# Information for Social Calendars

Prepare a list of upcoming events to post to social calendars that includes:

- A short name
- A description (that includes tags)
- Date
- Time
- Venue
- Contact name and email
- A list of tags

# Preparing Your Multimedia Items

- Gather all:
  - › Images you plan to share in media communities like Flickr
  - › Video clips you plan to share in media communities like YouTube
  - › Audio clips that can be used as podcasts
  - › Documents and presentations you plan to share on document sharing sites
- For each image, clip, and document above:
  - › Create a short list of tags
  - › Rename the file using at least one tag
  - › Create a short title and description using at least two tags

## Optimizing File Names

It is important that you rename multimedia files with descriptive names before you upload them to media communities like Flickr or YouTube.

The name of a multimedia file can often get the file better exposure than its title or description. With that in mind, try to rename files using at least one of your best tags. For example, you might change a logo file name from SMLogo1.jpg to SocialMediaPowerLogo.jpg.

# Gathering Content for Blog Posts

- Gather information you may already have at your disposal to use as blog posts, including:
  - › Excerpts from your existing Website
  - › White papers you may have written
  - › Articles you may have published
  - › Book excerpts
- For each bit of information that will become a blog post:
  - › Prepare a list of tags
  - › Prepare a list of links that will go into the body of the post
  - › Prepare a short title using at least two tags
  - › Prepare a short description using as many tags as you can

# This Chapter on the Resource CD

- Linkable Resources
- Fillable Forms:
    › Preparation Worksheet

# 3 RSS Feeds & Blogs

## RSS Feeds

RSS stands for Really Simple Syndication. An RSS feed is a way of syndicating (sharing) information across the Internet. Think of a feed as a subscription. Imagine that instead of getting your local paper delivered to your door each day, every story within the paper was delivered to your desktop. This is what happens when you subscribe to a news site's RSS feed. RSS has become so popular and is so easy to implement that most Websites have a feed of some sort available to its visitors. You'll want one too, because an RSS feed is an essential tool to build your presence on the Social Web.

Generally, the process works as follows:

- Content (like news stories, blog entries, or press releases) in the form of a properly prepared file is generated from a Website as an RSS feed.
- The "feed" is made available for subscription to visitors who have access to a "feed reader."
- The subscriber can read each story that is added to the Website's feed without ever having to return to the original site.

- A subscriber can have as many subscriptions as they like. Each time they open their feed reader they will be informed of new stories that are available for each of their subscriptions.

Web 2.0 is about sharing and interactivity. Having an RSS feed that offers a way for visitors to easily access your content accomplishes both of these goals.

# The Feed Reader

In order to subscribe to an RSS feed, you need access to a feed reader or "aggregator," as they are also called. There are a number of Web-based feed readers available, as well as readers you can install on your desktop.

Figure 3.1 shows Google Reader,[1] a Web-based feed reader. From here you can subscribe to feeds, read entries from your current feed subscriptions, search available feeds, and more.

## Figure 3.1. Google Feed Reader

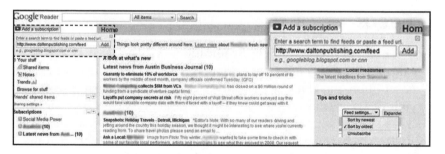

Figure 3.1 also shows how to add a new subscription by entering the feed's URL if you know it. Figure 3.2 shows the items from one of the feeds this user is subscribed to.

The next section discusses how you can subscribe to a feed using your preferred feed reader from any Website that has an RSS feed in place, and how to offer your own feed for subscription. Refer to the resource CD for a list of popular feed readers.

---

[1] http://www.google.com/reader

## Figure 3.2. Feed Subscription in Google Reader

Desktop feed readers are convenient if you do not always have access to the Internet. FeedReader3[2] and RssReader[3] are two good ones.

# The Feed

An RSS feed is an XML file that is formatted so that any feed reader can decipher and organize the contents of the file. The result is a file containing many stories (called items) that is kept up-to-date by the feed's author. Read more about how this is done in Appendix B, "Creating Your Own RSS Feed."

**A blog *is* an RSS feed.** Since blogging platforms have built-in RSS feed technology, each blog post becomes an item of the blog's RSS feed. This is very convenient if you do not need to have too much control over the functionality of your RSS feed.

---

[2] http://www.feedreader.com
[3] http://www.rssreader.com

Figure 3.3 shows the blog for the site, Social Media Power.[4] Figure 3.4 shows the same blog as it appears as a subscription in Google Reader.

You can subscribe to Social Media Power's RSS feed in a few different ways. One way is to look for the RSS icon. In Figure 3.3, the icon is just to the right of the "Social Media Power" title at the top of the page (the square icon with the dot and two curved lines). Clicking on this icon, you get the screen in Figure 3.5. From here, you can subscribe to this feed using any number of feed readers.

### Figure 3.3. Social Media Power's Blog

### Figure 3.4. Social Media Power's Blog Feed in Google Reader

---

[4] http://www.socialmediapower.com

## Figure 3.5. Subscribing to a Feed via Feed Readers

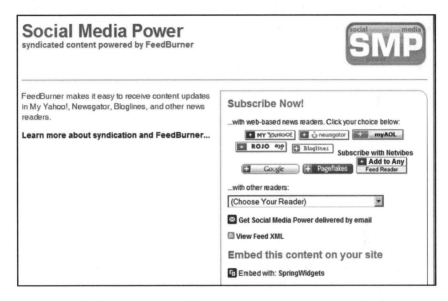

You can also enter your email address (to the right of the RSS icon) and receive this site's latest feeds in an email once a week (see Figure 3.6).

## Figure 3.6. Subscribing to a Feed via Email

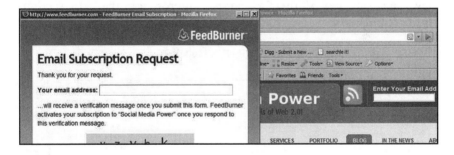

The other place to subscribe to the site's feed is to click on the button that says "Subscribe" on the right side of the page in Figure 3.3 (notice it also displays a small RSS icon). Figure 3.7 shows the screen that results when that button is clicked.

From here, you can choose to subscribe to this site's feed using any number of feed readers. This functionality is made possible by a feed widget called AddtoAny (see page 265).

## Figure 3.7. Subscribing to a Feed via AddtoAny

Blogging platforms are not the only applications that have built-in RSS technology. Content Management Systems (CMS) like Drupal[5] and Joomla![6] also have this feature, as do many other commercial Web publishing applications.

Figure 3.8 shows the RSS feeds offered by *The Austin Chronicle.*[7] Note that they have several feeds available. This is a common practice for larger news sites since not all their readers are interested in the same sections of the publication.

## Figure 3.8. The *Austin Chronicle's* RSS Feeds

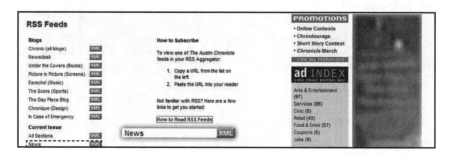

---

[5] http://www.drupal.org

[6] http://www.joomla.org

[7] http://www.austinchronicle.com

To subscribe to one of these feeds, you can click on the XML button to the right of the feed. Depending on your browser, this results in a page like Figure 3.9.

## Figure 3.9. Subscribing to the *Austin Chronicle* Feed

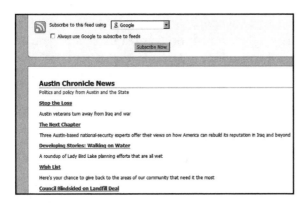

Choosing Google Reader as your reader of choice results in Figure 3.10. Clicking on "Add to Google Reader" adds the feed to your Google Reader account. Figure 3.11 shows how the feed is displayed in Google Reader.

## Figures 3.10 & 3.11. *Austin Chronicle* Feed in Google Reader

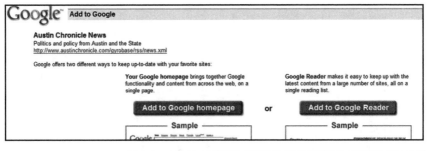

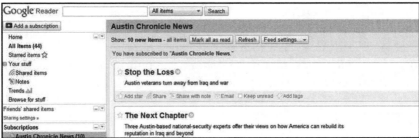

As you can see, different Websites may offer their feeds differently, but the ultimate result is the same.

# Displaying Feeds on a Website

You don't need a feed reader to access RSS feeds, only to subscribe to them. Many Websites display feeds from other sites that allow you to click through to the original story. Figure 3.12 shows the home page of Plumb Social,[8] a sister site to Social Media Power. In the right sidebar of this site is an area that displays the latest stories from Social Media Power's RSS feed. Clicking on one of the story titles brings you directly to the full story on Social Media Power's site.

### Figure 3.12. Displaying Feeds on a Website

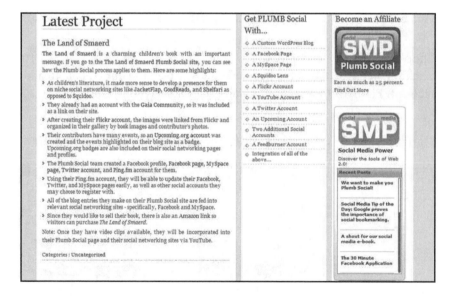

## On a Blog or CMS

Blogging and CMS platforms also have built-in functionality for displaying RSS feeds. Figure 3.13 shows the built-in RSS plugin in the WordPress backend. To add an RSS feed to your sidebar, you enter the

---

[8] http://www.plumbsocial.com

feed's URL, a title for the feed, and select some other display settings, and you are good to go. Read more about plugins and WordPress in Chapter 4: "Building a WordPress Powered Website." Each CMS platform has its own version of this plugin that allows you to add RSS feeds to your site easily.

### Figure 3.13. Adding an RSS Feed to a CMS

## On a Traditional Website

Even if your Website is not powered by WordPress or another CMS, there are still ways of offering feeds on your site. You can use a service like Google AJAX API[9] to generate code to place on your Website, or ask your Webmaster to do it for you.

Figure 3.14 shows the Dynamic Feed Control Wizard for Google AJAX API. This wizard can help you create custom feeds that you can display on your site. You can display a single feed or several feeds in their "Vertical Stacked" format. You can enter the URL of a feed you already know or enter key terms that generate a series of feeds based on those terms.

Once you have your feed just the way you want it, click the "Generate Code" button and copy the generated code.

---

[9] http://code.google.com/apis/ajaxfeeds/

## Figure 3.14. Using Google Feed Control Wizard

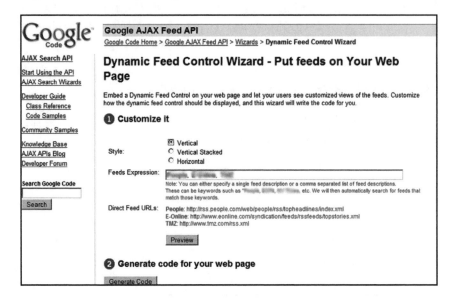

Figure 3.15 shows part of the generated code for the Social Media Power feed. You can then paste the code within the HTML of your Website. See Chapter 9: "Widgets & Badges" for more instruction on placing code on a Website.

## Figure 3.15. Generated Code from Feed Control Wizard

Copy and paste the following where you want your dynamic feed control to appear. Do not place it within the <head> ... </head> section of your page unless you plan on relocating the <div id="feed-control"></div> elements out of this chunk of code.

```
<!-- ++Begin Dynamic Feed Wizard Generated Code++ -->
<!--
// Created with a Google AJAX Search and Feed Wizard
// http://code.google.com/apis/ajaxsearch/wizards.html
-->

<!--
// The Following div element will end up holding the actual feed control.
// You can place this anywhere on your page.
-->
<div id="feed-control">
```

## Using Feed Widgets

The Social Media Power feed that is displayed on the Plumb Social Website in Figure 3.12 on page 60 was created using a feed widget from Widgetbox.[10] There are a number of nice widgets like this for offering or displaying your feeds. See Chapter 9: "Widgets and Badges" for more information.

# Options for Creating an RSS Feed

## Creating Your RSS Feed from an XML File

As mentioned above, an RSS feed is nothing more than an XML (extended markup language) file that can be read by feed readers. Appendix B demonstrates how to build your own RSS feed using XML. It is recommended that you take a look at this appendix even if you do not plan on building your own RSS feed, because it will help you gain a better understanding of how RSS feeds work.

## Using Software to Create Your RSS Feed

There is software available to help you build RSS feeds with little effort. However, it is recommended that you are familiar with the structure of an RSS file and the options available for building one before using the software. Again, Appendix B can help you gain this understanding.

Figure 3.16 shows one of the screens used to create an RSS feed using FeedForAll.[11] Refer to Appendix B for clarification on the options listed in the figures, specifically: Title, Description, URL, and Pub Date.

The end product of this process is an XML file that you upload to your site and make available for others to subscribe to. Figure 3.17 shows the resulting file, and Figure 3.18 shows how the feed will look to the subscribers.

---

[10] http://widgetbox.com
[11] http://www.feedforall.com

## Figure 3.16. Creating an RSS Feed with FeedForAll

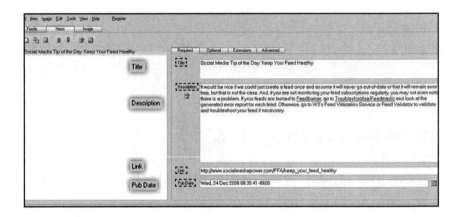

## Figure 3.17. XML File Created by FeedForAll

```
<?xml version="1.0" encoding="UTF-8"?>
<rss
    xmlns:content="http://purl.org/rss/1.0/modules/content/"
    xmlns:dc="http://purl.org/dc/elements/1.1/"
    xmlns:sy="http://purl.org/rss/1.0/modules/syndication/"
    version="2.0">
    <channel>
        <title>Social Media Power</title>
        <description>Discover the Tools of Web 2.0!</description>
        <link>http://www.socialmediapower.com/FFA</link>
        <docs>http://blogs.law.harvard.edu/tech/rss</docs>
        <lastBuildDate>Wed, 24 Dec 2008 10:43:35 -0600</lastBuildDate>
        <pubDate>Wed, 24 Dec 2008 08:47:42 -0600</pubDate>
        <generator>FeedForAll v2.0 (2.0.2.9) unlicensed version
http://www.feedforall.com</generator>
        <image>
            <url>http://www.socialmediapower.com/images/SMPWeb.jpg
</url>
            <title>Social Media Power</title>
            <link>http://www.socialmediapower.com/FFA</link>
            <description>Social Media Power Logo</description>
        </image>
        <item>
            <title>Social Media Tip of the Day: Keep Your Feed Healthy
</title>
            <description>It would be nice if we could just create a
feed once and assume it will never go out-of-date or that it will
remain error free, but that is not the case. And, if you are not
monitoring your feed subscriptions regularly, you may not even notice
there is a problem. If your feeds are burned to Feedburner, go to
Troubleshootize/Feedmedic and look at the generated error report for
each feed. Otherwise, go to W3€™s Feed Validation Service or Feed
Validator to validate and troubleshoot your feed if necessary.
</description>
            <link>
http://www.socialmediapower.com/FFA/keep_your_feed_healthy</link>
            <guid isPermaLink="false">B9709467-A518-4BF1-ABC3-
FF033D9BAA0C</guid>
            <pubDate>Wed, 24 Dec 2008 08:35:41 -0600</pubDate>
        </item>
    </channel>
</rss>
```

for Help, press F1

## Figure 3.18. Resulting FeedForAll Feed

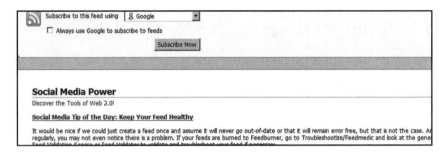

Armed with a basic understanding of the information in Appendix B, you can build a feed like this in as little as an hour. Once the feed is in place, you will only need to add new items or stories as they become available. You can add as many stories as you need at one time and postdate the publication dates as well.

There are also a number of services available that can help you create your feed and host it for you.

# Using a Blog as Your RSS Feed

Starting a blog is probably the easiest way to create an RSS feed. Blogging platforms like WordPress have built-in RSS technology so that each blog entry becomes an "item" of the feed, complete with titles, descriptions, links, and categories that you add to each blog entry. Continue on to the "Blogs" section of this chapter for more information.

# Planning Your Feed

## How will you create your feed?

- Create your own XML file
- Use software or a service to create your feed
- Use a CMS to serve as your feed
- Start a blog to serve as your feed

## How many feeds will you have?

If you have a lot of content, you may want to create several feeds: one for news, one for press releases, one for events, and so forth. If you have a news site, you may even break your feeds up by category like the *Austin Chronicle* feed in Figure 3.8 on page 58.

As another example, Dalton Publishing creates social media newsrooms for some of its authors. See Chapter 10, "Social Media Newsrooms." The newsrooms include sections for new releases, media coverage, book reviews, and events. Figure 3.19 shows how these newsrooms break out the RSS feeds accordingly.

**Figure 3.19. Feeds on a Social Media Newsroom**

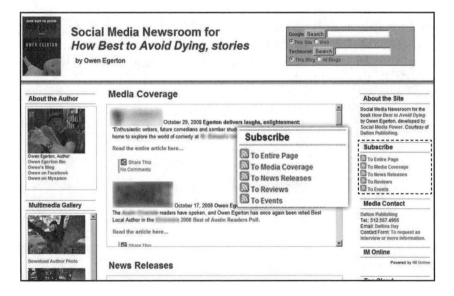

This is convenient not only for the press or others interested in subscribing to specific information about this author, but for the author as well. Authors can offer links to their latest media coverage, events, etc. by featuring the respective feed on their own Website or blog (see Figure 3.20).

**Figure 3.20. Social Media Newsroom Feed on a Website**

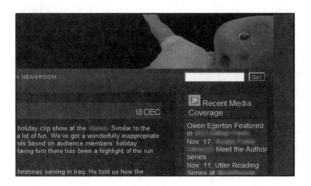

# Titles, Descriptions, Categories, and Links

You have a title and description for your main feed or "channel" (see Appendix B), as well as titles and descriptions for each individual feed item. Plan these titles and descriptions so they use some of your best key terms every time (see Chapter 2: "Preparation" to learn about key terms).

Your item descriptions may be the only thing a potential reader sees before they make a decision to read the full story. Make sure these descriptions do a good job of hooking the reader while still accurately describing each story.

Each feed item is assigned categories (see Appendix B). Assigning relevant and meaningful categories to each feed item is important. Categories allow feed directories to properly categorize your feed and helps others find it easier in searches. Compose a category list of your best key terms, and draw mostly from this list. We discuss categories in more detail on pages 74 and 78.

Each of your feed items should have a unique link that brings the reader directly to the full story.

## Content for Your Feed

It is important to keep your feed items fresh and plentiful. Even if you don't have a lot of content, good planning can make it go further.

- Gather any existing content you have available. This may include:
  › Print articles
  › E-zine articles
  › Newsletter stories
  › Press releases
  › Media coverage
  › Upcoming events
  › White papers
  › Informative sections of your Website
  › Book trailers
  › Book excerpts
  › Podcasts
  › Video clips
- Make a list of external links. These may include:
  › Industry blogs you are reading
  › Articles of interest to your industry
  › Websites of interest
  › News sites
  › Other RSS feeds
- Make a list of people in your industry who may be willing to contribute to your feed.
- Make a list of possible topics. These may include:
  › Article or story topics
  › Interviews
  › Reviews of books, tools, or Websites relevant to your industry
  › Top 10 lists
  › Tips

Once your content is gathered and your lists complete, start a calendar of entries for your feed. Mix up selections from the general areas mentioned above.

**Existing Content:** Try and get as much mileage out of your existing content as you can. Some of your existing articles, white papers, or other content can probably be broken down into many smaller entries.

**External Links:** Use these links for story ideas, sites to review, or blogs for starting possible dialogues.

**Other People:** Invite industry leaders to contribute to your feed.

**Possible Topics:** Writing top 10 lists and tips is a good way of quickly adding content to your feed to keep it fresh. Mix them up with beefy, informative articles.

Use a sheet like the one in Figure 3.21 to prepare your feed entries. See the resource CD for a fillable worksheet like Figure 3.21, as well as a worksheet for planning your entire RSS feed.

## Figure 3.21. RSS Feed Entries Worksheet

Feed Name: Social Media Power

| Pub Date | Title | Description | Link | Categories |
|---|---|---|---|---|
| 08/28/08 | The 30 Minute Facebook Application | Demonstrate a way for anyone with an RSS feed to painlessly build a Facebook application in only 30 minutes. | http://www.socialmediapower.com/2008/08/28/the-30-minute-facebook-application/ | Facebook, Facebook Applications, Social Media, Web 2.0, RSS feeds, Bebo |
| 09/01/08 | Social Media Tip of the Day: Keep Your Feed Healthy | Social Media Power's tips on keeping your RSS feed fresh, indexed, and error free. | http://www.socialmediapower.com/2008/08/20/social-media-tip-of-the-day-keep-your-feed-healthy/ | RSS feeds, Social Media, Web 2.0, Feedburner, Feed Validator |

## Optimizing and Promoting Your Feed

Read the section "Optimizing and Promoting Your Blog and RSS Feed" at the end of this chapter (see page 78).

# Blogs

In its simplest form, a *blog* is a tool for posting information chronologically and allowing others to comment. Blog posts can be organized into categories and indexed using tags that are read by blog indexes (much the same way as key terms are read by search engines). Users then use tags to search blog indexes on subjects that interest them.

But remember from the previous section that a blog is also an RSS feed. It is because of this that you should not buy into the stigma that is often associated with blogging. For our purposes, we focus on how blogging serves a vital role in accomplishing social media and Web 2.0 optimization, and how you can use WordPress to maximize the exposure of your blog, not only in blogging and RSS feed indexes, but in search engines as well.

If you need more information on how to blog in general, refer to the "Linkable Resources" and "Further Reading" sections for this chapter on the resource CD.

## The Thread that Binds Your Social Web Presence

As we have said, social media and Web 2.0 optimization can be broken down into three general areas: interactivity, sharing, and collaboration. Adding a blog to your Web presence covers each of these areas. You are freely sharing information, encouraging interactivity through visitor comments, and offering an atmosphere of collaboration for all of your visitors.

Many of the sites and tools that you implement in your social media strategy allow you to integrate blogs and RSS feeds directly into them. For instance, both Facebook and MySpace have applications that allow you to pipe RSS feeds or blog entries directly onto your page or profile. See Chapter 6: "Social Networking & Micro-Blogging" and Chapter 12: "Pulling It All Together" for more information.

Having an informative and engaging blog or RSS feed gives you an edge over many of your competitors in more places than just on your Website or in the blogosphere.

## Know Your Audience, Know Your Blog

A blog, like an RSS feed, can serve many purposes. Knowing the audience you want to target is the best starting place to determine your blog's purpose. Like any good media provider, knowing what your audience wants to read is imperative to your success.

As an example, the blog at Social Media Power[12] is dedicated to providing a resource for those interested in social media and Web 2.0 optimization. If I suddenly started blogging about Wolfgang, my eccentric problem cat, I would likely lose some readers. Instead, we keep our posts consistently on topic: writing informative articles, tips, and reviews on the topics of social media and Web 2.0.

The blog for Dalton Publishing,[13] however, caters to a different audience. They are writing for their current and prospective authors, their distributor, their authors' readers, and others in the industry. Therefore, their blog tends to be more of a hodge podge of information: upcoming events, media coverage, announcements, kudos, industry news, etc.

So it isn't that your blog shouldn't have different types of posts, just that you should keep your audience in mind when posting.

Types of blogs you might consider:

- A corporate RSS feed covering company news, articles, press releases, and the like.
- An educational or how-to blog offering articles and resources on a particular topic.
- An industry blog offering news, interviews, and resources within a particular industry.
- A blog about a particular product, author, or book.
- A straight news or entertainment feed.
- A traditional blog that is more conversational and casual than a news feed or corporate blog.

If you have content that falls into several distinct categories like events, news, press releases, or reviews, you can use categories to define several feeds within the same blog. Offer your readers the option of subscribing to specific parts of a feed rather than the entire feed. See "Optimizing and Promoting Your Blog and RSS Feed" on page 78 for more information.

---

[12] http://www.socialmediapower.com
[13] http://www.daltonpublishing.com/blog

# Options for Starting Your Blog

## Starting a Free Blog

You can start a free (or nearly free) blog at WordPress.com, Typepad, or Blogger. These blogs have limited capabilities, but you can upgrade to premium services that will open up more options.

## Starting a Blog on Your Website

Many hosts have one-click installs of WordPress or other blogging platforms. Check with your hosting company to see if they have this option available. If not, you can install WordPress in a folder on your Website. Refer to Appendix A: "Installing WordPress," and be sure to follow the instructions for installing WordPress in a folder on your site, not in the root directory of your site.

## Using WordPress to Power Your Website

You can use WordPress to power your entire Website and have your blog built in to your site. Refer to Chapter 4: "Building a WordPress Powered Website." Or, instead of replacing your main Website with a WordPress powered site, you can build a "Blog Site" or "Social Media Portal" with WordPress that has its own domain name and hosting account (if necessary). This site can be dedicated to hosting your blog and highlighting all of your areas of interest in the Social Web. An example of this is the service called PLUMB Web Solutions.[14]

# Main Elements of a WordPress Blog Post

Figure 3.22 shows the most basic elements of a blog entry in WordPress:

**Title:** The title is how your blog appears to others in your blog listings, as well as being the first thing subscribers see about a post when receiving your RSS feed or when they see your post in a directory.

**Permalink:** This is the permanent link to this blog entry. In WordPress settings, you can define the default style for permalinks. You can also override the default permalink for any blog entry. In our example, the default permalink structure is nameofblog.com/year/month/day/title. If

[14] http://www.plumbwebsolutions.com

## Figure 3.22. Elements of a Blog Post, Top

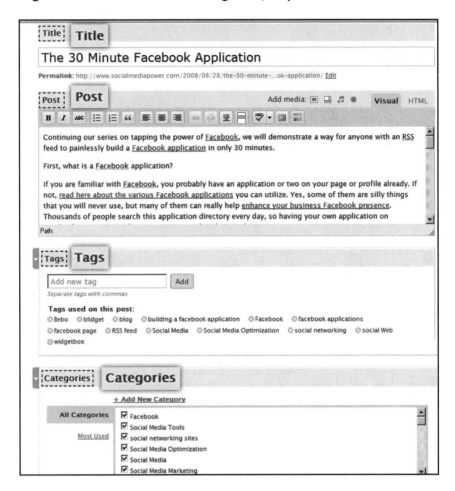

we choose, we can change the title portion of the permalink to make it shorter or have no dashes. Permalink structure is important. Read more about permalinks in the "Optimizing and Promoting Your Blog and RSS Feed" section of this chapter beginning on page 78.

**Post:** This is where the body of your blog entry is composed. Above this box are functions for you to format your blog entry, including text styles, bulleted lists, block quotes, inserting images and other media, and much more. Check this chapter's section on the resource CD for links about using WordPress.

**Links:** Figure 3.23 shows how to insert a link into a post by highlighting text and clicking on the closed chain link. How you do this is important. Read more about links within your posts on page 79.

## Figure 3.23. Creating Links in Blog Posts

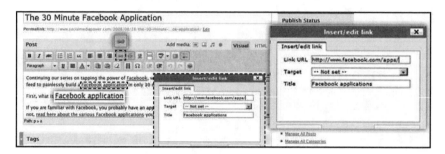

**Categories:** Categories help you group your posts by similar topics. They also have a hierarchy, so you can have parent and child (or sub) categories. When a visitor clicks on a category while viewing your blog, they will be able to view each post that is assigned to that category. Choice of categories is also important to blog optimization. See "Optimizing and Promoting Your Blog and RSS Feed" on page 78.

**Tags:** Tags are similar to categories in that they help group blog posts by similar topics, but tags have other uses as well. Tags are used by many plugins, including tag cloud plugins, that give users a visual representation of your blog posts. Tags do not have a hierarchical structure like categories. Tags are also used by RSS feed and blog directories as key terms, so you want to use these wisely. See "Optimizing and Promoting Your Blog and RSS Feed" on page 78.

**Categories vs. Tags:** Tags are used more than categories to classify individual posts in blog and RSS indexes. A good rule of thumb is to use categories to organize your posts for easy navigation on your site, but to use tags as key terms that will help others find your posts off your site. This keeps you from having too many categories, yet as many tags as necessary to get good placement in the directories.

**Excerpts:** Excerpts are used to summarize your post, and to use as a good "hook" to get readers interested in your entire post when they stumble upon it in a blog directory. WordPress defaults to the first 55 words of the original post if you leave the excerpt blank, so if your lead is good in the original post, you may want to leave this alone. Excerpts are also used in trackbacks, explained below.

**Trackbacks:** A trackback is a method of notification between Websites. They are a way for you to comment on someone else's blog from your own site, and have your entry show up on their site as a comment or as a notification on their WordPress dashboard. So, if you want to comment on someone else's blog post, but you want your readers to see your comment, you can post a blog entry, cite the blog you are commenting on, and send a "trackback" to the blog you are citing. Your post will then show up as a comment on the "trackbacked" blog post. The comment will show up as the excerpt of your post with a link back to your entire post. Figure 3.24 shows where this is done.

Note: This section has demonstrated the most basic elements of a blog post. If you are not an experienced blogger, please reference the resource CD to learn more.

## Figure 3.24. Elements of a Blog Post, Bottom

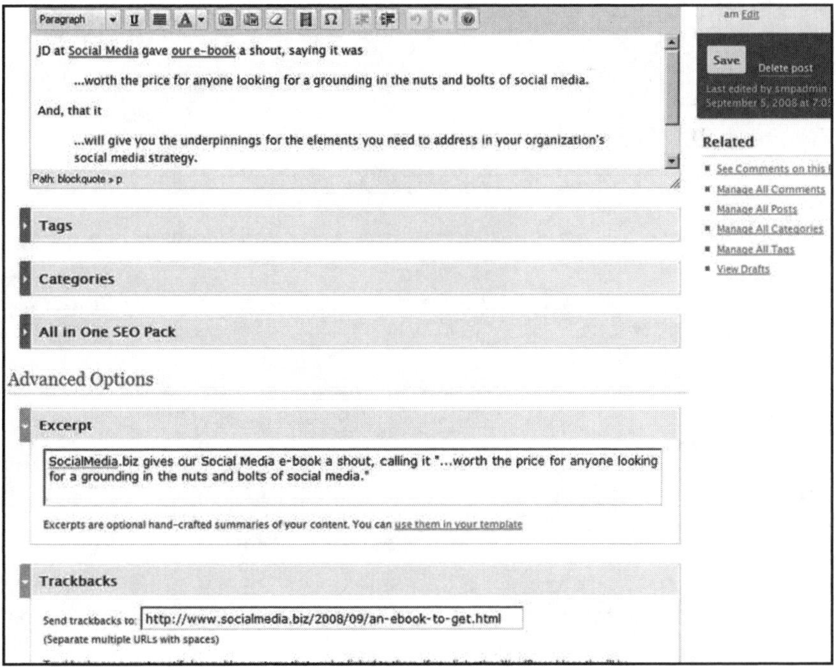

# Planning Your Blog

## Content

Read "Content for Your Feed" on page 68 above. The same principles apply to gathering and preparing content for your blog.

## Categories and Tags

Categories and tags are important elements of your plan, since they are what help others find your blog in the feed indexes and blog directories.

Choose your categories from the top level key terms you prepared in Chapter 2: "Preparation." Recall that you use categories to organize your posts, so make these quite broad.

Use all of your key terms as tags, even the ones you chose for categories. The nice thing about tags is that you can have a lot of them without adding too much clutter to your site (unlike with categories).

## Frequency and Delegation

Planning your blog entries ahead of time can help keep your blog populated with fresh content. Using a posting calendar like the one in Figure 3.25 can help this process. You can also use it for delegating the

## Figure 3.25. Blog Entry Worksheet

Blog Name: Social Media Power

| Pub Date | Title | Excerpt | Post (link text is underlined, followed by link to use) | Categories | Tags |
|---|---|---|---|---|---|
| 08/28/08 | The 30 Minute Facebook Application | Demonstrates a way for anyone with an RSS feed to painlessly build a Facebook application in only 30 minutes. | Continuing our series on tapping the power of Facebook (http://www.facebook.com), we will demonstrate a way for anyone with an RSS feed to painlessly build a Facebook application (http://www.facebook.com/apps/) in only 30 minutes... | Facebook, Facebook Applications, Social Media, Web 2.0, RSS feeds, Bebo | Bebo, blidget, blog, building facebook application, Facebook, facebook application, facebook page, RSS feed, Social Media, Social Media Optimization, social networking, social Web, widgetbox |
| 09/01/08 | Social Media Tip of the Day: Keep Your Feed Healthy | Social Media Power's tips on keeping your RSS feed fresh, indexed, and error free. | It would be nice if we could just create a feed once and assume it will never go out-of-date or that it will remain error free, but that is not the case. And, if you are not monitoring your feed subscriptions regularly, you may not even notice there is a problem. If your feeds are burned to Feedburner (http://www.feedburner.com), go to Troubleshootize/Feedmedic and look at the generated error report for each feed. Otherwise, go to W3's Feed Validation Service (http://validator.w3.org/feed/) or Feed Validator (http://feedvalidator.org/) to validate and troubleshoot your feed if necessary. | RSS feeds, Social Media, Web 2.0, Feedburner, Feed Validator | Feed Validation Service, Feed Validator, FeedBurner, healthy rss feeds, RSS Feeds, Social Media, Social Media Optimization, Web 2 |

| Trackbacks | SEO Title | SEO Description | SEO Keywords | | |
|---|---|---|---|---|---|
| http://docs.widgetbox.com/developers/blidget/ | How to build a Facebook application in around 30 minutes. | This post will show you how to create a simple RSS feed application for Facebook and Bebo using widgetbox.com. | social media, facebook, facebook applications, building facebook applications, widgetbox, widgets, blidgets | | |
| | Social Media Tip of the Day: Keep Your Feed | Keep your RSS feed healthy using Feedburner and feed validators. Part of Social Media Power's tips and tools for Web | social media, rss feed, feedburner, healthy rss feed, error-free | | |

actual posting to others. You can even enter your posts ahead of time and postdate the publication dates. This form is available on the resource CD.

# Comments and Commenting

## Comments on Your Posts

Allowing others to comment on your blog posts is what makes blogging a vital part of Web 2.0 optimization. However, this does not mean that you should allow anyone and everyone to say whatever they please or to spam you with comments. Always set the most stringent settings on your blog discussion settings in WordPress and be particular on which comments you approve.

From your WordPress admin panel, go to Settings/Discussion to change these settings (see Figure 3.26). Checking all of these boxes ensures that all comments on your blog need to be approved by you before they appear on your site. This means you will be contacted via email each time a comment is posted and will need to approve all new comments, but that is a small price to pay to make sure your blog maintains its integrity.

## Figure 3.26. Controlling Comments on a Blog

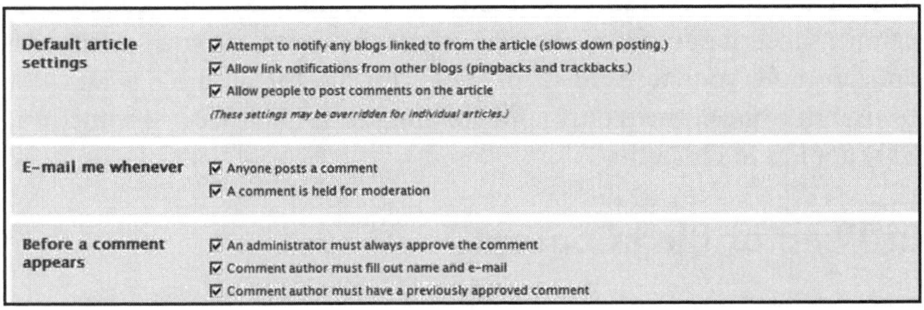

## Commenting on Other Blogs

Becoming part of the conversation is important to building a healthy Social Web presence. However, do not comment for the sake of commenting—that is considered spam.

The following strategy can save you time and help to optimize your efforts:

- Click through to the bloggers who leave good comments on your blog. If there is something on their site that interests you, leave a comment.
- Try to use trackbacks to comment on others' blogs when appropriate.
- Search Technorati[15] and Google Blog Search[16] for a handful of blogs that you feel you could comment on regularly and subscribe to them in a reader.
- Periodically search blog directories using your best key terms to find blog posts to comment on.
- Always use your real name, a valid email address, and your complete URL (a complete URL includes "http://www." at the beginning) when posting a comment, even if they are not required.
- Use a comment management tool like IntenseDebate[17] or DISQUS[18] to help manage and track comments on your own blog, as well as the comments you make on others' blogs.

# Optimizing and Promoting Your Blog and RSS Feed

Your RSS feed or blog will do you little good if nobody knows about it or cannot subscribe to it. This section highlights ways for you to optimize and promote your feed. Most of these tips are for both blogs and RSS feeds, but some of them only apply to blogs. It is made clear if something only applies to blogs.

## Your Feed or Blog Content

### Edit Your Content

Edit and proofread your feed or blog entries for accuracy every time you post. If you or your staff do not have the time or skills to do so, consider hiring a professional editor. If you write your posts ahead of time as

---

[15] http://technorati.com/
[16] http://blogsearch.google.com/
[17] http://intensedebate.com/
[18] http://disqus.com/

suggested in the previous section, you can save money since editors usually have a minimum charge and can get a lot done in one session.

## Titles

Always use at least one or two of your best key terms in your blog or feed titles. This gives you better placement in the directories as well as better search engine placement.

## Categories and Tags (tags only apply to blogs)

When posting blog entries, you should assign categories and tags to them *every* time. Most blog indexing sites use categories and tags to index blog entries. Draw from your top level key terms for categories and all of your key terms for tags.

## Links

Link to as many other blogs or Websites from within each of your posts as you can and trackback to them whenever possible (see the "Blogs" section beginning on page 69).

When creating links within a post, **use key terms as the link text**. Figure 3.27 shows an example of this. Each link in this post uses key terms as the link text. So, "Facebook" links to Facebook.com, "Facebook application" links to the Facebook application page, Facebook.com/apps, and so

### Figure 3.27. Text Links in Blog Posts

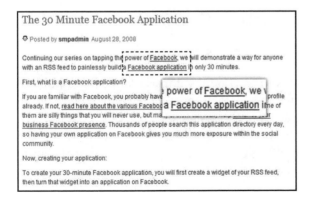

forth. Each link in the post also contains a key term that is used as a tag and/or category for the post. This tactic gives each of your posts more relevance in directories and search engines.

## Signatures

Attaching a signature at the end of each of your posts can encourage visitors to subscribe to your feed and aid in promoting your other sites or products. Figure 3.28 shows the signature at the end of one of the Social Media Power posts. This is also a good place for a copyright statement if you need one. Notice that there are three pound signs before this signature. It is best to keep your signature clearly separate from the post content.

### Figure 3.28. Blog Post Signature

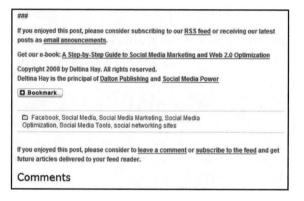

# Search Engine Optimization (SEO)

## SEO for Your Blog (only applies to blogs)

Since WordPress produces PHP as opposed to HTML, posts and pages do not necessarily have the metadata in their source that is required for search engine robots (read more about metadata on page 25). However, there are ways around this problem. A good SEO plugin for WordPress is The All in One SEO Pack.[19] This plugin lets you assign proper metadata to each of your posts and WordPress pages so that they get good placement

---

[19] http://wordpress.org/extend/plugins/all-in-one-seo-pack/

in search engines. You input the metadata from the same interface that you enter the post. The title, description, and keywords entered here become the metadata for that post (see Figure 3.29).

This plugin also helps you assign metadata for your site as a whole.

## Figure 3.29. SEO All In One Pack Plugin in Action

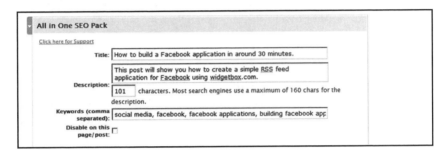

## Permalinks (only applies to blogs)

As discussed in the previous section, permalinks are the direct link to each of your blog entries. You want to use a permalink structure that does not use any special characters (these are often called "pretty" permalinks). Since WordPress is written using PHP, the default permalinks look something like this: http://yoursite.com/?p=6. Search engines often ignore links that contain characters like the ones in "?p=6." Choose a permalink structure that does not use them. To change the structure, go to the backend of WordPress; go to Settings/Permalinks. Figure 3.30 shows the common permalink settings. To make your permalinks "pretty," choose any of these options except the default.

## Figure 3.30. Defining Permalinks in WordPress

| Common settings | |
| --- | --- |
| ○ Default | http://www.socialmediapower.com/?p=123 |
| ⦿ Day and name | http://www.socialmediapower.com/2008/12/30/sample-post/ |
| ○ Month and name | http://www.socialmediapower.com/2008/12/sample-post/ |
| ○ Numeric | http://www.socialmediapower.com/archives/123 |

## External Links or "Link Baiting"

This is actually an SEO tip you can use for any Website. Use meta keywords in any link text that points back to your Website. These are the meta keywords that are in your site's header (see page 25 of the Introduction), not just arbitrary key terms. Whenever you can use text as links back to your site, use these terms to do so. As an example, we use the following blurb at the end of each article we submit to e-zines and the like for Social Media Power:

*Deltina Hay is the principal of Social Media Power, a Web 2.0 development firm in Austin. Ms. Hay's graduate education in computer science, applied mathematics, and psychology led her naturally to social media consulting. Find out more about using social media and Web 2.0 tools from her new straight forward, easy-to-follow e-book on social media marketing and Web 2.0.*

The term "social media" links to SocialMediaPower.com and "social media marketing" links to the e-book page on that site. We are also careful not to clutter these bios with links—two is a good limit. Search engine robots consider external links that are similar to meta keywords very relevant and will increase your page rank accordingly.

# FeedBurner

FeedBurner[20] is a free service offered by Google that helps you manage your feed subscriptions, submit your feed to directories, promote your feed, troubleshoot your feed, and advertise your feed.

### Burning Your Feed

By "burning" your feed to FeedBurner, all you are doing is creating an alternate URL for your feed that looks something like: "http://feeds. feedburner.com/YourBlogName." Doing this allows you to use the services that FeedBurner offers. This does not, however, negate your original feed URL—you can use either one of these URLs to represent your feed. If you choose to create a FeedBurner URL, you should use it to represent your RSS feed as much as possible—as opposed to the original feed URL—since the FeedBurner service will only record stats for subscriptions to the URL they create for you.

---

[20] http://www.feedburner.com

To burn your feed, first get an account with Google, then while logged in to your Google account, go to the FeedBurner site. Figure 3.31 shows the FeedBurner screen where you can then enter your feed URL to burn. If you are using a WordPress blog for your feed, then your feed URL is "http://www.yourblogURL.com/feed." The next screen lets you change the name of your feed URL (see Figure 3.32). Once your feed is activated, you can start using the FeedBurner services.

## Figures 3.31 & 3.32. Burning a Feed to FeedBurner

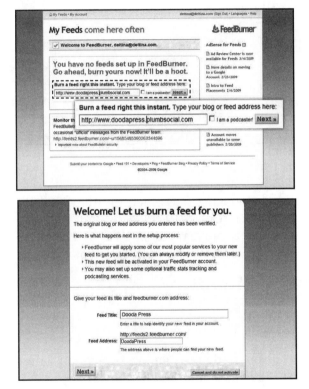

## Analyze Menu

Figure 3.33 shows the FeedBurner Analyze screen. From here you can see statistics on all of the subscriptions to your feed or blog broken down by feed reader and type of subscription. There is also a nice map overlay feature that shows where your subscribers are located.

## Figure 3.33. FeedBurner Analyze Menu

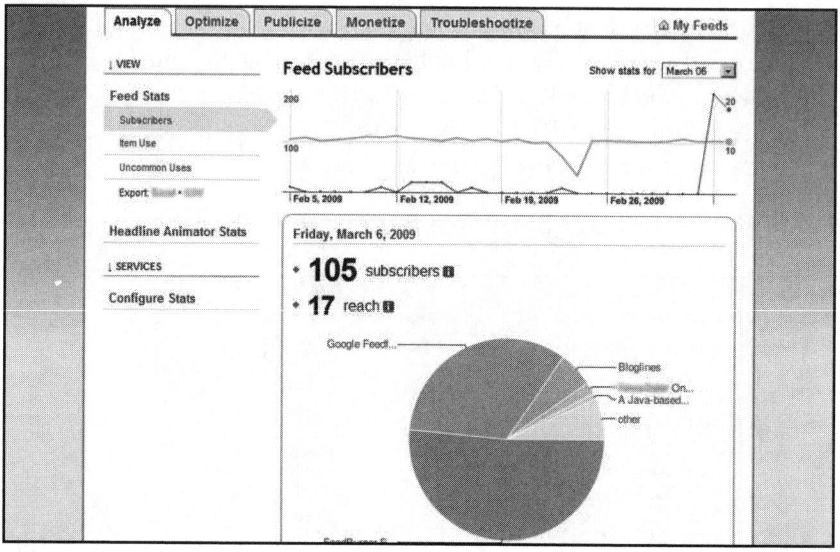

## Optimize Menu

From the Optimize menu (see Figure 3.34), activate the following services: "Browser Friendly," "Smart Feed," "FeedFlare," and "Geotag." These services help get your feed maximum exposure in the Social Web and make subscribing to your feed much easier for your visitors.

Activate "Link Splicer" if you have a lot of links saved to a social bookmarking site like Delicious.com.

Add your logo to your feed with "Feed Image Burner."

Activate the "Event Feed" if you have an Upcoming.org account, or use Google Calendar to keep track of upcoming events.

## Publicize Menu

"Headline Animators" are nice for advertising your feed as a banner on other sites and in emails. You can create any number of banners or email signatures.

Use "BuzzBoost" to show your feed on other sites—you can even combine more than one feed using this feature. This works great for cross-promoting your feeds if you have multiple feeds and/or blogs.

## Figure 3.34. FeedBurner Optimize Menu

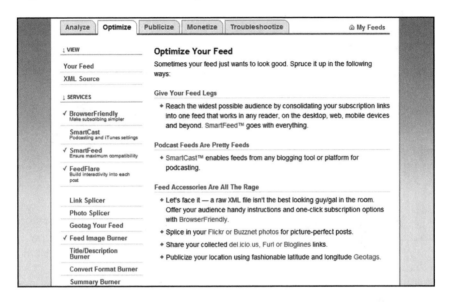

Using "Email Subscriptions," you can design custom emails of your feed entries along with a form to place on your site so that users can subscribe. Figure 3.35 shows how FeedBurner generates code for you to copy and paste onto your blog or Website so that visitors can easily subscribe to your feed via email. Figure 3.36 shows this code in action.

## Figure 3.35. Creating a FeedBurner Email Widget

"PingShot" should be one of the first things you do once you burn your feed. FeedBurner will automatically ping (notify) some of the most important feed services each time you update your feed. See "About Pinging" in the "Directories" section below.

### Figure 3.36. FeedBurner Email Widget on Website

Once you have a substantial number of feed subscriptions, use "FeedCount" to add a feed count chicklet to show it off.

"Chicklet Chooser" offers some nice feed subscription icons to place on your blog or Website. You should do this as soon as you burn your feed, so you make your feed available to your site visitors right away. Figures 3.37 and 3.38 show the different options for your "chicklet." Once you choose your chicklet, you can copy the generated code and place it on your blog or Website.

### Figure 3.37. FeedBurner Chicklet Chooser, Top

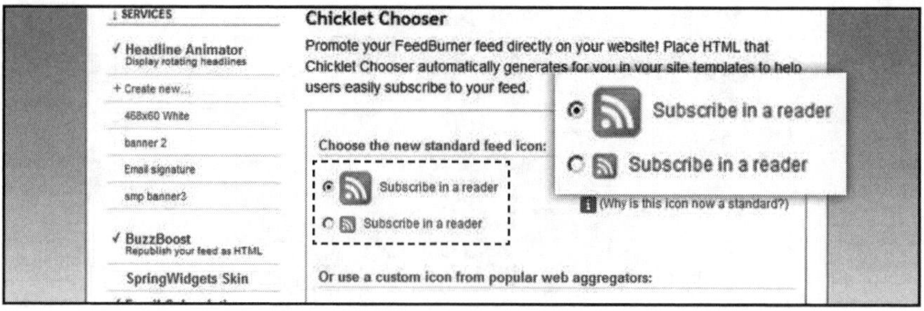

## Figure 3.38. FeedBurner Chicklet Chooser, Bottom

## Burning More than One Feed

You can burn as many feeds as you like on FeedBurner. In previous sections we discussed breaking your feeds up by topic using categories. If you are using WordPress, you can burn more than one feed based on categories. Each blog category in WordPress (version 2.7.1 and greater) has its own feed URL, based on the following structure: "http://www.YourBlogURL. com/category/categoryname/feed" where "categoryname" is the category name in WordPress. So, using the category name, you can burn a feed containing only the posts that are assigned that category. Figure 3.39 shows the Social Media Power feed that only includes posts assigned to the category "chapter."

## Figure 3.39. Feed URL for Specific Category

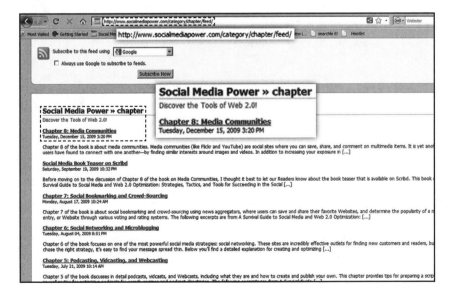

# RSS Feed and Blog Directories

These sites are called many things: blog directories, RSS feed indexes, blog and RSS feed search engines, etc., but they all have the same thing in common. They are all places you want your blog or RSS feed to show up if someone searches with your chosen key terms.

To avoid confusion, they will be referred to only as "directories" from here on. You can assume a directory is for both blogs and RSS feeds unless specified otherwise.

## About Pinging

One of the things that makes blogs and RSS feeds so accessible is their pinging system. Pinging means that when you post an entry to your blog or RSS feed, certain directories and aggregators are automatically notified or "pinged" that your blog has a new entry. This keeps the directories up-to-date and eliminates the need for you to ping them yourself.

WordPress notifies Ping-O-Matic[21] each time there is a new post to your blog. You can use the service to ping your blog manually, too. Figure 3.40 shows the directories that Ping-O-Matic notifies.

### Figure 3.40. Ping-O-Matic Pinging Service

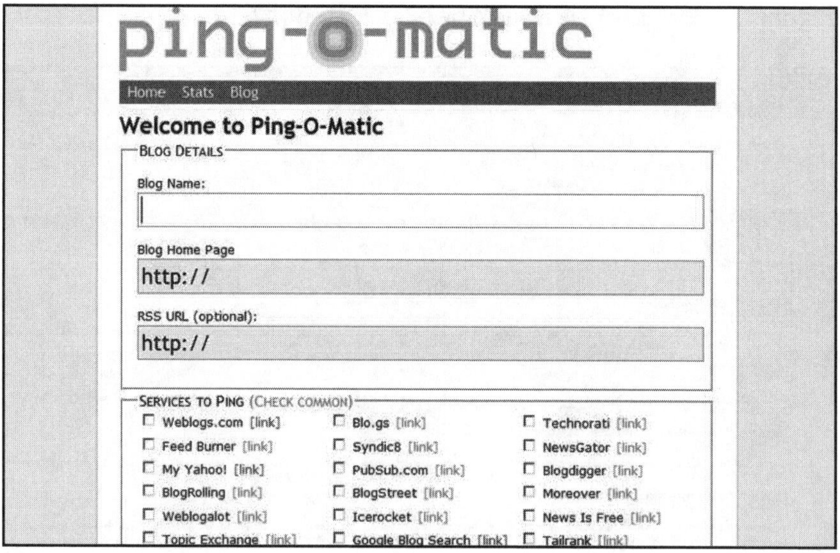

[21] http://pingomatic.com/

If you have burned your feed to FeedBurner and activated "PingShot" (see page 86), each service shown in Figure 3.41 will be notified each time you have a new feed or blog entry.

## Figure 3.41. FeedBurner's PingShot Service

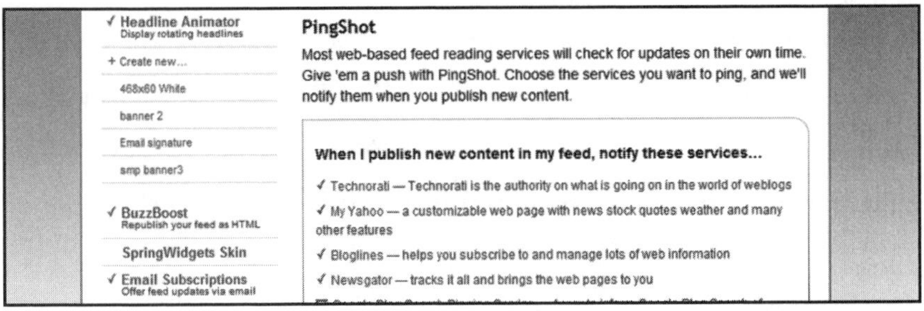

This does not mean, however, that you do not need to manually add your blogs and feeds to these directories. The pinging system only notifies a directory that your blog has a new entry; it does not list your blog for you in the directory. Besides, you want to do this manually so that you can put in place good tags and descriptions using your best key terms.

## Submitting to Directories

When submitting your blog or feed to directories, complete the submission forms thoroughly. Use a cheat sheet like the one in Figure 3.42 so you have the necessary information on hand to copy and paste

## Figure 3.42. Blog Directory Cheat Sheet

RSS Feed/Blog Information Sheet
For Submitting to Directories

Feed Name: Social Media Power

Feed URL: http://feeds.feedburner.com/SocialMediaPower

Feed Description: Tips and tools for social media marketing, Web 2.0 optimization, building WordPress sites, social networking, social bookmarking, crowd sourcing, and social media newsrooms, including social media ebooks and wordpress themes.

Feed Image URL: http://www.socialmediapower.com/images/smpWeb.jpg

Feed Tags/Categories: social media, social media marketing, web 2.0, social media ebooks, wordpress sites, social networking, social bookmarking, wordpress themes, social media newsrooms

when submitting, as well as a sheet like Figure 3.43 to keep track of your submissions. These forms are also available on the resource CD.

## Figure 3.43. Blog Directory Submission Tracking Form

| Date | Site or Service Name | Site URL | Type of Service | Notes | Upkeep |
|---|---|---|---|---|---|
| RSS Feed and Blog Directory Submissions for: Social Media Power | | | | | |
| 1/02/09 | Google Reader | http://www.google.com/reader | Reader | Opened an account and added feed to personal page. | None |
| 1/02/09 | Technorati | http://www.technorati.com | Blog Directory | Claimed blog and completed profile. Added description and tags. | Return and check that blog is being updated regularly and how others are saving, tagging, and commenting on posts |
| 1/02/09 | RSS Network | http://www.rss-network.com/submitrss.php | RSS feed index | Needed to choose category and sub-category. Chose Internet Feeds/Marketing | None |

## An Example

Technorati is probably the most popular blog directory. In order to "claim" your blog, you need to get an account. Once you have an account, you can claim all of your blogs. Figure 3.44 shows how to create a good description and tags. Again, use your best key terms both as tags and in your blog's description.

## Figure 3.44. Claiming a Blog in Technorati

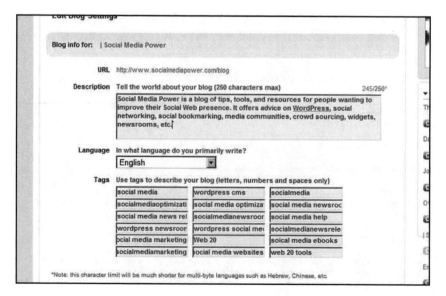

Fill out your profiles completely when joining these sites. If a potential reader or customer discovers your blog or feed on one of these sites they may want to learn more about you by exploring your profile. Don't rob yourself of the opportunity to put your best foot forward.

Always read a directory's submission guidelines before submitting your feed or blog. Some directories are strictly news-based or have themes or regional appeal that may not be a good fit for your blog or feed.

## Finding Directories

There are many feed and blog directories out there. Some of them are more important than others, but it is never a bad idea to get your blog initially listed in all of the directories that are good fits.

To get you started, RSS-specifications[22] has a good list of RSS feed directories, and Blog-connections has a nice list of blog directories[23]. Refer to the resource CD for an extensive list of directories.

If you want to know the most important directories, check which sites Ping-O-Matic or FeedBurner submit to. See Figures 3.40 and 3.41 on page 89.

## Submission Services and Software

To save time, and perhaps get more exposure, you can use submission software like RSS Submit from Dummy Software,[24] or a submission service like FeedShot.[25]

If you do go with a service, be certain it is a reputable company. You can hurt your standing with directories by submitting spam without even realizing you are doing it. Some services use "bots" to submit your information, and that is a violation of the terms of many directories.

---

[22] http://www.rss-specifications.com/rss-submission.htm

[23] http://www.blog-connection.com/submit-blogs.htm

[24] http://dummysoftware.com

[25] http://www.feedshot.com/

# Other Ways to Promote Your Blog or Feed

## Add Your Feed to Feed Readers

The best way to get your feed listed in the top feed readers is to get an account with them and subscribe to your own feed. See "The Feed Reader" section on page 54. Be sure to get accounts with NetVibes,[26] PageFlakes,[27] Google Reader,[28] iGoogle,[29] My.Yahoo,[30] and My.MSN.[31]

## Social Networking and Other Social Sites

In Chapter 12: "Pulling It All Together" we discuss integrating as many of your social tools as possible. For instance, you can pipe your feeds or blogs directly into your LinkedIn account, Facebook page and profile, Twitter account, Squidoo Lens, etc.

Whenever you implement a new social tool or get an account with a social networking site, check to see if adding one or more feeds or blogs to your account is an option.

## Feed Widgets

Figure 3.45 shows part of Social Media Power's front page. From here visitors can subscribe to their feed using the "Subscribe" button, which is an "AddtoAny" feed widget placed on their site (see page 58). Visitors can also subscribe to the Social Media Power feed by clicking on the Widgetbox[32] widget that says, "Get my blog as a widget from Widgetbox." Clicking on this box reveals a stylized feed that can be customized by the user. Read more about feed widgets in Chapter 9: "Widgets & Badges."

[26] http://www.netvibes.com/
[27] http://www.pageflakes.com/
[28] www.google.com/reader
[29] http://www.google.com/ig
[30] my.yahoo.com
[31] http://msn.com
[32] http://www.widgetbox.com

## Figure 3.45. Feed Widgets on SocialMediaPower.com

## Feed Widgets

Figure 3.45 shows part of Social Media Power's front page. From here visitors can subscribe to their feed using the "Subscribe" button, which is an "AddtoAny" feed widget placed on their site (see page 58). Visitors can also subscribe to the Social Media Power feed by clicking on the Widgetbox[32] widget that says, "Get my blog as a widget from Widgetbox." Clicking on this box reveals a stylized feed that can be customized by the user. Read more about feed widgets in Chapter 9: "Widgets & Badges."

## Figure 3.46. Sharing Sites Using Social Bookmarking Widgets

[32] http://www.widgetbox.com

### Figure 3.47. Sharing Posts Using Social Bookmarking Widgets

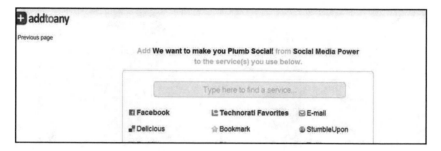

## Keeping Your Feed Healthy

It would be nice if you could create a feed once and assume it will never go out-of-date or that it will remain error free, but that is not the case. And, if you are not monitoring your feed subscriptions regularly, you may not even notice there is a problem.

If your feeds are burned to FeedBurner, go to the "Troubleshootize" menu to troubleshoot any problems with your feed. Running the "Feed Medic" utility (see Figure 3.48) on each of your feeds periodically can help avoid problems.

### Figure 3.48. FeedBurner's Feed Medic

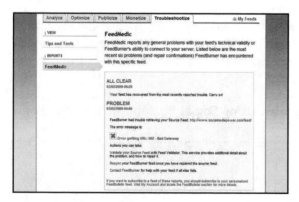

You can also go to W3's Feed Validation Service[33] to validate and troubleshoot your feed if necessary.

---

[33] http://validator.w3.org/feed/

# An Optimization Plan for Your Blog or RSS Feed

- Your Content
  - › Edit your content
  - › Optimize titles, categories, tags, and links
- Attach signatures to your posts
- Search Engine Optimization (SEO)
  - › Implement "The All In One SEO" pack in WordPress
  - › Use pretty permalinks
  - › Optimize external links to your site
- FeedBurner
  - › Burn your feed or blog
  - › Activate services
    - Browser Friendly
    - Smart Feed
    - FeedFlare
    - Feed Image Burner
    - Email Subscriptions
    - PingShot
    - Chicklet Chooser
- Directories
  - › Submit feed or blogs to directories
  - › Use FeedBurner's PingShot
  - › Use feed submission software or service
- Other Ways to Optimize
  - › Submit to feed readers
  - › Advertise your feed
  - › Add to the rest of your social presence
  - › Use feed widgets
  - › Place social bookmarking buttons

This plan is recreated as a form on the resource CD.

# This Chapter on the Resource CD

- Further Reading
- Linkable Resources
- Fillable Forms:
  - › Planning Your RSS Feed Worksheet
  - › RSS Feed Entries Worksheet
  - › Planning Your Blog Worksheet
  - › Blog Entries Worksheet
  - › Blog Directory Cheat Sheet
  - › Blog Directory Submission Tracking Form
  - › Blog/RSS Feed Optimization Plan

# 4 Building a WordPress Powered Website

## Using WordPress as a CMS

If you are in a place where you can rebuild your Website or start a new one, it is recommended that you use a content management system like WordPress to build it. RSS feed and widget technology is already built into the WordPress platform, so social media and Web 2.0 optimization can be achieved easily and naturally.

This chapter will only cover *some* of the features WordPress has to offer. We will only focus on the essentials you need to create and maintain your site. You will find, however, a plethora of information in the WordPress documentation,[1] as well as on the WordPress forums.[2] There are many people on these forums who are more than happy to help you out.

The examples used in this chapter are based on WordPress version 3.0. Be sure to check WordPress.org for changes that have taken place in the latest version of WordPress.

[1]http://wordpress.org/
[2]http://wordpress.org/support/

## What Does It Mean to Use WordPress as a CMS?

By definition, a CMS is an application that is used to create, edit, manage, and publish content in an organized way. Web applications like WordPress, Joomla!,[3] and Drupal[4] do this by storing information in a database, and using scripting languages like PHP to access the information and place it on a Website.

Using a common scripting language like PHP makes it easy for developers to create add-ons or "plugins" for anybody to upload and use with a particular CMS. Plugins are applications that perform a specialized function that the original CMS may be lacking. Examples of plugins include search engine optimization applications, contact forms, survey applications, and image galleries.

CMS applications also use cascading style sheets (CSS) to make it easy for users to change the look and feel of their site, and for developers to contribute templates or themes that others can use to customize their sites. Theme developers also use PHP to control the overall functionality of a CMS.

WordPress is one of the easiest content management systems to learn and there are countless plugins and themes to choose from. The remainder of this chapter will be dedicated to showing you how to build a Website using WordPress, so many of these definitions will become more clear as we progress.

## On Open Source Etiquette

The CMS applications discussed in this section are all open source applications. What that means to you is that the applications are free, as are most of the plugins and themes developed for them. To a developer, it means that there is a vast community of people working together to create a quality application they can be proud of.

The developers have put a lot of time into these projects. Please show them respect by:

---

[3]http://www.joomla.org/
[4]http://www.drupal.org/

- Making donations to the open source developers whose plugins you use regularly
- Never deleting the credits from the footer of a theme or a plugin.

When using the support forums of an open source application:

- Always search the forums thoroughly for an answer to your question before posting.
- Give back if you can: Check the recent posts for questions from newcomers you might be able to answer.

# Diversity of WordPress Sites

Many people shy away from using a CMS because they fear their site will look too "templated." The figures throughout this chapter show a variety of sites that were all built using the WordPress platform. These sites seem to have little in common, but, as we will see in the next section, every site is composed of the same general content areas that are easily customized.

These sites began with an existing WordPress theme that was customized to fit their needs. Customizing a theme is not a difficult task, especially if all you want to change are colors and images. There are even themes that come with built-in options to change colors, header images, fonts, and other features.

## Figure 4.1. Deltina.com

## Figure 4.2. PureSoapbox.com

## Figure 4.3. RicWilliams.com

## Figure 4.4. PlumbWebSolutions.com, Part One

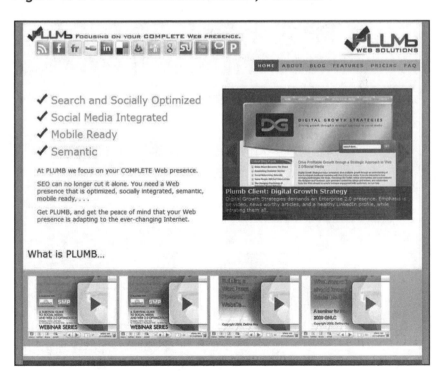

## Figure 4.5. ChavahAima.plumbsocial.com

## Figure 4.6. SocialMediaPower.com

## Figure 4.7. DaltonPublishing.com

## Figure 4.8. PlumbWebSolutions.com, Part Two

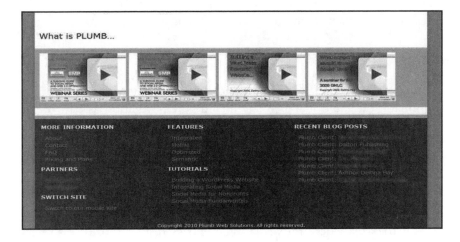

# The Anatomy of a WordPress Site

Before we go into specifics, let's look at the main elements of a WordPress site. Each example in this chapter has these general areas, though represented a little differently. Refer to the images on the previous pages.

## The Header

The header area is where the main header image is located, along with the title and tag line of the blog site. It is also where the navigation menu is typically located, if the theme has one.

The header can be as simple as the blog title and description as in Figure 4.3, composed of a custom header image like Figure 4.2, or a combination of both as in Figure 4.7. The header can contain other elements, too, like the search box in Figure 4.6, or the rotating images in Figure 4.5.

The header is usually the first element you want to customize to suit your own needs. For instance, you could easily replace the entire header with your own image and/or logo of the same dimensions. This is explained in greater detail when we discuss choosing themes and customizing.

## Navigation Menu

The navigation menu is usually found near the header of the site, but is optional. You could just as easily include the navigation as part of the sidebar elements. As you can see in Figures 4.1 through 4.8, you have a lot of choices for styling your navigation menu. You can work with the navigation style that comes with a theme or create your own.

## The Main Body Area

This is the area where the actual blog entries reside. WordPress refers to this as the "content area." You can easily customize the content area by changing how many blog entries display on a page. There are many options on how to display blogs. A common method is to display snippets of a blog with a "read more" option.

You have the option of having either a static home page as your front page, or your blog entries as the front page. If you choose a static home page, your blog will become another page that you would add to your navigation menu, as opposed to the home page. Figures 4.3 and 4.5 on pages 101 and 102 show a site with blog entries on the front page. Figures 4.4 and 4.7 show a static home page.

The content area is usually located in the middle of the site as in Figure 4.2 on page 100. They also could be off to the side or on the top as in Figures 4.5, 4.6, and 4.7 (pages 102 and 103).

## The Sidebars

The columns on either side of the content area (or below in some cases) are called "sidebars." They hold many of the other elements of your site, such as links, categories, search tools, recent blog entries, archived entries, photos, video streams, RSS feeds, widgets, badges, advertisements, etc. Sidebars are also where you implement many of the plugins you add to the site.

Typically, sidebars are on either side of the content area, as seen in Figure 4.2 on page 100. Many themes get more creative with their placement. In Figure 4.6 on page 102, there is one wide sidebar on the top of the left area of the site and two smaller sidebars underneath the wider one. Figure 4.7 on page 103 shows three sidebars under the content area.

## The Footer

This is the area of the site where credit is given. Do not remove the credit to WordPress or to the theme designer from the footer of a WordPress site. There are a lot of people who have donated their time to this free, open source project, and it is never good form not to give them due credit. You should place your own copyright statement in the footer as well. Figure 4.8 on page 103 shows a footer area. Figure 4.8 also demonstrates a footer area containing three additional sidebars or columns of information.

## Sidebar Widgets

Sidebar widgets are the different elements or modules you can place on your sidebars. You can have as many of these widgets as you like and can arrange them however you choose.

Each widget performs a specific function. For example, in Figure 4.3 (page 101) on the left sidebar of the site, the widgets are:

- "Ric's Books"—graphical links to purchase the author's books.
- "Blog Categories"—a drop down list of blog categories.
- "Ric's Art"—a Flickr widget that displays the author's art and photos in a little flash "badge."
- "Share & Enjoy"—a series of widgets that allow visitors to share the site in the Social Web.

In Figure 4.1, on the right sidebar, some of the widgets are:

- A widget from FriendFeed (at top) showing all of the places this author is on the Social Web.
- A Facebook Fan Page widget that shows the fans of this author's page and a way for visitors to "like" or join her page.
- "Downloads"—links to a couple of external sites.

WordPress comes with a number of standard widgets that perform functions specific to the functionality of your WordPress site, such as listing blog categories (Figure 4.3), search features, recent posts (Figure 4.7), tag clouds, etc.

You can create your own custom widgets easily by placing text or HTML/Java code in what is called a "text" widget. This is how you create most of the widgets and badges you accumulate from the Social Web.

Some custom widgets in our examples include:

- The Flickr badge in Figure 4.3
- The buy-now buttons for books on Figures 4.2, 4.3, and 4.5
- The widgets for sharing on social sites in Figures 4.3 and 4.5
- The widgets used for banner advertisements in Figure 4.6

For a more detailed discussion of widgets and badges, go to Chapter 9: "Widgets & Badges."

# Static Pages

Static pages are the pages of a WordPress site that do not contain blog entries—just like a regular Website page. You can link to these pages from the navigation menu. Figures 4.9 and 4.10 demonstrate static pages. You can have as many pages as you like on your site and it is easy to add and populate them.

## Figure 4.9. DaltonPublishing.com, Static Page

## Figure 4.10. DigitalGrowthStrategy.com, Static Page

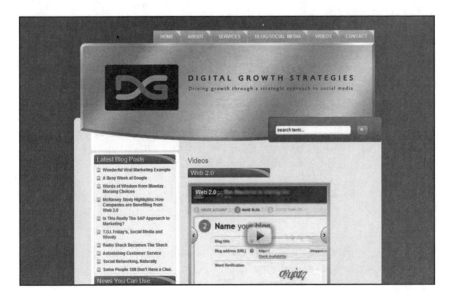

# Installing WordPress as a CMS

## Know the Difference Between Your *Domain* Account and Your *Hosting* Account

When you register your domain name, an account is created for you with the company that sold you the domain name. This account has its own user name and password that you can use to change settings or account information. Just owning the domain name, however, does not mean you have a place to put a Website. You need a hosting account for that.

If you get your hosting account with a different company than the one that sold you the domain name, you need to change what are called "name servers" in your *domain* account that tell the domain name to point to the proper *hosting* account. This is not difficult to do and most hosting companies have good instructions to show you how.

### Choosing a Hosting Account for Your WordPress Site

There are some minimum requirements[5] that your hosting account must have in order to run WordPress properly:

- PHP 4.3 or greater
- MySQL 4.1.2 or greater
- The mod_rewrite Apache module

Apache or Litespeed is also HIGHLY recommended.

Your host will be able to tell you whether or not they meet the requirements.

**A word of caution:** Some hosting companies may meet these requirements, but if yours is a free account (having shared servers), many WordPress features and plugins will not run properly. Godaddy.com's free account option falls into this category.

WordPress has a few hosting companies they recommend.[6] I use Westhost.com because of their reliability and exceptional tech support.

---

[5]http://wordpress.org/about/requirements/
[6]http://wordpress.org/hosting/

Their personal starter plan runs under $10 a month and is all you will likely need.

Once you have a hosting account that runs WordPress effectively, be sure to point your domain to your new hosting account by changing your name servers, if applicable. Your hosting company can give you instructions for your particular account.

## Be Careful of the One-Click WordPress Install Feature Offered by Many Hosts

Installing WordPress as a CMS means that you are going to install it into the root directory as opposed to a subdirectory of your hosting account. Most of the one-click install options offered by hosting companies install WordPress in a subdirectory and preassign the database name. In order for WordPress to power your entire site, however, it needs to be installed into the root directory, and you also want to have more control over the name of your database for security reasons.

# FTP Access

FTP stands for File Transfer Protocol. FTP is the means by which you upload files to your hosting site. You need to use FTP to upload WordPress files if you decide to install it yourself, as well as to upload themes and plugins as we discuss later in this chapter. Luckily, there is a fantastic plugin for Firefox that makes it easy for you to gain FTP access to your site.

First, if you are not using it already, download and install Mozilla Firefox.[7] Next, download and install the plugin FireFTP.[8] Go to Tools on your Firefox task bar and open FireFTP. Create an account to connect you to your hosting account. Contact your host for that information. A good hosting company has tech support readily available to walk you through how to upload files using FireFTP.

One free desktop FTP application is Filezilla.[9] Two good (but not free) applications are WS_FTP[10] and CuteFTP.[11] WS_FTP is best for PCs, while CuteFTP is best for Macs.

---

[7]http://www.mozilla.com
[8]http://fireftp.mozdev.org/
[9] http://filezilla-project.org/
[10]www.ipswitch.com/WS_FTP
[11]http://www.cuteftp.com/products/ftp_clients.asp

## Installing WordPress

Some of the preliminary steps required to install WordPress can be a bit involved, so we have reserved that topic for Appendix A: "Installing WordPress." This appendix provides a step-by-step installation guide for the do-it-yourselfer. Once WordPress is installed, continue on to the next section of this chapter.

# A Brief Look at the WordPress Dashboard

Figure 4.11 shows a typical WordPress dashboard. From here, you post blog entries, create and edit pages, install plugins and themes, and manage all of the settings of your site.

From the "Posts" menu you can write or edit blog posts and manage blog categories and tags. You can upload and organize images, audio, and video files from the "Media" menu. From the "Links" menu you can add and organize your links. The "Pages" menu is where you create or edit your static pages. The "Comments" menu is for viewing and approving other's comments to your blog posts. The "Appearance" menu is where you customize themes, manage your sidebar widgets, and create your navigation menu. You install and manage your plugins from the

**Figure 4.11. WordPress Dashboard**

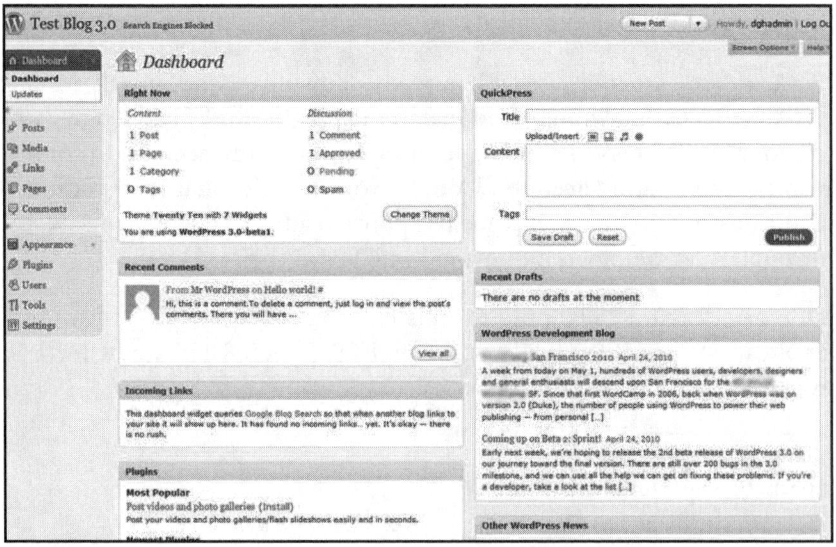

"Plugins" menu, and manage authorized users from the "Users" menu. The "Tools" and "Settings" menus are where you manage the overall settings of your site, as well as most of the plugins you install.

# Important Initial Settings

Before you start to build your site, there are some important initial settings that should be in place, and tasks that should be performed.

## Security Settings

Open source platforms like WordPress can be a target for hackers, but there are precautions you can take to protect your site. We took a couple of these precautions when we first installed WordPress in Appendix A: We gave our database a name other than "wordpress" and gave our tables a prefix other than "wp." These safeguards are a good first step.

The next step is to always keep the latest version of WordPress installed. The developers are continuously adding security fixes and other features. Most of the time, this keeps your site secure—this and good password protection.

In the interest of security, you should change your administrative password as soon as you have installed WordPress. Sign in to WordPress using the user name and password that WordPress sent you during the installation. At the WordPress dashboard, go to "Users/Authors and Users," click on the admin user, and change the password.

The final step to securing your WordPress site is to install the WP-Security Scan plugin,[12] but we will cover that in the "Plugins You Will Want to Install Right Away" section on page 121.

## Other Settings and Tasks to Complete Right Away

### Permalinks

Go to "Settings/Permalinks" and set your permalink structure to anything but the default. See Figure 4.12 on the next page. This keeps your links

---

[12]http://wordpress.org/extend/plugins/wp-security-scan/

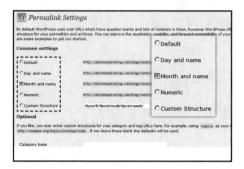

### Figure 4.12. Permalink Settings

optimized for search engines. If you are interested, you can read more about permalinks on the WordPress codex.[13]

### Creating a Static Home Page

If you want your front page to serve as a normal home page, you need to complete a couple of preliminary tasks. First, create two pages named "Home" and "Blog." Refer to the "Building Your Pages" section on page 124 if you do not know how to create pages yet.

Once you have these two pages created, go to "Settings/Reading" and change the settings according to Figure 4.13.

### Figure 4.13. WordPress Settings

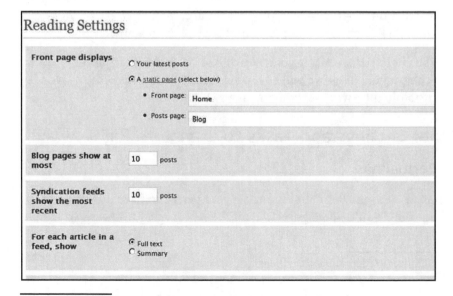

[13]http://codex.wordpress.org/Using_Permalinks

There are many other settings to examine and set to your needs, but the ones discussed here should be done before you start testing themes or populating your site.

# Planning Your Site

Make an *ambitious* list of what you would like to have on your site. Don't hold back on any idea you may have for your site based on an assumption that it will be too difficult or too expensive to implement. Chances are that even if the function is not built into WordPress, somebody has written a plugin to accomplish it.

Search the plugins available for WordPress.[14] They can give you ideas on the types of things you can add to your site. You will discover that you can easily utilize plugins to accomplish seemingly difficult tasks.

Beyond the normal functionality of a Website, I find these are pretty typical functions most entrepreneurs, small businesses, authors, and publishers are looking for:

- Image galleries
- Streaming video
- E-commerce
- Amazon widgets
- Blogs/Podcasts/Vidcasts
- Random quote generators
- Newsletters
- RSS feed subscription sign up
- Bookmarking/crowd-sourcing buttons
- Surveys and Polls
- Mailing list sign-up
- RSS feeds from other sources
- Events listings

---

[14]http://wordpress.org/extend/plugins/

- Forms for submissions
- Banner advertising
- Widgets from other social sites like Facebook and Twitter
- Social media newsrooms

You should also make a list of the types of widgets you want to have on your sidebars (see the discussion on sidebar widgets on page 105).

Once you have the list of features and widgets you want on your site, draw out a plan for where each of them will be placed on your site. This helps you know what to look for in a theme.

Next, make a list of the static pages your site needs to start. These may include an "about" page that tells visitors about you or your site, a gallery or portfolio page, a contact page, etc. You can add as many pages as you need, whenever you like, so just outline the ones you know you need right out of the gate.

**Refer to the resource CD for a series of forms to help you plan and map out your WordPress Website.**

# Themes

Armed with a thorough plan, move on to choosing a theme. WordPress themes control more that just the look and feel of your site—they ultimately determine your site's functionality.

Look at the figures throughout this chapter. They demonstrate how themes control the number and placement of the sidebars, the placement and behavior of the navigation menus, the layout of the pages, the fonts and colors, and so forth.

It is important that you understand that you can change the theme you use for your WordPress site and that it will not affect the content on your site. This is one of the features that is so appealing about a CMS: You can easily change or update a Website with little effort.

## Choosing a Theme

You can search the WordPress theme directory and install themes right from the WordPress backend. Go to "Appearance/Themes" and click on the "Install Themes" tab. Figure 4.14 shows the resulting screen. The search feature allows you to search the WordPress theme directory using many standard parameters including colors, special features, position of sidebars, number of columns—or you can just as easily enter your own search terms. Note: Total columns include the sidebars and the content area, so a theme with three columns would have two sidebars.

### Figure 4.14. Finding and Installing a WordPress Theme

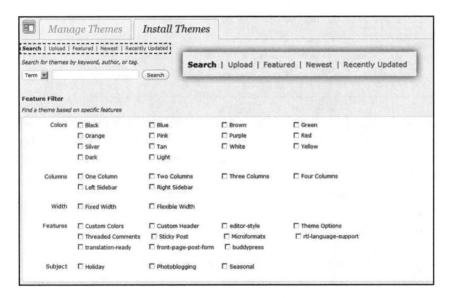

Figure 4.15 shows the resulting screen with a search for themes with built-in options. From here, you can preview themes, see how others have rated them, and get more details about them. You can also install the themes you like right from this screen.

Use your plan to decide whether you need a one, two, or three-column theme (there are also four-column themes). When in doubt, decide on one more column than you think you need. It is easier to populate an extra column (or remove it) than it is to try and cram too much onto too few columns.

## Figure 4.15. Finding and Installing a WordPress Theme

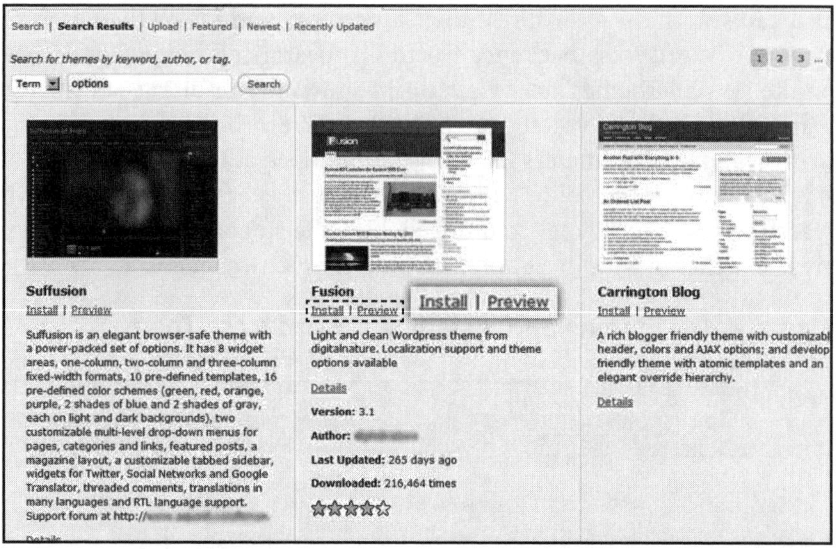

Choose at least 12 themes that you like. You may find that for various reasons you will not be able to use many themes that you choose. Try to make your choice based only on the overall look and feel of a theme, with the idea that the colors, fonts, images, and most anything else can be customized to fit your needs.

## Installing Your Theme

If your theme is within the WordPress directory, all you do is click "Install" when searching themes as mentioned in the previous section. If you downloaded your theme from somewhere else, click on the "Upload" tab under the "Install Themes" tab as seen in Figure 4.14.

Once your theme is installed, go to "Appearance/Themes" and click on the "Manage Themes" tab. You will see the theme is now listed as an available theme for you to select. Simply click on the theme you want to make current.

You can read more about installing and using themes at WordPress. org.[15]

---

[15]http://codex.wordpress.org/Using_Themes

## Customizing Your Theme

You may find that you would like a theme if only it had different colors, or the font were larger, or it had different images, etc. Many of those things are easily remedied, so do not give up on a theme too quickly.

Many themes automatically come with options that let you change the colors, fonts, or header images. This is demonstrated in Figure 4.16, which shows how you can customize the header in the WordPress default theme.

Even if a theme does not come with such options, all that is required to customize most themes is a little knowledge of cascading style sheets (CSS). Usually, the changes to a CSS file that you would want to make are minor, so don't be put off by this prospect.

There are good tutorials[16] for using CSS, and the forums at WordPress. org[17] are a fantastic resource. WordPress has a good section on the topic as well.[18]

### Figure 4.16. Theme Options in WordPress

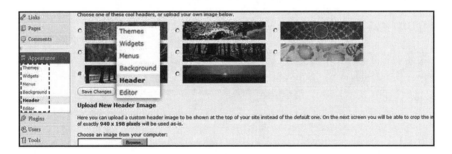

---

[16]http://www.w3schools.com/css/
[17]http://wordpress.org/support/
[18]http://codex.wordpress.org/CSS

# Plugins

Plugins are what give WordPress its tremendous power and flexibility. Most plugins can be found on the WordPress site[19]. As you browse these plugins, you soon realize that there is little you will not be able to do with your new Website.

Refer to your plan to decide the types of plugins you want to install. For instance, if your plan includes an image gallery, search for a plugin that displays images to your specifications. Sometimes it takes several tries before you find the best plugin for the job. If you cannot find the perfect plugin on the WordPress site, you can do a Google search for plugins to purchase as well.

## Choosing a Plugin

The "Plugins/Add New" screen is shown in Figure 4.17. From here, you can search for plugins using any search term. The most commonly searched terms are shown as a tag cloud. Figure 4.18 shows the resulting screen when a search for "statistics" is implemented. You can usually get a good feel for how a plugin fits your needs by its description. Pay

**Figure 4.17. Choosing a WordPress Plugin**

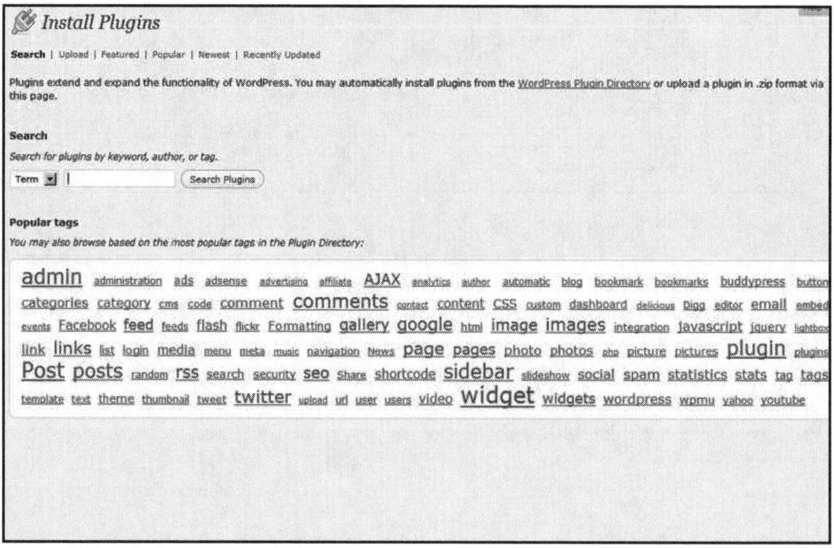

[19]http://wordpress.org/extend/plugins/

attention to the rating, how many times a plugin has been downloaded, and whether it is compatible with your version of WordPress.

## Installing and Setting Up Your Plugins

To install a plugin that is in the WordPress directory, just click on the "Install Now" button. See Figure 4.18. You can upload and install plugins that are not in the directory from the "Plugins/Add New/Upload" tab. See Figure 4.17.

**Figure 4.18. Installing a WordPress Plugin**

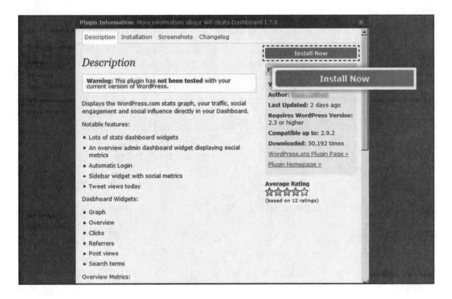

Figure 4.19 shows a version of the "Plugins/Installed" screen. Here is where you can manage your plugins by activating, deactivating, upgrading, etc. Note the options available under the "Plugins" and the "Settings" tabs. This is typically where the options for your installed plugins can be found. On this screen, you see options for the "WordPress. com Stats" and "Akismet Configuration" plugins under the "Plugins" tab, and for the "All in One SEO" and "IntenseDebate" plugins under the "Settings" tab.

Once a plugin is activated, read its documentation to learn how to integrate it into your WordPress site. A plugin should not be too complicated to implement. A general rule of thumb is this: If you can't get the plugin to work on the second try, get another plugin to accomplish the task at hand.

### Figure 4.19. Managing Plugins in WordPress

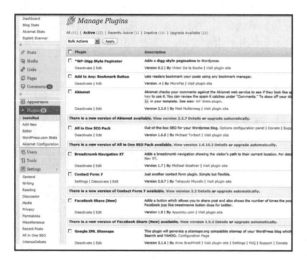

## Creating Your Navigation Menu

You can customize your navigation menu from the "Appearances/ Menus" screen. Figure 4.20 shows this screen. From here, you can create menu tabs for your site that link to pages, go to custom links anywhere on the Internet, or link to lists of posts by category. Note: The screen shot shown here is from the beta version of WordPress 3.0. Your version will likely look different, but the idea is the same.

In our example, we created a custom link to Deltina.com, and a tab that goes to our About page. Figure 4.21 shows the resulting custom navigation menu.

## Plugins You Want to Install Right Away

- Akismet: This plugin comes with WordPress and is used as a spam filter for blog comments.
- WordPress.com Stats:[20] This plugin tracks your blog statistics.

---

[20]http://wordpress.org/extend/plugins/stats/

**Figure 4.20. Custom Menu Feature in WordPress**

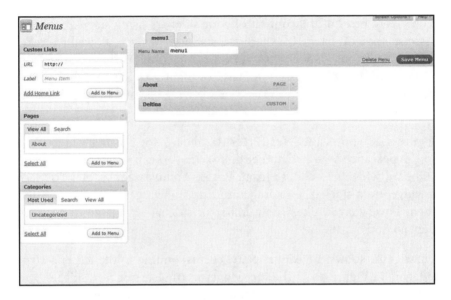

**Figure 4.21. Custom Menu in WordPress**

- WP-Security Scan:[21] This is the plugin that was mentioned in the section above on security. It is highly recommended that you install and activate this plugin.
- WordPress Exploit Scanner:[22] This plugin searches the files on your Website and the posts and comments tables of your database for anything suspicious.
- All in One SEO Pack:[23] This optimizes your site for search engines.

---

[21]http://wordpress.org/extend/plugins/wp-security-scan/

[22]http://wordpress.org/extend/plugins/exploit-scanner/

[23]http://wordpress.org/extend/plugins/all-in-one-seo-pack/

# Setting Up Your Sidebars

You create most of the content of your sidebars using sidebar widgets. As discussed on page 106, there are standard widgets as well as "text" widgets that you can populate with your own content. These text widgets can contain HTML, JavaScript, Flash, or plain text. Some of the plugins you install may also come as ready-made widgets you can place on your sidebars.

Figure 4.22 shows the WordPress dashboard for placing widgets (go to "Appearance/Widgets" to get there). As you can see, there are many standard widgets to choose from: Pages, Archives, Links, etc. To place a widget on a sidebar, just drag and drop the widget. You can position them however you like. The number of sidebars available to you will depend on your theme.

Figure 4.22 shows the widget panel corresponding to the left and right sidebars in Figure 4.23. The top widget in the left sidebar (Sidebar 1 in Figure 4.22) is a text widget containing HTML code that displays the title "Register for a Webinar!" along with its corresponding image. The second widget in that sidebar is a text widget that contains the code to display the Widgetbox.com widget (the "Get my blog as a widget from widgetbox" button). The next widget is a standard "Links" widget that displays the list of links that appear underneath the Widgetbox widget.

In the right sidebar of Figure 4.23 (Sidebar 2 in Figure 4.22), there are a number of text widgets that display content from other sites or perform functions.

Figure 4.24 shows the admin area where the HTML code is placed to create the "text" widget that displays the social media book with CD banner at the top of the sidebar (see Figure 4.23). We discuss this process at greater length in Chapter 9: "Widgets & Badges."

## Figure 4.22. Managing Widgets in WordPress

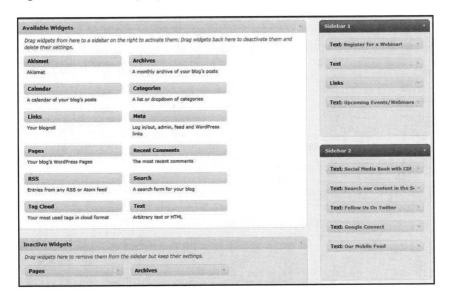

## Figure 4.23. Sidebar Widgets on a WordPress Page

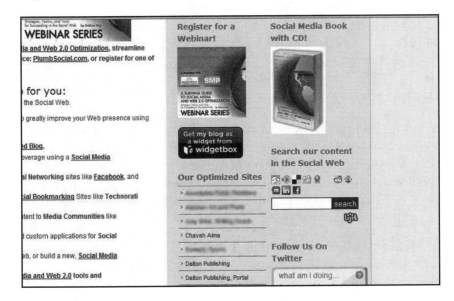

## Figure 4.24. Setting Up Sidebar Widgets in WordPress

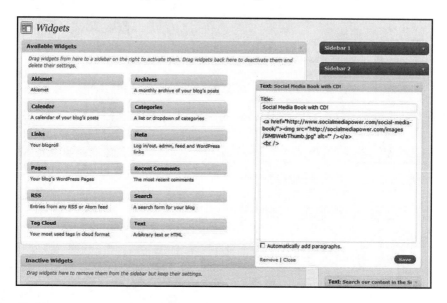

# Building Your Pages

The static pages of your WordPress site can contain the same content as any regular Website page (HTML page). You can create pages that contain simple text or pages as complex as fully interactive image or video galleries, and beyond.

## A Basic Page

Creating the pages of your WordPress site is a simple process. For a page that only contains text, go to "Pages/Add New." Put the name of your page as the title, the content of the page in the body area, and click "publish." Figure 4.25 shows the "About" page depicted in Figure 4.26. Note that the page is automatically added to your navigation menu, if your theme has one.

The above is really an oversimplified example of a WordPress page. There are many customization settings you can use to get your page closer to how you would like it to look or behave, such as whether you will allow comments, the order of the page in the navigation menu, whether it will

## Figure 4.25. Creating a Page in WordPress

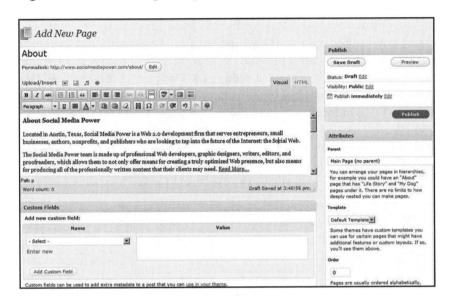

have images, or what its title and description will look like to search engines. Again, refer to WordPress[24] for more complete documentation.

## Figure 4.26. SocialMediaPower.com, Static Page

[24] http://codex.wordpress.org/Pages

## More Advanced Pages

As mentioned before, a WordPress page can accommodate just about anything a regular HTML page can. The example on page 101 demonstrated how using plugins can transform a WordPress page into anything from a gallery to a shopping cart. Figure 4.27 shows the HTML view of a WordPress page. You could, therefore, design your page in a WYSIWYG editor like Dreamweaver, and paste the resulting code into your WordPress page. The code in Figure 4.27 produces the home page shown in Figure 4.28.

### Figure 4.27. Creating an HTML Page in WordPress

### Figure 4.28. SocialMediaPower.com

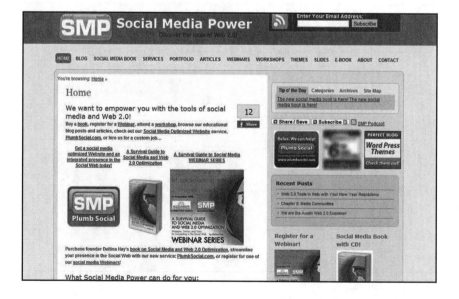

## Custom Page Templates

Notice how each of the pages we have demonstrated so far has the same sidebars, headers, etc. as the rest of the site. But what if you want a page that is different, like one with no sidebar, a different sidebar, or a different page header? That is not a problem with most themes as long as you are willing to do a little bit of coding.

Figure 4.29 shows a page from the same site as Figure 4.28, but with no sidebar. This page required a wider body area to accommodate the portfolio and was accomplished by creating a custom page template that did not include the PHP code that included sidebars. To learn how to create custom page templates go to the WordPress documentation.[25] There are also many themes that come with their own custom page templates.

### Figure 4.29. SocialMediaPower.com, Static Page

---

[25] http://codex.wordpress.org/Pages#Creating_Your_Own_Page_Template

## Posting Blog Entries

Now that your site is in place, you can start adding blog posts to keep it dynamic and interactive. Add blog posts by going to "Posts/Add New." Refer to Chapter 3: "RSS Feeds & Blogs" for following good blogging guidelines and creating optimized blog posts.

## This Chapter On The Resource CD

- Further Reading
- Linkable Resources
- Fillable Forms:
    › Planning Your WordPress Website, with Diagrams

# 5 Podcasting, Vidcasting, & Webcasting

A podcast is a series of audio or video files that is distributed over the Internet. What distinguishes a podcast from just any audio or video file you can download or stream from the Internet is that a podcast can be syndicated and subscribed to. This is because a podcast, like a blog, is an RSS feed. A podcast is really just a blog composed of episodes of audio or video entries rather than text, and can be subscribed to like any blog/ feed. You can even add podcast entries to an existing blog, rather than having a stand alone podcast.

Read Chapter 3: "RSS Feeds & Blogs," before proceeding, since most of the tools and tactics covered in that chapter apply to podcasts as well. Chapter 4: "Building a WordPress Powered Website" also provides a review of RSS feed and blogging technology.

Podcasts can include both audio and video files. There are other terms like vidcast and vlog that refer to video feeds, but in this book the term podcast refers to both types of files. All of the examples in this chapter are for audio files, but the same process applies equally to video files unless stated otherwise.

The general plan for creating and promoting your podcast looks something like this:

1.  Record and prepare a podcast episode (either audio or video).
2.  Upload the episode to the Internet.
3.  Publish the episode to a blog, Website, or service.
4.  Create your podcast feed.
5.  Burn your podcast feed to FeedBurner.
6.  Promote your podcast on your Website or blog, and in podcast directories.
7.  For each new podcast episode, repeat steps 1, 2, and 3.

# What Will Your Podcast Be About?

Before you create your first episode, you should be clear about the purpose of your podcast. Will you be recording interviews, lectures, or panel discussions? Clips of your own music? Reciting excerpts from your book? Reading stories for children? Or just recreating existing blog posts as podcast episodes? What is the premise of the podcast?

When people subscribe to your podcast they will have an expectation of consistency as to the topics your episodes will cover. So planning ahead at this stage is important.

# Publishing Options for Your Podcast

## Using a Blogging Platform

If you have an existing blog, this is a natural choice for publishing your podcasts. All you need to do is add podcast episodes in a way similar to how you add blog posts. Even if you only post podcasts and not blog posts, a blogging platform like WordPress is still the best solution, since all of the technology is already built in. There are also many good podcasting plugins for WordPress[1] that will help you streamline the process.

---

[1] http://wordpress.org/extend/plugins

## Publishing to Your Website

A podcast is an RSS feed, so to publish a podcast to your Website, you need to know how to create an RSS feed. Read about this in Chapter 3: "RSS Feeds & Blogs" and in Appendix B: "Creating Your Own RSS Feed," which also includes a section on podcasts.

You can also use software like FeedForAll to create your podcast feed. See the "Using Software to Create Your RSS Feed" section on page 63.

## Using a Service

There are a number of good services out there that can help you record, publish, and promote a podcast. Audio Acrobat[2] is one of them; HipCast[3] is another.

If you do not plan to have a blog any time soon, but still want to publish a podcast, using a service is a good solution.

# Creating and Uploading Podcast Episodes

## Preparing the Script and Key Terms

Below is a typical podcast script. You can get royalty-free music for your podcast episodes at a number of sites on the Internet.[4] Always make sure that the music you use is royalty-free and offered freely for use in podcasts, and give the author credit. This script outline can also be found on the resource CD.

- Opening (30-60 seconds)
  - › Introduce the podcast as a whole.
  - › This should be the same for each episode.
  - › Mention the name of the podcast, what its purpose is, and the URL where it can be found.
  - › Introduce yourself and who you are.
  - › Introduce the topic of the episode.

---

[2] http://www.audioacrobat.com/
[3] http://www.hipcast.com/
[4] http://www.podsafeaudio.com/

- › Mention the episode number.
- › Introduce guests if you have any.
- Opening Jingle (30 seconds)
- Main Topics (6 to 12 minutes)
  - › Depends on the type of episode you are recording.
  - › An informational podcast is typically only six minutes long.
  - › A panel or interview could be as long as 12 minutes.
- Intermission (30 seconds)
  - › Break up longer episodes with an intermission.
  - › Use music for the intermission.
- Closing (2 minutes)
  - › Thank your guests if you have any.
  - › Thank the audience for listening.
  - › Announce the next episode topic.
  - › Repeat the podcast URL.
- Closing Jingle (60 seconds)

Make a list of the best key terms for each episode and repeat these key terms at every opportunity that feels natural in your script. Of course, you can write the script first and extract the best (most repeated) key terms for use in the metadata and landing page of the episode (more about that later).

## Recording Episodes

There are many programs you can buy or download for audio or video recording. Audacity®[5] is a good freeware choice for recording audio. You can download, install, and begin using this software in about 30 minutes. You need to get a decent microphone for your computer first or the quality of your podcasts will suffer. USB microphones seem to have higher ratings than others.

Once you have your script written, start Audacity, and record your podcast. Figure 5.1 shows an example script open in one window, and Audacity in another. It really is as easy as hitting the record button and talking into your mic. You can monitor your voice levels with the graphics and pause at any time and resume.

[5] http://www.audacity.sourceforge.net

## Figure 5.1. Creating a Podcast Episode Using Audacity

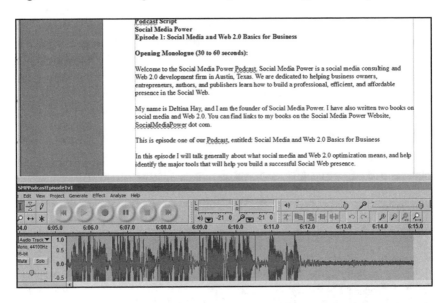

Adding music is easy, too. Figure 5.2 shows our finished podcast episode in one Audacity window, and a royalty-free music MP3[6] in another. To copy part of the music into your podcast, just select the portion you want and paste it into your podcast where you want it to play.

## Figure 5.2. Adding Music to a Podcast Episode Using Audacity

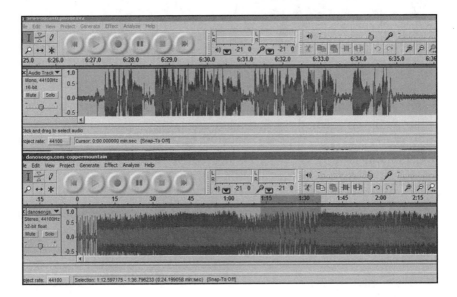

[6] http://danosongs.com/

Once your podcast episode is recorded, save it as an MP3 file. Go to File/ Export as MP3 to do this in Audacity. Figure 5.3 shows the resulting screen. Be sure and complete every option in this box. This is the "metadata" of your audio file and is important for optimization. See the "Optimizing Your Podcast" section on page 138. You want to repeat the key terms you generated in the "Preparing the Script and Key Terms" section on page 131. Repeat key terms in Title, Artist, Album, and Comments.

## Uploading Episodes

### Figure 5.3. Creating a Podcast Episode Using Audacity

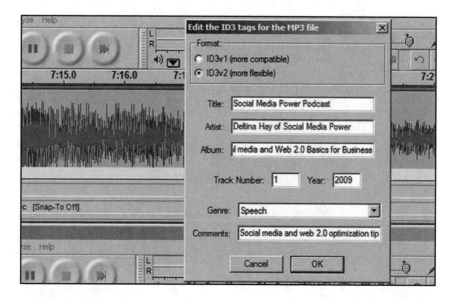

The next step is to upload your MP3 file to your hosting site. Using FTP is the preferred method for getting your files onto your site (see page 109). Figure 5.4 shows how we have uploaded our example podcast to a folder on our hosting site called "podcasts." We created this folder at the main level of our site, so that the direct link to our podcasts will always be    http://www.socialmediapower.com/podcasts/nameofpodcast.mp3. (Whenever you create a folder on a hosting site, and place a file in the folder, you are also creating a link to that file that can be accessed via the Internet, as demonstrated in the previous example.)

**Figure 5.4. Uploading a Podcast Episode**

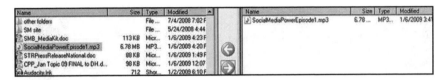

If you are using a service to create and host your podcast, however, they may have different uploading procedures.

# Publishing Your Podcast

If you are using a service like Audio Acrobat (see the "Publishing Options For Your Podcast" section on page 122), you should follow their guidelines for publishing your podcast episodes.

## To a Blogging Platform

Figure 5.5 shows the WordPress posting interface. Click on the audio icon to the left of "Add media" as shown. From here you can post your podcast episode just like you would a regular blog post, only you provide the link to the actual episode file (see Figure 5.6). You created this link when you uploaded the podcast episode in "Uploading Episodes" page 134.

**Figure 5.5. Publishing a Podcast to a Blogging Platform**

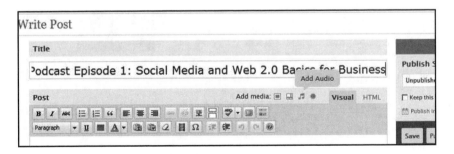

Part of optimizing your podcast is to have its landing page (in our case the blog entry) contain the key terms associated with the podcast episode

## Figure 5.6. Publishing a Podcast to a Blogging Platform, 2

See the "Optimizing Your Podcast" section on page 138. Once the link to the podcast episode is posted, include a description that uses these valuable key terms. Use the key terms as tags and utilize whatever SEO plugins you have in place to optimize the entry. Remember that this is still a blog post, so apply all of the optimization skills you learned in Chapter 3: "RSS Feeds & Blogs." See Figure 5.7.

Note that on Figure 5.7, one of the categories that is assigned for this post is "podcasts." This is how we distinguish the podcast episodes from the other posts in WordPress. Recall in Chapter 3 how to use categories to generate separate feeds (see page 87). This "feed" constitutes the entire

## Figure 5.7. Publishing a Podcast to a Blogging Platform, 3

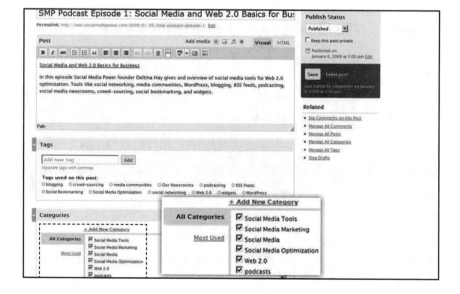

podcast, so that every time a post is saved with that category assigned, it will become an episode of the podcast.

Figure 5.8 shows how this method of posting will look on your site. When a visitor clicks on the link they will be able to download or play the episode. There are other ways of displaying your podcast, though. For instance, you can use plugins[7] that allow you to embed audio or video players directly into your posts.

## Figure 5.8. Podcast as a Blog Post

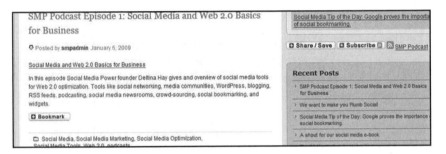

## To a Website

For SEO purposes, each episode of your podcast should have its own landing page. That is, each episode should reside on its own HTML or PHP page, so that it has a unique URL. On this landing page, you want to write a description of the podcast episode that includes all of the key terms you established in "Preparing the Script and Key Terms" on page 131. Your landing page, then, will look very similar to the blog post created in the previous section (Figure 5.8), with a description and a link to the podcast episode.

Once your landing page is created, you need to add the episode to your RSS feed by adding a new item with an enclosure element (see Appendix B: "Creating Your Own RSS Feed") or to FeedForAll if you are using it to manage your feeds.

---

[7] http://wordpress.org/extend/plugins/podcasting/

# Optimizing Your Podcast

First, read the "Optimizing and Promoting Your Blog and RSS Feed" section on page 78. Since your podcast is also an RSS feed, apply most of the tactics discussed in that section.

Podcasts can be optimized for search engines and podcast directories by consistently using the same key terms within the podcast itself, in the metadata (see the "Recording Episodes" section on page 132) of the audio and video files, and on the page that the podcast resides (the landing page). As you create your podcast and podcast episodes, keep these three optimization points in mind:

1. Many audio and video search engines now use speech recognition to identify key terms within podcasts. So make sure you write each episode to include your best key terms, and that you use these same key terms in the file's metadata and on the landing page of each podcast episode.

2. You add the metadata for each podcast episode when you save it as an MP3 file (see the "Recording Episodes" section on page 132). Repeat key terms from the actual spoken episode in this metadata.

3. The page where each podcast episode resides is called its landing page (see the "Publishing Your Podcast" section on page 135). Again, make sure you repeat your best key terms on this page, and especially repeat terms that are spoken in the podcast episode.

## Burning to FeedBurner

Once your podcast is published, you want to burn it to FeedBurner and optimize it. Go to your FeedBurner account, or create one if you don't have one yet. Before proceeding, read the entire "FeedBurner" section on page 82.

Figure 5.9 shows how we burn our Social Media Power podcast feed example. The feed URL we use is based on the WordPress category ID for "podcasts" that we assigned to our podcast entry above. Refer to burning feeds using WordPress categories on page 87. Note that the box is checked that reads "I am a podcaster." This lets FeedBurner know to look for an audio or video file at this feed URL. In the next step, you are

## Figure 5.9. Burning a Podcast to FeedBurner

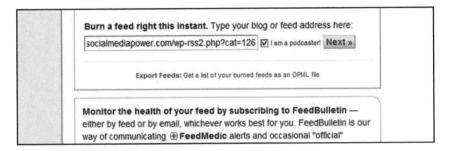

given an option to change the name of the feed FeedBurner creates for your podcast (see Figure 5.10).

## Figure 5.10. Burning a Podcast to FeedBurner, 2

Figures 5.11 shows the screen in the next step toward burning your podcast feed. This step is very important—this is where you optimize the feed for iTunes and Yahoo!. Do not skip anything in this step and use your best key terms in the summaries and search keywords areas.

## Figure 5.11. Burning a Podcast to FeedBurner, 3

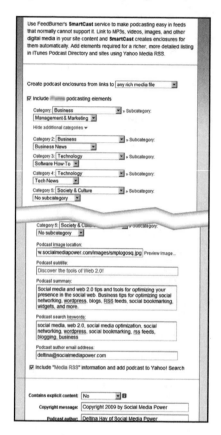

Since FeedBurner knows that this is a podcast, some of the settings are different than the settings covered in the previous chapter. For instance, Figure 5.12 shows the "PingShot" options for our podcast feed. The services listed here are specifically for podcasts, so select all of them.

## Figure 5.12. Burning a Podcast to FeedBurner, 4

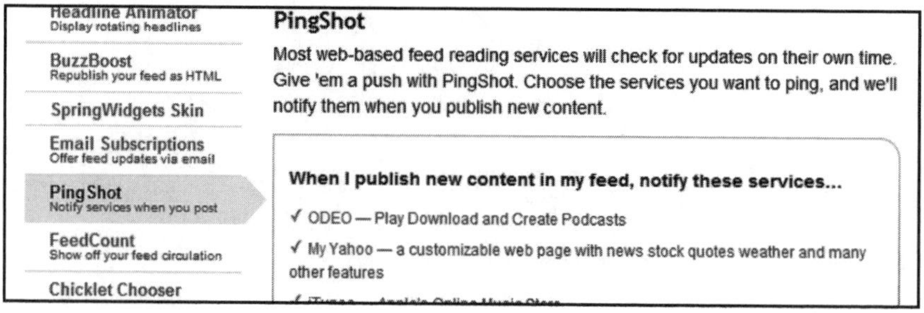

**Headline Animator**
Display rotating headlines

**BuzzBoost**
Republish your feed as HTML

**SpringWidgets Skin**

**Email Subscriptions**
Offer feed updates via email

**PingShot**
Notify services when you post

**FeedCount**
Show off your feed circulation

**Chicklet Chooser**

**PingShot**

Most web-based feed reading services will check for updates on their own time. Give 'em a push with PingShot. Choose the services you want to ping, and we'll notify them when you publish new content.

**When I publish new content in my feed, notify these services...**

✓ ODEO — Play Download and Create Podcasts

✓ My Yahoo — a customizable web page with news stock quotes weather and many other features

## Helping Visitors Subscribe

People subscribe to podcast feeds the same way they subscribe to any other RSS feed. See Chapter 3: "RSS Feeds & Blogs." You can subscribe to a podcast using the usual feed readers (Google Reader, MyYahoo, Pageflakes, etc.), but also through specialized readers called "podcatchers." These services specialize in indexing only podcasts.

Make it easy for visitors to your Website or blog to find your podcast feed. Figure 5.13 shows the FeedBurner "Chicklet Chooser"—read more about this in the "FeedBurner" section on page 86. Create a separate button for your podcast feed on your site (separate from your regular blog or RSS feed).

### Figure 5.13. FeedBurner Chicklet chooser

Once you have generated and copied the code from the Chicklet Chooser, place it onto your Website or blog, and make it clear that this feed is to your podcast (see Figure 5.14).

### Figure 5.14. Podcast Chicklet on a Website

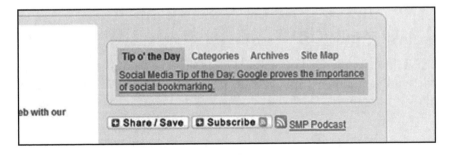

Figure 5.15 shows what a visitor sees when they click your FeedBurner chicklet. Notice that there are a number of podcatchers as choices. As you can see from Figure 5.16, the process for subscribing to your podcast feed using Google Reader is no different than subscribing to a regular feed. What *is* different is that Google recognizes the feed as a podcast, so subscribers can play it in an embedded player from their Google Reader account (see Figure 5.17).

## Figure 5.15. Subscribing Using a Chicklet

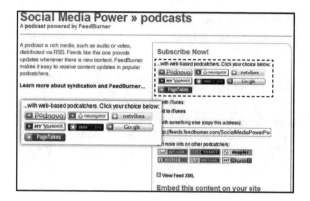

## Figure 5.16. Subscribing to a Podcast

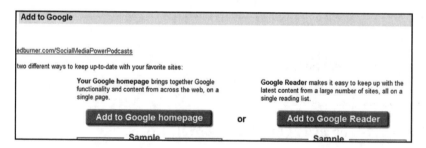

# Podcast Directories

In addition to the feed directory sources listed in the previous chapter, there are a number of podcast directories for submission of podcasts. Check the resource CD for an extensive list of podcast directories.

## Figure 5.17. A Podcast Subscription in Google Reader

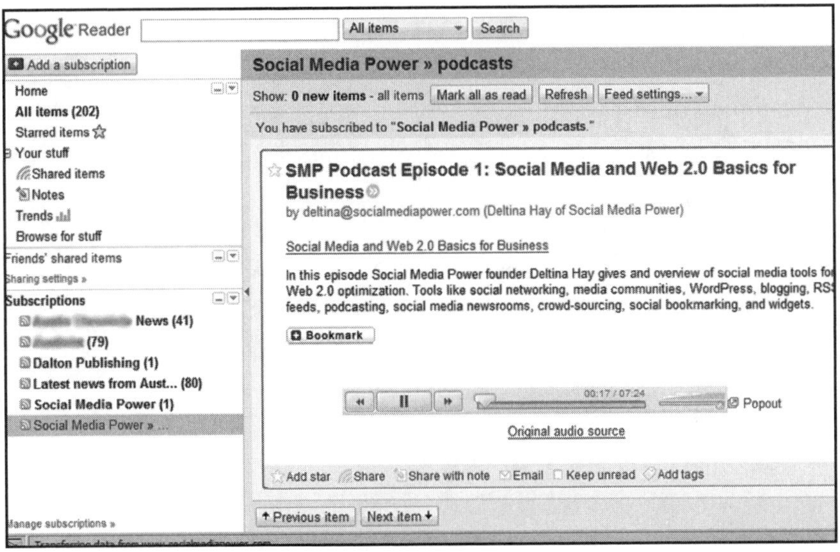

# Webcasting

A Webcast is an online broadcast, and usually consists of a series of uploaded videos. They can be viewed either on Webcasting sites or embedded into your Website or blog.

Webcasts are also called channels. YouTube lets you create channels (collections of videos) that you can regularly add videos to. See Chapter 8: "Media Communities" for information on how to create these channels.

Some popular Webcasting sites are blogTV[8] and blip.tv.[9] Note that these are also social networking sites, so use the tactics from Chapter 6: "Social Networking & Micro-Blogging" to optimize your presence in these sites.

Services such as Webcast2000[10] and Webcasting.com can help you create and maintain your own Webcast as well.

---

[8] http://www.blogtv.com/
[9] http://www.blip.tv/
[10] http://www.webcast2000.com/

# This Chapter On The Resource CD

- Further Reading
- Linkable Resources
- Example Podcast
- Fillable Forms:
    - › Podcast Script Outline

# 6 Social Networking & Micro-Blogging

Social networking can be one of the most powerful social media strategies you can implement. Most social networking sites allow you to create a personal profile page to post information about you or your business, invite people to join your network, join groups, blast messages, post events, connect with other people, and much more.

Micro-Blogging (Twitter) is a combination of blogging and social networking where you post short, frequent entries and gain followers around those entries.

Networking and micro-blogging sites are effective outlets for finding new customers and readers, but it is easy to find your message spread thin if you don't choose the right strategy. Many businesses settle for sparse profiles on various sites, never discovering the other powerful marketing tools many of these social networking platforms have to offer—most of them for free. To avoid the scattershot approach, choose two or three social networking sites that best fit your business and invest the time to maximize your presence in them.

In this chapter we first take a thorough look at Facebook, currently the fastest growing social networking site, and an ideal first choice for anyone or any business wanting to get a solid foothold in the Social

Web. We also highlight the professional networking site, LinkedIn, and the popular micro-blogging tool, Twitter. We then discuss other social networking tools, building custom social networks, and the future of social networking. Finally, we outline a plan that you can implement for whichever sites you choose to add to your social networking and micro-blogging strategy.

# Facebook

Below is an overview of the most basic features of the Facebook platform. Most social and professional networking sites have these same functionalities in one way or another. You access these features from your Facebook home page. See Figure 6.1.

## The News Feed

Often called a mini-feed, this is where you can view lists of posts that others in your network have added to their profiles (and where they view yours). This is also where you can connect with others by commenting on their posted entries. You can even filter your feed by friend lists, photos, links, etc. The News Feed is found on your Facebook home page. See Figure 6.1 on page 148.

## The Wall

This is where all of your own posts reside. Recent activity such as who you have "friended," which groups you join, or what you have recently "liked" on Facebook or on the Internet in general shows up here. You can see your friends' walls by visiting their profile page. You can also leave messages on people's walls. The Wall is on your Facebook profile page. See Figure 6.5 on page 151.

## Posting

Posting is what you do to add items to your News Feed or Wall. Posts can include a brief status update (a quick "What's on your mind?" post), photos, videos, events, links, etc. See Figures 6.1 and 6.2.

# Applications

Applications are add-ons that Facebook or other developers have created to work within the Facebook platform. There are many types of applications. They range from book sharing applications to games to RSS feed imports. You can use applications to help connect with other people within the Facebook community.

# Groups

Facebook groups are a way to connect with other people around a common interest. With so many people on the network now, it is important to connect with groups to increase your reach.

# People Search

This feature lets you search Facebook for people you may know. Facebook also recommends people you may know based on your existing friends and geographic region.

# Marketplace

Marketplace is an area where Facebook friends can sell things and post jobs. It is not intended to be a commercial or consumer outlet, it is meant to be more of a community marketplace like Craig's List.

# Messages and Requests

People can leave you messages, send requests to be their friends, join groups, attend events, and more.

# Pages and Advertising

You can create Facebook pages for your business or book (see the "Facebook Pages" section on page 155), or place highly targeted ads within the Facebook community. It is important to note that Facebook *pages* are meant for businesses, while your Facebook *profile* should be created for you, as an individual.

# The Facebook Home Page

Figure 6.1 shows my Facebook home page. From this page, I can:

- Post status updates (see the "What's on you mind?" box in Figure 6.1)
- Read and send messages or invitations
- View and post events
- View my friend's photos or upload my own photos and video
- View my friends, search for friends, or add friend lists that I can filter my news feed by
- Add or browse applications and games
- Add Facebook pages and ads, or see stats on my existing pages
- Browse, join, or create groups
- Browse the marketplace
- Manage my installed applications

## Figure 6.1. A Facebook Home Page

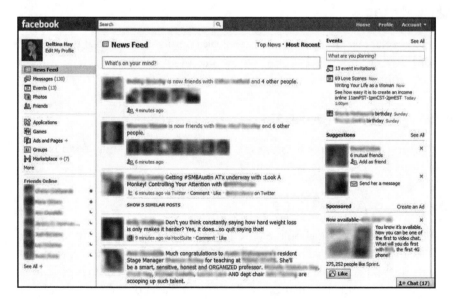

From the "Account" menu in the upper right of the page (Figure 6.2), I can:

- Edit Friends: View and search for friends, and add friend lists to filter my News Feed by (Figure 6.3)
- Manage my Facebook pages
- Change my account and privacy settings (see the "Facebook and Privacy" section at the end of this chapter)
- Manage Application settings (Figure 6.4)

## Figure 6.2. Facebook Account Menu

## Figure 6.3. Facebook Friends Options

Also from my Facebook home page, I can see and comment on what my network of friends and colleagues are up to (see Figure 6.1). Through the news feed, I can see the photos, links, videos, events, and other items they have posted. In addition to being able to filter the feed by photos, links, and other items, I can also filter this feed using my own friend lists (on Figure 6.3 those are "Personal" and "Business").

## Figure 6.4. Facebook Application Settings

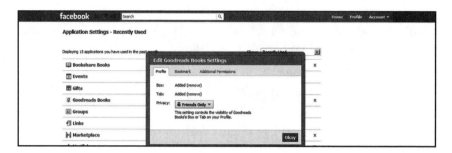

I can post many types of items to my page easily. See the "Posting Status Updates" section on page 153.

# The Facebook Profile

Figure 6.5 shows my Facebook profile page. From this page, I can:

- Publish stories; add links, photos, videos, and notes to my own "wall"
- Update my profile and add events
- View links, notes, and events I have posted
- Add additional tabs to my profile, (depending on which applications I have added). See Figure 6.6.

This is also where others can see what is on my wall, leave me messages, comment on my entries, or write to my wall.

Your profile page will likely look different, including the applications and tabs you have added, but the basic options remain the same. Be certain to fill out your profile completely.

## Setting Up Your Profile

Figure 6.7 shows a completed Facebook profile—when you click the "Info" box from your profile page.

Use the following guidelines when completing a "professional" and optimized profile:

## Figure 6.5. A Facebook Profile Page

## Figure 6.6. Facebook Profile Page Tabs

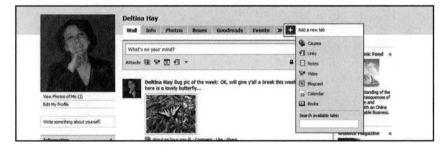

- Use and reuse your best key terms
- Avoid the "Relationship" section altogether
- Keep the "Likes and Interests" section professional
- Fill out the remaining sections completely

There are a number of settings you can control on your Facebook profile (click the "Options/Settings" button), including how friends and others are allowed to interact on your wall. See Figure 6.8.

## Figure 6.7. A Facebook Profile

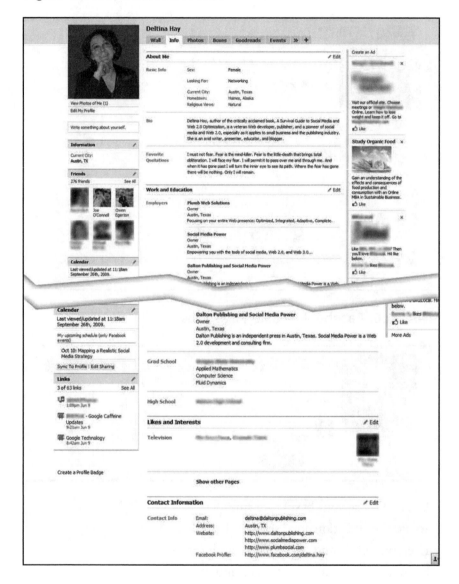

## Figure 6.8. Facebook Settings

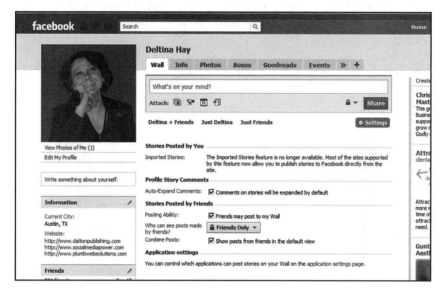

# Posting Status Updates

Keep your audience in mind when posting. Try to stay on topic. However if you are posting a lot of promotional material, offset them with lighter updates. Be sure to use key terms frequently within posts and in the file names of uploaded images and video clips.

Figure 6.9 shows some of the posting options available from your Facebook profile page. You can post images, video, links, and events. The "more" tab will show your posting options from your installed applications.

## Figure 6.9. Facebook Posting Options

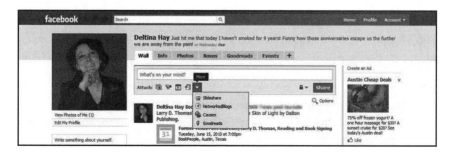

When posting links, just enter the link and click "Attach." Figure 6.10 shows how Facebook automatically grabs information from the link location and even allows you to choose an image to display from the link source.

Another nice feature is that you can upload images and video clips instantly from your iPhone or Webcam. See Figure 6.11.

## Figure 6.10. Posting Links in Facebook

## Figure 6.11. Posting Images and Video in Facebook

# Facebook Groups

Joining groups is particularly important now that there are almost 500,000 people on Facebook. Groups can help you get in front of your target audience easier.

You can find groups using search terms or join groups that your friends already belong to. Join groups that may contain your target market, or groups formed within your industry. Always post promotional updates to groups sparingly.

Create your own group only if you have the time and resources to maintain it. Try to find a niche in your industry to fill rather than creating a group based on a business. For instance, Figure 6.12 shows a local literary group started by a small press.

## Figure 6.12. Example of a Facebook Group

# Facebook Pages

Facebook pages are specifically for marketing a business, product, or personality. They offer a way for a business to represent itself to the Facebook community in an authentic way. Facebook users can search pages the same way they search for people within the network community. Facebook offers these pages to businesses at no charge.

Figure 6.13 shows the search results for "social media wordpress." A Facebook search shows all search results, or a breakdown of results by people, pages, applications, or groups. Our search yields Social Media Power's Facebook page as well as their application.

As an added bonus, Facebook pages are indexed in search engines. Figure 6.14 shows a Google search for "Dalton Publishing." Notice their Facebook page listed second, as well as their MySpace page listed fourth.

## Figure 6.13. Facebook Search Results

## Figure 6.14. Google Search Results With Facebook Pages

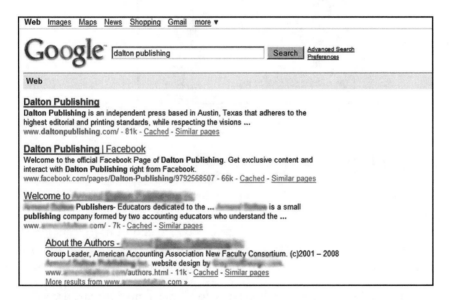

# Creating Facebook Pages

Once you have an account and have completed your profile, log in to Facebook and go to the "Advertising" link at the bottom of your Facebook profile page, or go directly to the Facebook pages link.[1]

Choose the best category for your business, book, or product (see Figure 6.15). The three main categories are: local business; brand, product, or organization; and artist, band, or public figure. You can choose a subcategory as well. If you offer a number of different services or products,

[1] http://www.facebook.com/pages/

## Figure 6.15. Facebook Page Categories

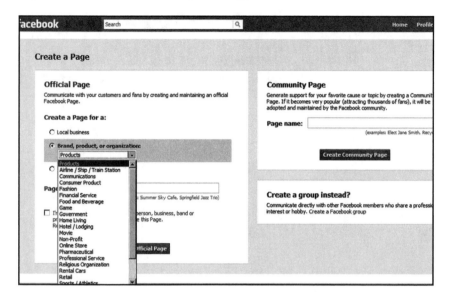

you may want to create several pages. For instance, if you are a publisher, you may want to create a main page for your publishing company using the "brand or product" category and individual pages using the "Artist, Band, or Public Figure" category for each of your authors.

Choosing the name of your Facebook page is very important. You are limited to around 65 characters, so make them count. The name of your Facebook page determines how well your page performs in searches, so put some thought into the key words you choose to include in it.

Figure 6.16 shows a newly created Facebook page. The next step is to input detailed information about your business or product. Click on the "Info" tab on your new page to do this (see Figure 6.16).

The category you chose in the previous step determines what type of information you can enter. Figure 6.17 shows the information options for the "Artist, Band, and Public Figure" category, whereas Figure 6.18 shows the "Brand or Product" options.

Regardless of the category you choose, prepare the information you enter here ahead of time. Use your preparation worksheet (refer to Chapter 2:

## Figure 6.16. Creating a Facebook Page

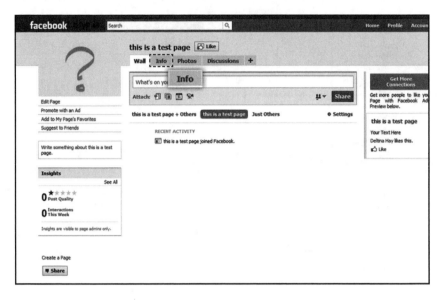

## Figure 6.17. Facebook Page: Detailed Information

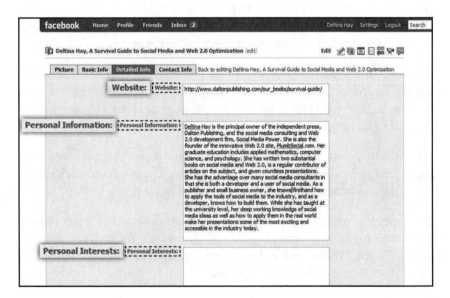

"Preparation" or the "A Social Networking Strategy" section at the end of this chapter on page 190) to populate your page with all of your best information and key terms. You may only have a few seconds to get a reader's attention, so put your best key terms forward.

## Figure 6.18. Facebook Page: Detailed Information, 2

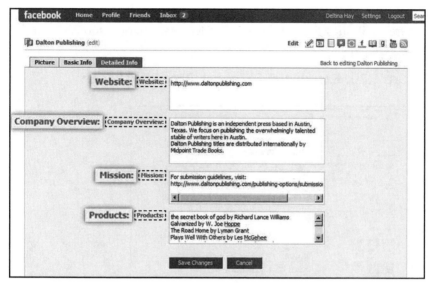

Figure 6.19 shows the screen for editing the page information (click on the "Info" tab and choose "edit information"). From here, click on every tab and fill each box thoroughly, reusing your key terms often. Be certain

## Figure 6.19. Editing Info on a Facebook Page

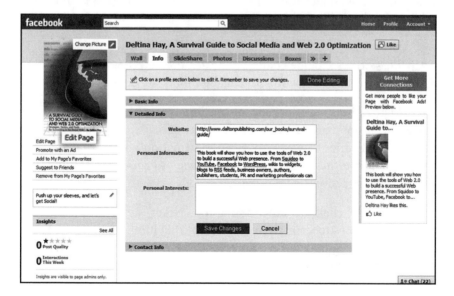

to upload a logo by clicking "Change Picture" in the upper left corner of the page.

Figure 6.20 shows what good, detailed information looks like on a Facebook page.

### Figure 6.20. Example of Facebook Page Information

## Settings and Applications

Once you input your detailed information, you can change the settings of your page and manage applications by clicking on "edit page" in the left sidebar as seen in Figure 6.19. Figures 6.21 and 6.22 show the resulting page.

Available settings include changing the default view of your page, setting up options for updating your page using mobile devices, etc.

The "Applications" section shows the built-in applications as well as any applications you have installed. Clicking on "edit" beside any one of these applications gives you more information about what they are and how to use them. Click on "view page" to see these settings and applications in action on your page.

As an example, click on "edit" beside the "Notes" application. You can add manual notes to your page or, as seen in Figures 6.23 and 6.24, you can import a blog that feeds your latest blog posts onto your Facebook page using this application.

## Figures 6.21 & 6.22. Facebook Page Settings and Applications

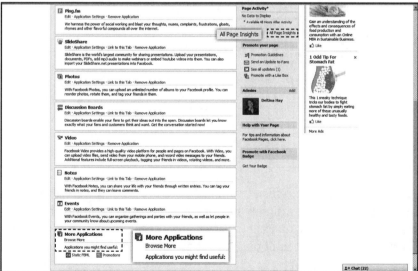

There are many more applications you can add to your page. Click on "More Applications" at the bottom of the edit page (Figure 6.22) or go to the Facebook application directory. Add applications that help represent your company and/or your products in your own unique way.

### Figure 6.23. Importing a Blog to Facebook Notes, 1

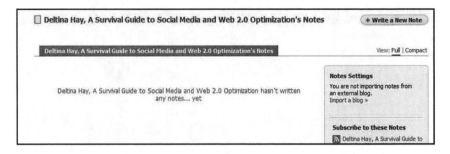

### Figure 6.24. Importing a Blog to Facebook Notes, 2

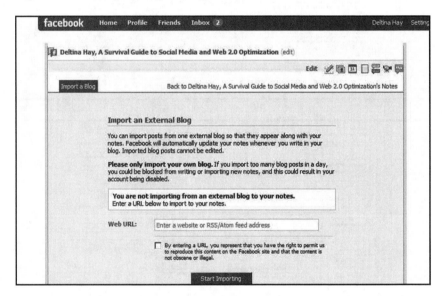

Applications are not difficult to install and are usually very easy to set up. A general rule of thumb when choosing an application is that if you can't figure out how to set it up after the second try, find another one. There is often more than one application out there that can accomplish the same task.

Browse or search the application directory for applications that make sense to implement for your business or product.

## Figure 6.25. Facebook Page Tabs

Figure 6.25 shows Dalton Publishing's Facebook page. On this Facebook page, Dalton Publishing utilizes the following applications:

## Book Share Books[2]

This application (see the pull-down tab called "books") lets readers share their favorite books with their friends, as well as rate them and comment on them. This is a perfect application for a publishing company wanting to showcase their books.

## My Flickr[3]

Display photos from your Flickr account using this application (see the tab called "My Flickr"). These photos can include logos, book covers, photos from author events, etc. You are provided many options of how to display the photos, too.

---

[2] http://apps.facebook.com/bookshare/dashboard.php
[3] http://apps.facebook.com/myflickr/

## Social RSS[4]

This is a nice application (see the "RSS/Blog" tab) that allows you to display RSS feeds on your Facebook page. It is a convenient way for Dalton Publishing to display the feeds from their main site, as well as to their authors' newsroom feeds.

## ShopTab[5]

Dalton also uses the application ShopTab. See Figure 6.26. This application offers a nice way for Dalton to sell their books within Facebook. There is a fee to use this application, though.

### Figure 6.26. ShopTab Application

By implementing these applications, Dalton Publishing has created an interactive page that also gives their visitors a personable look into their business. You can find many applications that can do the same for your business.

---

[4] http://apps.facebook.com/social-rss/tabsettings.php
[5] http://www.facebook.com/ShopTabApp

Once your page is ready, don't forget to publish it. You will see a message in the upper right corner as you prepare your page that says "This Page has not been published…" Click on "publish this Page" in that box so that your Facebook page can be seen by others.

Figure 6.27 shows the "wall" of Dalton's Facebook page. This is similar to a regular Facebook profile in that Dalton can post items and others can comment on them. This is also where most of the built-in applications appear (see page 145). Also, from here you can send updates to all the fans of your page, promote your page with an ad, and manage page settings.

## Figure 6.27. The Wall of a Facebook Page

## Promoting and Analytics

In the right sidebar of the settings screen (Figures 6.21 and 6.22) there are options for promoting your page and viewing analytics.

Promotional options include sending updates to existing page fans, and creating a "Like" box to place on your blog or Website (these options are under "Promoting Your Page"). Before promoting your site or contacting your fans, read the "Promotional Guidelines" that is also an option in this section. Further down the page is an option for creating a badge that you can also place on a blog or Website. We discuss Like boxes and badges in more detail in Chapter 9: "Widgets and Badges."

You can also view your page analytics by clicking on "All Page Insights" from the settings screen (Figure 6.22). Figure 6.28 shows some of the features of Facebook's page Insights. These stats can be very useful for determining what types of posts have been most successful and whether you are reaching your target market.

**Figure 6.28. Facebook Insights**

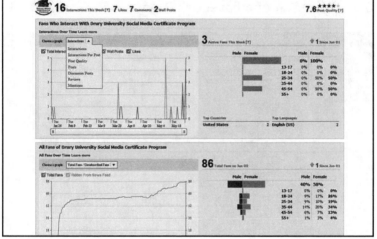

# Facebook and Privacy

Facebook's privacy policies are a touchy subject, and something you should be aware of. Facebook does not always make it clear how their members' information is shared on the Internet outside of the Facebook platform. This results in members often becoming surprised and angered when they discover their photos or names appearing across the Internet via Facebook plugins and widgets utilized by other sites.

Figure 6.29 shows the initial privacy settings screen. From here, members can manage most of their privacy settings within Facebook, but to control how their information is shared outside of Facebook, members need to

## Figure 6.29. Facebook Privacy Settings

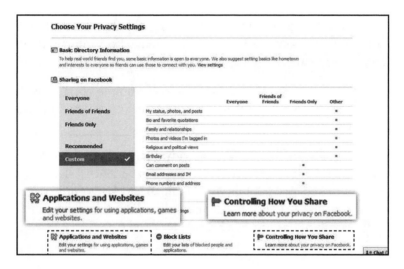

## Figure 6.30. Facebook Privacy Settings, 2

continue on to the "Applications and Websites" option at the bottom of the screen. That screen is shown in Figure 6.30.

Also at the bottom of the main privacy settings screen (Figure 6.29) is the option "Controlling How You Share," which gives an explanation of all of the settings and how a user's information is shared across the Internet.

# LinkedIn

LinkedIn[6]is more of a professional networking site than a social one. As you can see from Figures 6.31 and 6.32, a LinkedIn profile is more focused on professional experience and expertise.

This networking site is a great tool for people wanting to connect with other professionals, or for those seeking professional positions. It is also ideal for consultants and service firms seeking clients.

When completing a LinkedIn profile, take advantage of the ample room this tool offers for a nice summary, your work experience, all of your businesses, groups and associations you belong to, etc. Use your best key terms throughout your profile and edit all of the content you add. Think of this profile as a mini resume. See Figures 6.31 and 6.32.

## Figure 6.31. A LinkedIn Profile

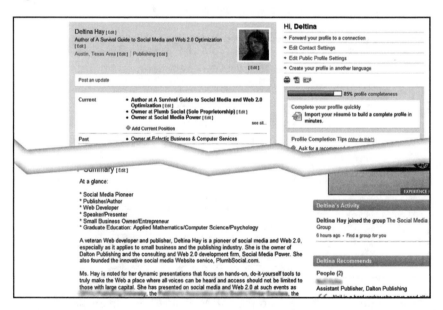

Just like other networking sites, you can add applications, join groups, post quick updates, and search for and interact with other people. One thing that is more specific to LinkedIn, however, is the ability to

---

[6] http://www.linkedin.com

## Figure 6.32. A LinkedIn Profile, continued

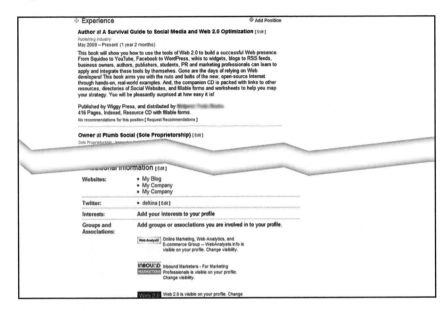

recommend others in your network. You can ask others to recommend you and your services, or others may ask the same of you. See Figure 6.33.

## Figure 6.33. LinkedIn "Recommend" Feature

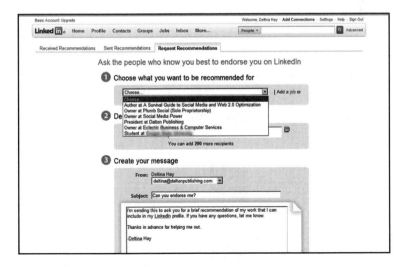

Not surprisingly, LinkedIn groups are much more focused on doing business than anything else (see Figure 6.34). You should join groups relevant to your business, or start groups where there is a niche to fill. Always read a group's guidelines before posting. LinkedIn allows group administrators to send members email updates, so involvement in many targeted groups can pay off nicely.

## Figure 6.34. LinkedIn Groups

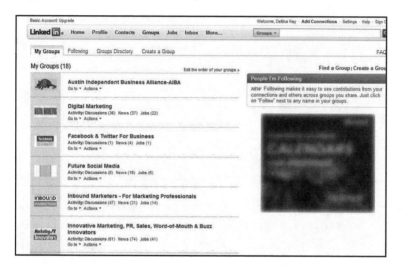

## Figure 6.35. LinkedIn Applications

Though LinkedIn doesn't have many applications, they are all very targeted to helping you enhance your professional message to other members. See Figure 6.35. Figure 6.36 shows the SlideShare and Blog Link applications as they appear in our example profile.

## Figure 6.36. LinkedIn Applications In a Profile

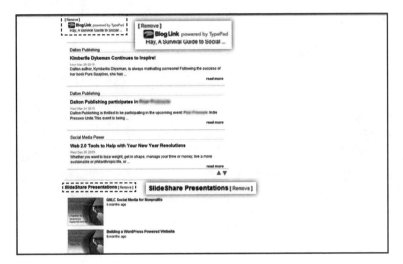

# Twitter

Twitter is a micro-blogging site, which means it is a tool for making short (up to 140 characters) updates or "Tweets" on a regular basis. You can post updates from your computer or from a mobile device. Others then follow those updates in a real-time stream called a "Timeline." Followers can also comment on updates so that conversations can ensue around them. This makes a micro-blogging site a hybrid between a blog and a social network.

The Timeline on your Twitter home page lists all the real-time updates from you and your followers. Figure 6.37 shows a Twitter profile page, which shows only the Timeline that includes your own updates. Note that your profile Timeline can also be accessed as an RSS feed as well. See Figure 6.38.

## Figure 6.37. A Twitter Profile Page

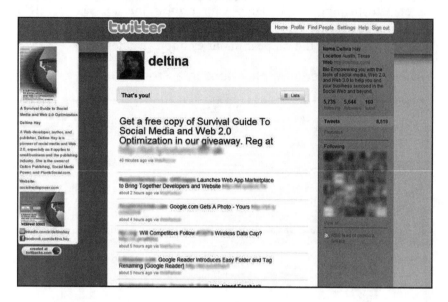

## Figure 6.38. A Twitter Timeline as an RSS Feed

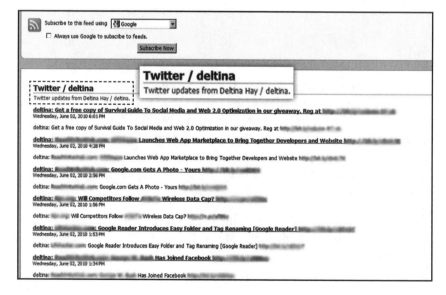

# Setting Up Your Account

Twitter prides itself on keeping its platform simple, and does a good job of living up to that claim. There are only a few options on the main menu aside from Home and Profile: Find People, Settings, and Help. From the Settings menu you can set privacy, notification, location, and mobile preferences. You can also manage which applications can access your account under the "Connections" screen.

Figure 6.39 shows the "Settings/Profile" screen. Make the best of the 160 characters allowed for your bio by using as many key terms as possible without sacrificing clarity.

## Figure 6.39. Twitter Profile Screen

Figure 6.40 shows the "Settings/Design" screen. From here, you can change your background image or upload a custom image. You can make up for the short bio space in your profile by adding a custom background image.

## Figure 6.40. Twitter Design Screen

A custom background image allows you to customize your Twitter profile with your own branding, Website, and contact information. Figure 6.41 shows such a background image. Keep this image simple. Your purpose should be to provide additional information about you or your business, not overwhelm visitors with graphics or information.

## Figure 6.41. Twitter Background Image

Luckily, you don't have to be a designer to create nice background images. Use a service like Twitbacks[7] to create a background with the proper specifications.

# Finding People

Figure 6.42 shows the "Find People" screen. There are a number of ways to search people out within Twitter, whether you know them or not. You can browse through Twitter categories to find people to follow, or look to your own lists, either through email or direct searches. See the "External Tools" section on page 185 for services that can help you find more people to follow.

---

[7] http://www.twitbacks.com

## Figure 6.42. Twitter Find People Screen

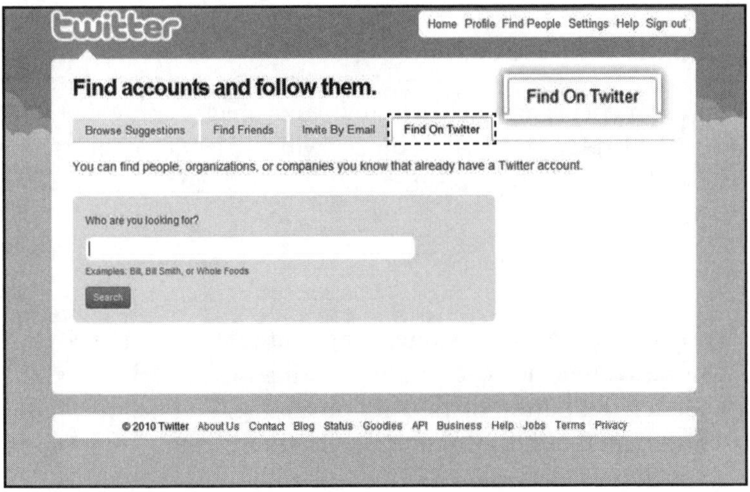

# Posting Updates or Tweets

Twitter updates are called "Tweets." They are 140 characters, including embedded links. A 140 character space is not a lot to work with, but there are ways to help you make the most of the limited space. (Note: We use the terms "tweet," "post," and "update" interchangeably here.)

## Shortening Links

When posting a link, use a URL shortening service. These services provide you with a shorter version of any URL you want to share. A couple of URL shortening services are http://bit.ly and http://ow.ly. You can see examples of "short URLs" in Figure 6.43. The second update in

## Figure 6.43. Shortening URLs

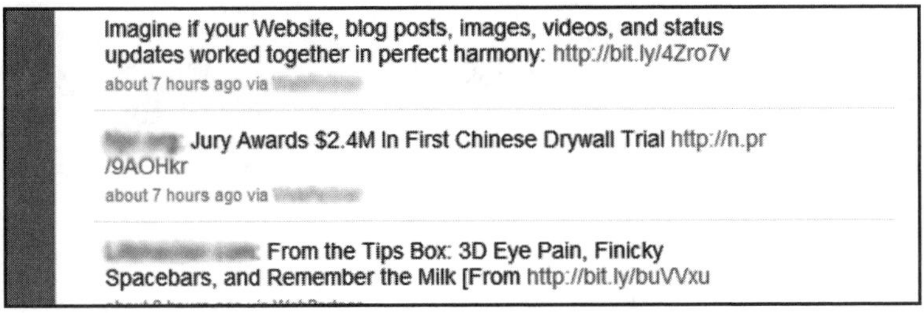

this example shows how NPR uses their own URL shortening method. This is a good strategy for large organizations or media companies.

## Posting Images and Video

You need to use media sharing sites to pull your images and video into Twitter so they display properly. Some Twitter-friendly choices are Twitpic[8] and Plixi[9] for image posting and Vimeo[10] and YouTube for posting video.

## Retweeting

Sharing tweets or "retweeting" is one thing that makes Twitter a viral tool. You can retweet entries you find interesting to your followers just by clicking the retweet button of an entry on another's Timeline. Figure 6.44 shows an original tweet from another Twitter account, and Figure 6.45 shows how it is retweeted on our Timeline.

### Figure 6.44. Retweeting in Twitter

### Figure 6.45. Retweeting in Twitter, 2

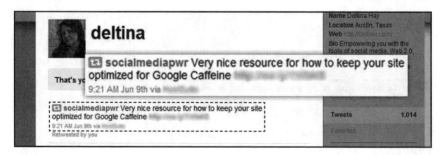

---

[8] http://twitpic.com/
[9] http://plixi.com/
[10] http://vimeo.com/

You can view your retweets, your followers' retweets, and which of your updates have been retweeted by clicking on the "Retweets" option in the right sidebar of your home page. See Figure 6.46.

## Figure 6.46. Viewing Retweets in Twitter

Retweeting can substantially increase the exposure of your own Tweets, so keep this in mind when you are posting by frequently posting content that will have a good chance of being passed on. See the "External Tools" section on page 185 for tools that can help you find interesting posts to retweet.

## Tweeting Your Location

Twitter's "Tweet With Your Location" feature allows you to add location information to your Tweets. This feature can be handy if you are targeting regional markets or for hooking up with your followers. You can add a location to individual Tweets as you create them, but the device you are using to post (your mobile device or Web browser) must be set to transmit location information. See the Twitter Help Center[11] to learn more.

## @Replies and Mentions

An @reply is any Twitter update that begins with @username. This means that the update is meant for that particular user. It is like sending another user a message right in their timeline. Figure 6.47 shows how to reply while viewing someone else's timeline, and the resulting reply in our timeline. When we click on "Reply," we are taken to our own account to complete the reply, as shown in Figure 6.47.

---

[11] http://support.twitter.com/

## Figure 6.47. Sending an @Reply in Twitter

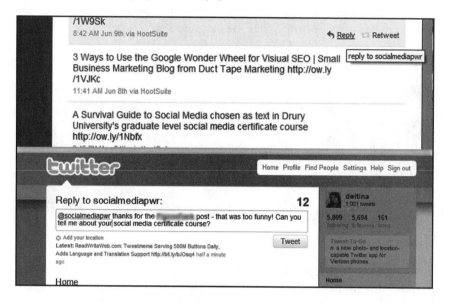

A "Mention" is a Twitter update that contains @username anywhere within the tweet (not just at the beginning).

When you click on your @username stream in the right sidebar (@socialmediapwr in our example), you can view all of the @replies and Mentions that include your username. See Figure 6.48.

## Figure 6.48. @Replies in Twitter

## Direct Messages

You can also send followers private messages. However, you can only send direct messages to people who are following you. You can send or read direct messages from the "Direct Messages" option in the right sidebar of your Twitter home page. See Figure 6.49.

## Figure 6.49. Direct Messages in Twitter

## Hashtags

Hashtags are Twitter's version of tags or key terms contained within updates. If a hash mark (#) is placed before a word, that word will come up in searches based on the term the hash mark precedes. Traditionally, hashtags were added to the end of tweets, but it can save room to include them directly within your posts. The other significant thing about hashtags is that they are linkable within an update, so that creating hashtags for a specific event or business can result in a nice Twitter archive.

To demonstrate, Figure 6.50 shows an update with two hashtags: #socialmedia and #drurysmc. It is a post announcing a social media course offered by Drury University.

## Figure 6.50. Hashtags in a Twitter Post

Figure 6.51 shows the search results on Twitter Search using the search term #socialmedia. This search could easily prompt a user to click on the hashtag #drurysmc contained in our example post. Figure 6.52 shows the resulting list of all the tweets containing the hashtag #drurysmc.

## Figure 6.51. Twitter Search Results

## Figure 6.52. Twitter Search Results, 2

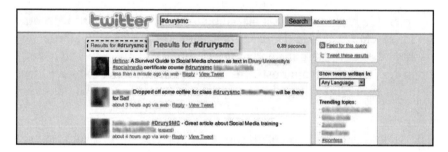

See the "External Tools" section on page 185 for more information on Twitter Search.

# Twitter Lists

Twitter lists let you organize people you are following into manageable groups. Lists are generally collections of people who have something in common, so that you can visit a particular list based on what type of updates you are in the mood for. You might make a list of friends and colleagues, or create lists based on interests.

Add lists by clicking on "Lists" in the right sidebar of your home page. See Figure 6.53. Create list names that are descriptive but not too long.

## Figure 6.53. Creating a Twitter List

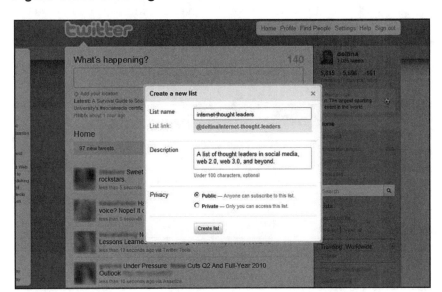

Give your lists good descriptions using key terms. It is best to make your lists public so you can leverage them.

One way to add people to your lists is to click on "Following" in the right sidebar of your home page. Figure 6.54 shows how you can add the people you are following to your lists, as well as the other options that are available to you on this screen (by clicking on the small "gear" icon). You can also follow people by visiting their profile page.

## Figure 6.54. Adding People to a Twitter List

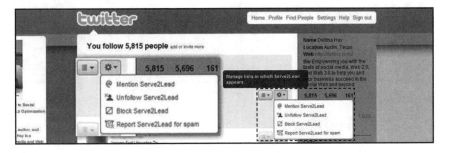

By perusing the public lists you have been added to (Figure 6.55), you can get good insight into how people tend to classify you. You can get to this screen by clicking on "Lists" in the right sidebar of your home page.

### Figure 6.55. Viewing Twitter Lists You are On

Assuming that others will be doing the same thing, you can leverage your own lists by adding influential tweeters. Another strategy is to investigate others' lists to help you decide whether to follow them or not, or to find new people to follow. See Figure 6.56.

You are limited to 20 lists, so use them wisely.

### Figure 6.56. Viewing Your Lists in Twitter

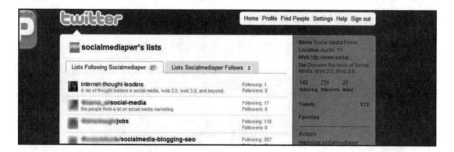

## The "New" Twitter

Though not fully rolled out at the time of this book's publication, we did manage to get some examples of the changes that Twitter has made to its platform. Luckily, none of the major features highlighted in this section have changed.

Figure 6.57 shows the new Twitter home page. One change to note is that many of the main features (like mentions, retweets and lists) can now be accessed as tabs just above the time line.

## Figure 6.57. New Twitter Home Page

The biggest change is to the right sidebar area. This area gives much more information about individual tweets and tweet sources when a specific tweet is clicked (see Figure 6.58).

## Figure 6.58. Tweet Details in the New Twitter

This sidebar also shows images and allows you to play video right in the Twitter platform. See Figure 6.59.

### Figure 6.59. Viewing Videos in the New Twitter

## Promoting Your Account

At the bottom of your home page is a link called "Goodies." From this screen, you can create Twitter widgets that can stream your timeline, your favorite content, or tweets based on search terms. See Figure 6.60. We discuss widgets and badges in more detail in Chapter 9: "Widgets and Badges."

### Figure 6.60. Twitter Widgets

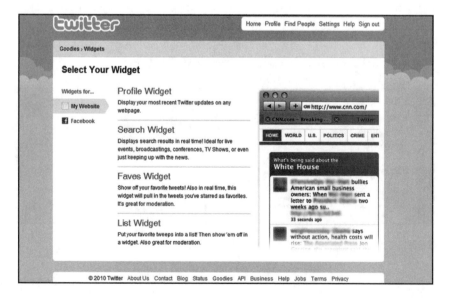

## @Anywhere

Much like Facebook's social plugins, @Anywhere is a series of widgets using the Twitter API that can be placed on a Website to personalize your site visitor's experience.

# External Tools

Twitter itself may seem simple, but there are many tools that tap into the Twitter API enhancing its functionality and making it a more powerful tool.

Here are some examples of tools you may want to add to your Twitter arsenal right away:

- HootSuite[12] is a must-have tool that helps integrate your other social accounts with Twitter, imports blog posts into your timeline, post-dates your tweets, manages more than one account, manages lists, and more. We discuss this tool in more detail in Chapter 12: "Pulling It All Together."
- Tweetmeme[13] is a way to find interesting Tweets and retweet them on the spot.
- TwitterSearch[14] can help you find people to follow based on search terms.
- TwitterFeed[15] is another way to link your blog posts with Twitter and other social accounts.
- Klout[16] is a tool for measuring your effectiveness as a tweeter. Their formulas seem sound in determining how much reach and influence you are achieving through your updates.
- Twittercounter[17] can help you keep track of your list of growing followers.

---

[12] http://hootsuite.com/
[13] http://tweetmeme.com/
[14] http://search.twitter.com/
[15] http://twitterfeed.com/
[16] http://klout.com/
[17] http://twittercounter.com/

These are just a few of the useful tools you can find to help manage your Twitter account. See the resource CD for a list of many more, or do a Google search to find popular tools.

# Other Social Networking Tools

## Social Bookmarking and Media Communities

Though considered social bookmarking sites (see Chapter 7: "Social Bookmarking & Crowd-Sourcing"), Delicious.com and other bookmarking sites like StumbleUpon.com naturally evolve into social networking sites. As conversations and connections develop around common bookmarks, so too does your network within these communities.

The same evolution happens within media communities like Flickr and YouTube. See Chapter 8: "Media Communities." Since conversations and connections develop around different multimedia items like images and video, communities naturally form as a result.

Apply the same tactics and strategies to these sites as you do to the other networking sites discussed in this chapter.

## Niche Social Networking Sites

If you are in an industry that tends to have a lot of its own niche social networks, you should consider adding one or more of those networks to your strategy. For instance, the publishing and tech industries have vibrant networking communities that could warrant such a strategy.

Joining these niche sites can put you in front of potential clients and affiliates in your area of expertise. You can find niche sites within your industry by searching Google or by researching where other people in your industry are putting their efforts.

Here are a few examples:

### Publishers and Authors

* LibraryThing[18]

---

[18] http://www.librarything.com

- GoodReads[19]
- Shelfari[20]

## Tech Consulting Firms

- Mashable[21]
- Slashdot[22]

## Entertainment Firms

- MySpace[23]
- Bebo[24]

# Social-Networking-Like Tools

There are many social tools that have social networking characteristics or can be considered social networking hybrids. These are nice tools, and may even be good additions to your strategy, but be careful not to fall into the trap of having more profiles or accounts than you can keep dynamic. Here are some popular examples:

## Google Buzz

Google Buzz is a social networking platform that is an extension of Gmail. Many people do not like the idea of linking social networking to their email accounts, however, so it has not taken off as well as Google would have liked.

## Posterous

Posterous is a nice tool for posting content quickly from email and has social networking features. It is a blogging tool as well as a social network. It is also a nice integration tool, which is why we also discuss it in Chapter 12: "Pulling It All Together."

---

[19] http://goodreads.com
[20] http://www.shelfari.com
[21] http://www.mashable.com
[22] http://www.slashdot.org
[23] http://www.myspace.com
[24] http://www.bebo.com

### FriendFeed

FriendFeed is a Lifestreaming tool and can also be used as a social network. Like Posterous, users can pull in updates, photos, videos, feeds, etc. to one central place. We discuss FriendFeed in more detail in Chapter 12: "Pulling It All Together."

### Tumblr

Tumblr is also a platform that users can post to easily. It also has social networking features. Tumblr encourages its members to connect through similar interests, which gives it social networking characteristics. We discuss this tool in more detail in Chapter 11: "More Social Tools."

### Geo-Tagging

Geo-tagging is a way for users to tag their location as they post updates. As we saw with Twitter, most social networking tools are starting to add geo-tagging features within their own platforms.

### Finding Social Networks in Unlikely Places

Pay attention to the types of social networking or other interactive features the tools of your industry have to offer (like associations). Take advantage of them, especially if they are not difficult to maintain.

An example is Amazon's Author Central[25]. Amazon offers this free service to authors, allowing them to have their own page within the Amazon platform, thus encouraging authors to interact with their readers. You can upload video, offer a lengthy bio, even blog right on the page, or import your existing blog. Plus, readers can start discussions with the author or other fans without leaving Amazon.

# Creating Your Own Social Network

If you have a large readership or following whose members tend to have a lot to say to each other, you might consider creating your own social network. Custom social networks are also handy for corporate teams and educational classes.

---

[25] https://authorcentral.amazon.com/

Maintaining a custom network can be time consuming, so consider alternatives before jumping in. Can your need be filled by a Facebook page, LinkedIn group, or Facebook group? Do you have the resources to keep your own community engaged and free of spam? Can a blog with author privileges serve the same purpose? Do you need a place for users to engage, or just share information that could be accomplished with a Wiki? These questions can help you decide whether a custom network is a viable solution.

There are a number of ways to create a social network. Joomla! and Drupal are two CMSs you can use to do so, and BuddyPress[26] is a solution that integrates well with WordPress. Ning[27] is probably the most established service, and their plans start at only $4/month. SocialGo[28] is a service similar to Ning that also offers a free option.

Using Ning, you can build a very functional Web-based social networking site, complete with forum, blogging, and file sharing capabilities in a few short steps. Figure 6.61 shows the features available for building and enhancing a custom network.

## Figure 6.61. Features of a Ning Network

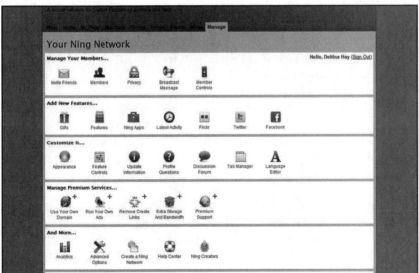

[26] http://www.buddypress.org

[27] http://www.ning.com

[28] http://www.socialgo.com

# The Future of Social Networking

With privacy concerns becoming more of an issue with social networking, people will be looking for alternatives to the more proprietary solutions that the most popular social networks currently offer.

The ultimate solution will likely have the following characteristics:

• Be open source so that anyone can contribute add-ons and enhancements without an expectation of harvesting personal information to use them

• Recognize that all personal information and individual content—including status updates, images, friend lists, etc.—belongs to the user, not to the service

• Can be linked to all other people who use the same platform, but can be hosted wherever the user chooses, along with all of their information

• Is part of the Linked Open Data cloud (we discuss the Linked Open Data cloud in Chapter 13: "Looking to the Future")

This type of solution is not as far off as you may think. One possible candidate is Diaspora[29]. They are building a social networking platform that will work much like WordPress. You create a "seed" like you would a blog in WordPress. This seed becomes your own personal social networking page. You can host your seed anywhere you want, just like you do a Website or blog. And when you want to move it, you can do so without leaving anything behind.

You would update your seed by adding status updates, images, video, or events the same way you do in Facebook, and other people who also have "seeds" and are in your network would get notified accordingly on their own seed. The main point is that all of your information is your own, and stays in your control.

It is rumored that Google is adding a "social layer" to its existing services that will be called "Google Me." Rather than create a stand-alone social network to compete with Facebook, Google would add social features to all of its existing services. Since Google is notorious for offering open platforms to developers, this could be a well-received addition.

---

[29] http://www.joindiaspora.com/

# A Social Networking Strategy

Follow these steps for each social/professional networking or micro-blogging site you join:

- Read and follow the site's Terms of Use.
- Complete your profile using prepared material, including your best key terms.
- Upload a profile image, logo, or custom background when available.
- Search for applications to enhance or customize your presence.
- Integrate other social tools and sites into your presence (like Flickr images or YouTube videos).
- Invite friends and colleagues to join your network. Do not invite people just for the sake of inviting them; only invite people you think can benefit from a specific community.
- Choose your friends wisely; do not just add anyone who asks; check out their profile first.
- Join groups relevant to your area of expertise or interest.
- Create and leverage follower lists.
- Promote your page or profile on your Website or blog.
- Add your account to Twitter Search and other search directories.
- Get to know the network features: Explore all of the features of the networking platform and implement each of them that make sense for you or your business.
- Do not turn your back on your investment: Keep your presence dynamic by contributing to it frequently.

If you have not competed the tasks in the "Preparation" chapter, prepare the following worksheet before you go forward with your strategy:

- Key Terms
    - › Start with a list of your best key terms and weave them into the rest of your worksheet items.
    - › Key terms are one, two, or three-word terms that you can imagine someone using as search terms if they were searching for your business or book in a search engine.

- General Information
  - › Your name
  - › Business or book name
  - › Email addresses
  - › URLs
  - › Instant Messaging screen names
  - › Other social networking profile URLs
- Biographical and Descriptive Information
  - › Short bio (50 words)
  - › Longer bio (100 words)
  - › Short company or book description (50 words)
  - › Longer company or book description (100 words)
  - › Business mission statement
- Products
  - › List of books and other products

These worksheet items are based on building a profile and a page in Facebook. For Twitter, you want to also prepare a succinct 160 character bio, whereas for LinkedIn you want to have expanded descriptions, bios, and professional experience prepared.

If you choose a different social networking or micro-blogging site, look at some completed profiles on which to base your worksheet items. This worksheet is also available on the resource CD.

# This Chapter on the Resource CD

- Further Reading
- Linkable Resources
- Fillable Forms:
  - › Social Networking Strategy Worksheet
  - › Social Networking Preparation Worksheet

# 7 Social Bookmarking & Crowd-Sourcing

## Social Bookmarking

Social bookmarking is a way for you to save your favorite blogs and Websites in a public space the same way you might save them using your own Web browser. The concept is simple, but its power is enormous.

Imagine that you have saved (or bookmarked) all of your favorite Websites and blogs to a central place online and tagged them with specific terms so you could easily search and find them later. Imagine further that you could then see how thousands of other users have tagged the same sites and that you could view all of the sites that they tagged. From this process we get "folksonomy"—the taxonomy of the Internet in terms of its users.

Instead of allowing search engines to provide you with the "supposed" best matches for your search terms, you can go to a social bookmarking site, search using those same terms, and find the top sites tagged (and commented on) by users just like you. You can pull up a site on one of these bookmarking sites and have access to everyone who has tagged the site, and if they have made their bookmarks public, you can even look at all of the other sites those users have tagged. There really is no end to the resources and readers you can access via social bookmarking.

## Social Bookmarking in Action

Figure 7.1 shows the front page of Delicious.com,[1] one of the most popular social bookmarking sites. This front page features some Websites people have recently saved to their own delicious bookmarking accounts.

### Figure 7.1. Delicious.com* Home Page

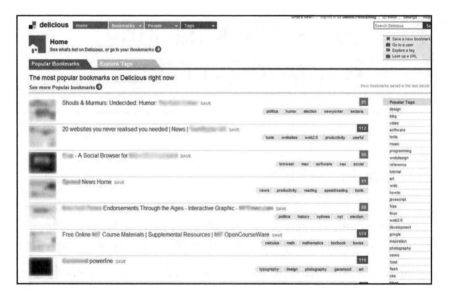

From here you can enter search terms that return resulting Websites that other members have "tagged" with those same search terms. Figure 7.2 demonstrates this. When the term "books" is searched, we get the results shown. All of these results were bookmarked by other users and tagged with the term "books." Click on any of these links, and you are taken to the respective Website, just like in traditional search engines.

*All Delicious.com images reproduced with permission of Yahoo! Inc. ©2009 Yahoo! Inc. Delicious is a registered trademark of Yahoo! Inc.

---

[1] http://delicious.com

The number to the right of each site listed shows how many people have bookmarked that site. If you click on that number you see a list of all of those people (see Figure 7.3). Figure 7.3 shows a general list, but if you click on the "Notes" tab, you see the comments that others entered when they originally bookmarked the site (see Figure 7.4). You also see a list of the most popular tags that users have used to describe the site.

## Figure 7.2. Searching Delicious.com

## Figure 7.3. Viewing Who Has Bookmarked a Site in Delicious.com

## Figure 7.4. Viewing Comments in Delicious.com

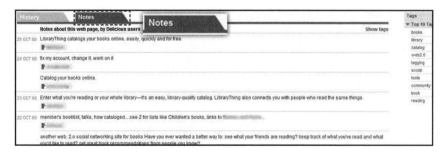

This is where the concept of "folksonomy" is demonstrated. You not only see the comments other people have made on a particular site, you also get the additional terms they used to tag it. You can further expand your search on those tags, so your search results are influenced by real people's classification of the Web, not a machine's.

Furthermore, you can click on another user to see all of the sites that he or she has bookmarked (as long as they have made them public). Figure 7.5 shows the bookmarks for Dalton Publishing, an independent press in Austin, Texas. We found their bookmarks, and hence their Website, only two clicks away from the very general search term "books" that we started with—this would be nearly impossible in a traditional search engine.

## Figure 7.5. Dalton Publishing's Bookmarks

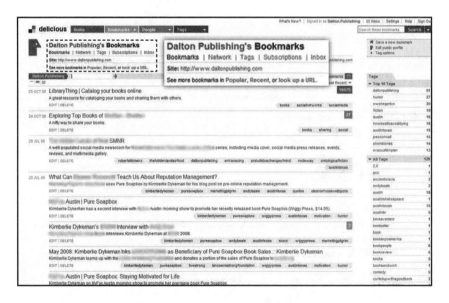

Hopefully, you see how powerful these sites can be in helping you reach millions of potential readers you may not have reached otherwise.

## Using Social Bookmarking Sites

To get started, get an account with Delicious.com. Once you have an account, the service walks you through how to add a button to your browser's task bar so you can bookmark sites easily.

Figure 7.6 demonstrates how you would bookmark a site using Delicious from a Firefox browser. When you come across a site you want to bookmark, just click on the "post to delicious" button on your browser's task bar—you then see a screen similar to Figure 7.6. Here is where you enter your chosen "tags" and your notes to the site you want to bookmark. Make these descriptive, since this is what attracts others to your account if they happen to come across your notes on this particular site.

### Figure 7.6. Bookmarking a Website to Delicious.com

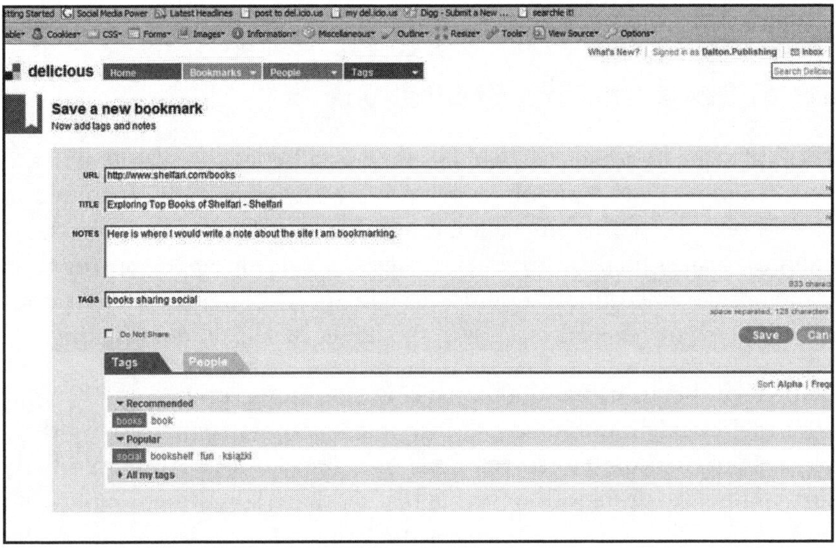

Once you have bookmarked many sites, you can search them just like you search the entire Delicious site—based on tags. Figure 7.5 shows the bookmarks for Dalton Publishing. Figure 7.7 shows only Dalton Publishing's bookmarks that are tagged with the term "humor."

## Figure 7.7. Dalton Publishing's Bookmarks, Tagged

# A Social Bookmarking Strategy

The first thing to do is get a good feel for a number of social bookmarking sites. There are some popular sites listed at the end of this chapter and on the resource CD. Choose a couple that represent your interests. If you do not feel inclined to do the research, I recommend starting with Delicious.com, Technorati, and StumbleUpon. Using these three sites should give you a broad reach into the world of social bookmarking.

Before you begin using a bookmarking site, however, become familiar with their guidelines. Some sites are much more stringent than others about bookmarking your own sites, or representing a business of any sort. It is best to go forward informed rather than risk getting a reputation for ignoring the rules, or worse, getting banned from a site.

As you develop your social bookmarking strategy, keep in mind that the Social Web is about interacting, sharing, and collaboration—not self promotion. Bookmark, tag, and comment on sites that interest you, and connect with others with similar interests. You will be amazed at how many people you ultimately reach. There is nothing wrong with bookmarking your own Web pages or blog posts, as long as the site allows it; just balance those contributions with others.

I know I sound like a broken record on this point, but fill out your profiles completely! You don't want to go through the trouble of bookmarking a bunch of sites, only to have others not even know how to find *your* Website if they find your bookmarks engaging enough to click through to your profile.

Create a list of your best key terms to use as tags and use them as often as they apply to the sites you bookmark. Use your best tags within the descriptions you give each of your bookmarked sites as well.

Many of the social bookmarking sites have developed social networking characteristics. If available, you should join groups that are relevant to your area of expertise or interest and subscribe to email updates for those groups.

## Purpose-Built Delicious Pages

When you create your Delicious.com account, the link to your bookmarks look something like this: http://delicious.com/your.account, where "your.account" is the username you chose when you created your account. When you bookmark a Website and "tag" it, you in essence create another URL that looks like this: http://delicious.com/your.account/tag.

For example, on Figure 7.7 notice the URL at the top of the browser: http://delicious.com/Dalton.Publishing/humor. This is there because we searched for all bookmarked sites in Dalton Publishing's account with the tag "humor."

Now, imagine that you can create a URL for any collection of sites you want by just bookmarking the sites in Delicious.com using a common tag. These are called "purpose-built Delicious pages."

Rather than tagging your favorite sites blindly, think about how you might tag them intentionally to create your own purpose-built pages that contain a collection of related sites. For instance, you could create links to several pages like this:

- delicious.com/your.account/company.name
- delicious.com/your.account/public.relations
- delicious.com/your.account/client.name

- delicious.com/your.account/competition
- delicious.com/your.account/book.title
- delicious.com/your.account/author.name

You can then use links to those URLs in the body of your Websites, blogs, news releases, etc.

Book publishers and companies with many advocates can especially benefit from these pages. A publisher could collect sites relevant to each of its authors and book titles, and use links in each author or title's respective press releases or media pages. The pages could be referenced by the authors themselves on their own Websites or blogs, too.

The best demonstrated use of purpose-built pages are within social media newsrooms and news releases—see Chapter 10: "Social Media Newsrooms."

# Other Popular Social Bookmarking Sites

## Technorati[2]

"Technorati was founded to help bloggers to succeed by collecting, highlighting, and distributing the online global conversation. As the leading blog search engine and most comprehensive source of information on the blogosphere, we index more than 1.5 million new blog posts in real time and introduce millions of readers to blog and social media content."

*—Technorati.com*

## StumbleUpon[3]

"StumbleUpon helps you discover and share great websites. As you click Stumble!, we deliver high-quality pages matched to your personal preferences. These pages have been explicitly recommended by your friends or one of 6 million+ other websurfers with interests similar to you. Rating the sites you like automatically shares them with like-minded people—and helps you discover great sites your friends recommend."

*—StumbleUpon.com*

---

[2] http://www.technorati.com
[3] http://www.stumbleupon.com

### Searchles[4]

"Searchles is a highly scalable 'social search' platform that showcases expertise, enables collaboration with peers and instantly captures it in searchable knowledge indexes. The platform is a hybrid, combining aspects of 'social bookmarking' and 'social networking' technology with analytical 'social search' capability. You decide who influences your discovery efforts, when and how through networks of trust you create— no other bookmarking or social search site lets you do that!"

*—Searchles.com*

# Crowd-Sourcing

A *crowd-sourced* news site allows its users to determine the popularity of a news story, blog entry, or Website through various types of voting or rating systems. Most of these sites also have certain social aspects, allowing users to connect to others with similar interests. Connections between users are usually made through the conversations that ensue around a particular story, blog post, or Website.

This system gives news-searchers an alternative to what is served up to them by the regular news sites. It offers a way for searchers to see how other people rate stories and what they have to say about them. This concept of user-rated content is what has been coined "crowd-sourcing."

## Crowd-Sourcing in Action

Digg[5] is an example of a crowd-sourced news site since it encourages people to "digg" the stories they like, which will in turn bring the most "dugg" stories or blog posts closer to the front page of the site. Each news site has its own unique twist on this concept.

---

[4] http://www.searchles.com
[5] http://www.digg.com

Figure 7.8 shows the front page of Digg. All of the stories listed have been added by users, and "dugg" by other users—some of the most popular of these stories will show up on this front page. Digg's front page offers a number of general areas to click on (like Technology, World & Business, Science, etc.) for more specific news to fit your interests. It also offers crowd-sourced videos and images.

### Figure 7.8. Front Page of Digg.com

Search crowd-sourced news sites the same way you search other news sites or search engines. Figure 7.9 shows the search results for the search term "business social networking." The search results will show stories,

### Figure 7.9. Search Results on Digg.com

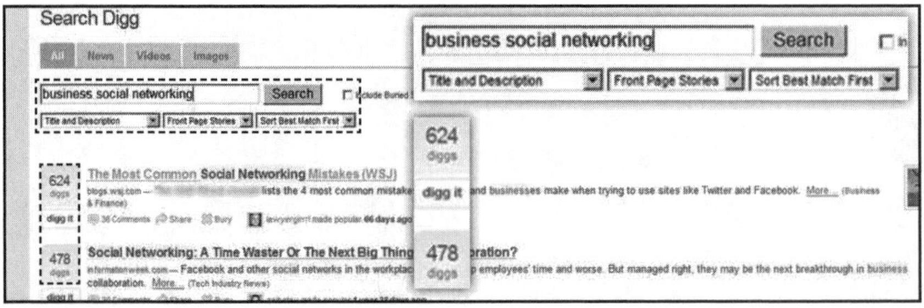

blogs, and Websites other users have added that fit the search criteria along with how many people have "dugg" each result—this number is to the left of each result in Figure 7.9.

You see a few additional ways to filter or sort your search results as well. For instance, you can choose to see only the stories that made it to the front page of Digg, or all stories, or you can order the search results by "the best match," "the most diggs," etc. (see Figure 7.10).

## Figure 7.10. Filtering Searches in Digg.com

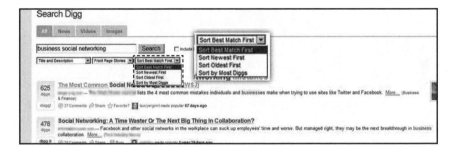

Once you find a story of interest, you can go directly to the story, read others' comments on the story, or see the other users who dugg the story. Figure 7.11 shows a few of the comments other users posted on the first

## Figure 7.11. Comments on Submissions to Digg.com

story listed in Figure 7.9. From here, you can connect with others by adding comments of your own or going to another user's profile (see Figure 7.12). If you find their profile interesting, you might want to visit one of their Websites or explore other stories they have dugg.

## Figure 7.12. User Profile on Digg.com

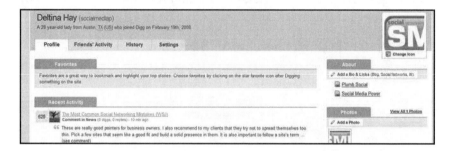

# Using Crowd-Sourced News Sites

Once you have an account with a crowd-sourced news site, you can add your own content and/or rate existing content. Continuing with Digg as an example, to add a story to the news site, you can go to Digg.com and click on the "Submit New" button at the top right of the page (see Figure 7.8 on page 202).

Figure 7.13 shows the first screen you see when you submit a new link to the site. Pay close attention to the submission guidelines listed to the left. Each crowd-sourced site has its own submission guidelines. Become familiar with them before you submit.

## Figure 7.13. Submitting to Digg.com

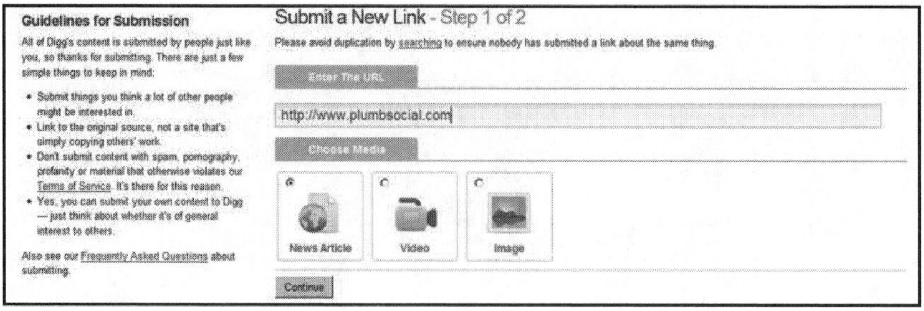

Figure 7.14 shows the next step, which is to enter a title and description for your submission. Just as you did with social bookmarking entries, use as many of your best key terms in each title and description as you can. You also need to choose a topic (category) to place your submission in during this step.

## Figure 7.14. Submitting to Digg.com, 2

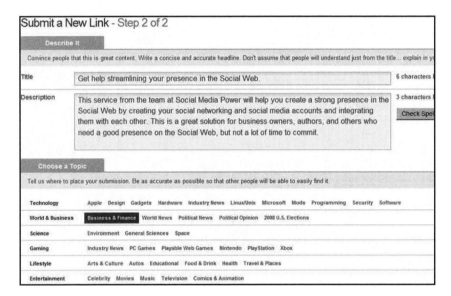

Once you submit your entry at the second step above, Digg then searches all of its existing entries for duplicates. It then presents a list of possible sites that might be a match to your submission. If it has already been added to Digg by another user, you can still digg it, but it will retain the title and description given by the original submitter. If your submission is original, you see a screen like Figure 7.15.

For convenience, you can digg stories on the fly right from your browser by installing a button on your browser's task bar.[6]

To digg a story that you find interesting while you are browsing the Digg site, just click on "Digg it" to the left of the story. Likewise, if you would like to comment on a story, click "comments" just under the story's title. See Figure 7.8.

---

[6] http://about.digg.com/downloads

## Figure 7.15. Submitting to Digg.com, 3

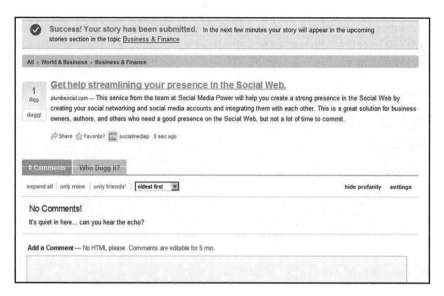

# A Crowd-Sourcing Strategy

Crowd-sourced news sites are different from social bookmarking sites in that they focus on sharing news and information *about* stories, Websites, and blogs, as opposed to sharing bookmarks *to* Websites or blogs. As a result, you want to use a different strategy for these sites than you would social bookmarking sites.

There are a lot of crowd-sourced news sites out there, so you may want to explore a number of the sites we mention at the end of this chapter or on the resource CD to get a feel for them. You should be able to choose a few sites that are good fits for your message.

As always, fill out your profiles completely so that others can find their way to you easily.

Add some of your more newsworthy blog posts, Web pages, or online press releases to each of your chosen crowd-sourced news sites. Pay close attention to each site's submission guidelines and do not add information that does not adhere to their guidelines or is not a good fit for the site. When considering whether to add something to one of these sites, ask yourself if it is something *you* would find newsworthy, and if you would *naturally* share it with others. Just like with social bookmarking sites, be sure to offset your own content by contributing other content as well.

You will get a natural following of readers from these sites if you contribute regularly and engage in the conversations that happen around topics of interest. The advantage to this strategy is that you can hone in on your target audience by seeking out and commenting on topics relevant to your product, book, or message.

Many of these sites have also added social networking features, so explore any additional ways the sites may offer to connect, such as groups.

## Other Popular Crowd Sourcing Sites

### reddit[7]

"[R]eddit is a source for what's new and popular on the Web—personalized for you. Your votes train a filter, so let reddit know what you liked and disliked, because you'll begin to see recommended links filtered to your tastes. All of the content on reddit is submitted and voted on by users like you."

*—reddit.com*

### Mixx[8]

"You find it; we'll Mixx it. Use YourMixx to tailor the content categories, tags, specific users and groups, and we'll deliver the top-rated content as chosen by you and people who share your passions. So go ahead and whip up your own version of the Web. Just tell us how you like it Mixxed and we'll deliver the best the Web has to offer—morning, noon and night."

*—Mixx.com*

# Preparation and Tracking Your Progress

Use a sheet like Figure 7.16 to list the Web pages and blog posts you plan to add to bookmarking and crowd-sourced news sites, along with some of your best key terms as tags, and descriptions that also include those key terms.

---

[7]  http://www.reddit.com
[8]  http://www.mixx.com

## Figure 7.16. A Form for Organizing Submissions

| Company Name: Social Media Power | | | |
|---|---|---|---|
| URL | Title | Description | Tags |
| http://www.socialmediapower.com/articles/social-media-news-releases-explained/ | Social Media News Releases Explained | A thorough explanation of social media news releases, with links to examples. | social media, social media newsroom, social media news release, social media optimization, Web 2.0 |
| Http://www.socialmediapower.com/2008/08/28/the 30-minute-facebook-application/ | The 30-minute Facebook Application | Learn how to further optimize your presence in the social Web by creating your own Facebook application in 30 minutes or less. | social media, social networking, facebook, facebook applications, web 2.0 |
| http://www.socialmediapower.com/2008/06/02/top 9-wordpress-plugins/ | Top 9 Most Useful Wordpress Plugins | A list of essential plugins for anyone looking to optimize their Wordpress site for social media and Web 2.0 | social media, wordpress, plugins, social media optimization, social bookmarking, SEO, social media tools, Web 2.0 |
| http://www.socialmediapower.com/articles/social-media-newsrooms-the-ultimate-web-20-tool-for- | Social Media Newsroom: The Ultimate | A social media newsroom is one place to send the media, prospective clients, book reviewers, or anyone who wants to know all about you, your business, or your book. It is the ultimate Web 2.0 | social media, social media newsroom, web 2.0, social media tools, web 2.0 tools, soc |

If you have a lot of content you plan to add, or if you are doing bookmarking and crowd-sourcing for your clients, you may want to keep a record of your additions to these sites (see Figure 7.17).

## Figure 7.17. A Form for Tracking Activity

| Company Name: Social Media Power | | | |
|---|---|---|---|
| Date | Original URL | Bookmarking Site | Bookmark URL |
| 1/11/08 | http://www.socialmediapower.com/artic les/social-media-news-releases-explained/ | Delicious | http://delicious.com/social.media.power/socialmedianewsrelease |
| | | Digg | http://digg.com/tech_news/Social_Media_News_Releases_Expla ed |
| 1/11/08 | Http://www.socialmediapower.com/200 8/08/28/the-30-minute-facebook-application/ | Delicious | http://delicious.com/social.media.power/facebookapplications |
| | | Digg | http://digg.com/tech_news/The_30_minute_Facebook_Applicati |
| 1/11/08 | http://www.socialmediapower.com/2008/06/ 02/top-9-wordpress-plugins/ | Delicious | http://delicious.com/social.media.power/wordpress |
| | | Digg | http://digg.com/tech_news/Top_9_Most_Useful_WordPress_Plu s |
| 1/11/08 | http://www.socialmediapower.com/articles/s ocial-media-newsrooms-the-ultimate-web-20-tool-for-your-business/ | Delicious | http://delicious.com/social.media.power/socialmedianewsrooms |
| | | | http://digg.com/tech_news/Social_Media_Newsrooms_A_Web_ |

Fillable versions of these worksheets are available on the resource CD.

# A Note on Making Your Content Sharable

Hopefully this chapter has demonstrated for you how important it is for you to make your own content easily shared on social bookmarking and crowd-sourcing sites. Refer to Chapter 3: "RSS Feeds & Blogs," Chapter 12: "Pulling It All Together," and Chapter 9: "Widgets & Badges," for more information on how to do this.

# This Chapter on the Resource CD

- Linkable Resources
- Fillable Forms:
    › Social Bookmarking Strategy
    › Crowd-Sourcing Strategy
    › Social Bookmarking & Crowd-Sourcing Submission Form
    › Social Bookmarking & Crowd-Sourcing Tracking Form

# 8 Media Communities

Media communities are social sites where you can save, share, and comment on multimedia items. It is yet another way Internet users have found to connect with one another—by finding similar interests around images, videos, and documents.

In addition to increasing your exposure in the Social Web, adding your images, video, and documents to media communities can have other advantages. There are many open source applications that tap into the power of these sites to offer you a host of features you can add to your blog or Website, features like image and video galleries, slide shows, portfolios, or sidebar widgets. With proper planning, you can even see better search engine placement for your images, video clips, and document files by adding them to media communities.

## Image Sharing Sites

Image sharing sites are a way for you to get some serious mileage out of your photos and other images. With the right strategy, you can maximize the ways in which potential clients and readers can find you through your posted images in the Social Web.

## Image Sharing in Action

Flickr[1] is probably the most popular site on the Internet for sharing images. Flickr offers a place for you to share your images with others, as well as a platform for organizing and linking to your images.

Figures 8.1 and 8.2 show the Flickr account for Dalton Publishing. This opening screen shows the most recently uploaded images.

Along the right are the sets of images Dalton has created. A "set" is a collection of related images. You can create up to three sets with a free Flickr account, or unlimited sets with a "pro" account. A pro account

### Figures 8.1 and 8.2. A Typical Flickr* Account With Sets

[1] http://www.flickr.com

*All Flickr images reproduced with permission of Yahoo! Inc. ©2009 Yahoo! Inc. Flickr is a registered trademark of Yahoo! Inc.

runs $25 a year. Dalton creates a set for each of their books, for each significant event they host, and for a few miscellaneous collections of images—like one for all of their book covers. Sets can be further organized into "collections." Figure 8.3 shows a set of images. You can reach this screen by clicking on any set.

## Figure 8.3. A Flickr Set

By clicking on a specific image, you can see more detail for that image, like the tags and descriptions assigned to it when it was uploaded (see Figure 8.4). If you click on a specific tag, you can view all the other

## Figure 8.4. Flickr Image Detail

images that Dalton Publishing associated with that tag. Figure 8.5 shows all of the images tagged with the term "dalton publishing."

### Figure 8.5. Tagged Images in Flickr

When you upload images, you can make them public so that anyone can view them, or private so that only people who are your "friends" on Flickr can see them. Public images can be viewed and commented on by anyone. Figure 8.6 shows how you might comment on an image.

### Figure 8.6. Commenting on an Image in Flickr

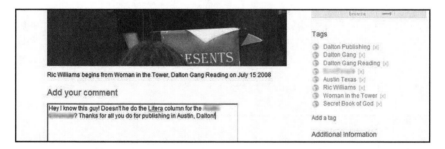

# Using Image Sharing Sites

## Uploading and Optimizing Your Images

Once you have an account, uploading images to sites like Flickr is easy. However, just because it is easy is no reason to go about it without a plan. Read the "Image Sharing Strategy" section on page 222, and go forward with a good plan so you can maximize the effectiveness of using these communities.

Figure 8.7 shows one of the options you can use to upload images to your Flickr account. You can reach this menu by signing in to your account and clicking "Upload Images and Video." There are three steps to this process:

1. Choosing your images

2. Uploading your images

3. Giving your uploaded images good titles, descriptions, and tags.

You can upload several images at a time as shown in Figure 8.7. Just select each image you want to upload and click "open."

## Figure 8.7. Uploading Flickr Images

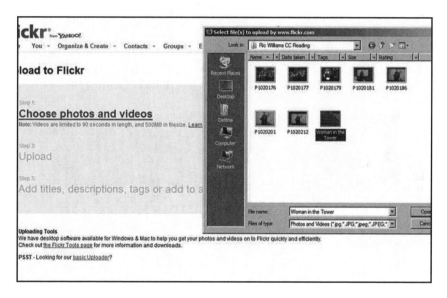

On the next screen (Figure 8.8), you can perform batch operations, like assigning tags to each image, adding all the images to a specific set, even adding a new set on the fly. In our example, we are uploading photos taken from one of Dalton Publishing's author events. Therefore, we want to "tag" each image with the author's name, the book title, and the event name.

## Figure 8.8. Batch Operations on Uploaded Flickr Images

## Figure 8.9. Assigning Titles and Descriptions to Images

Figure 8.9 shows the titles and descriptions that we assigned to each image. We make a point to use the author's name, the venue and event name, and the book title in each title and description. Note that when you upload an image, Flickr will automatically use the name of the file as the title. You want to be sure and change the title to one that uses several good key terms as we did in our example. Figure 8.10 shows Dalton Publishing's "photostream," along with the new set to the right, and the recently uploaded images.

### Figure 8.10. Uploaded Images in Flickr Photostream

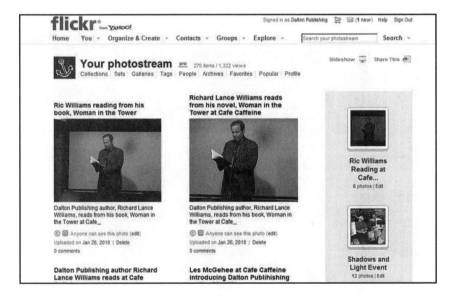

There is a great tool called the "Flickr Uploadr" that you can download to your desktop. The tool allows you to upload to Flickr right from your desktop by dragging and dropping images into the tool. Figure 8.11 shows

### Figure 8.11. Flickr Tools Menu

the download screen used to access the tool. You can reach this screen by clicking on "help/tools" at the bottom of your main photostream page, or by going to this link: http://www.flickr.com/tools/.

## Creating Badges

From the tools menu in Figure 8.11, you can create a Flickr badge. A Flickr badge is a widget that you can place on your Website or blog that displays images from your Flickr account as a small gallery. Figure 8.12 shows a Flickr badge in the right sidebar.

### Figure 8.12. Flickr Badge and Gallery on Website

On the right sidebar of the tools screen (Figure 8.11) is a link to "build a badge" (not visible). There are a few steps to creating your badge: First, choose what type of badge you want, then choose which images to include; then you choose layout options and colors; finally, copy the code to place on your site or blog.

The first step is to choose whether you want to create an HTML badge or a Flash badge (Figure 8.13). A Flash badge offers some movement to an

## Figure 8.13. Creating a Flickr Badge

otherwise static site, while an HTML badge is static, but takes less time to load.

Figure 8.14 shows the next step, which is to choose which images you want in your badge—all of them, images tagged with a certain key term, or images in a specific set.

## Figure 8.14. Creating a Flickr Badge, 2

If you chose to create an HTML badge, the next screen (Figure 8.15) allows you to choose certain layout options like number of images, size of images, etc. If you chose a Flash badge, you go directly to the color options screen.

## Figure 8.15. Creating a Flickr Badge, 3

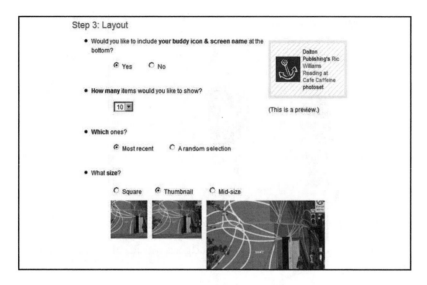

Figure 8.16 shows the color options screen. You can enter hex numbers for your colors if you know them, or use the color picker.

Finally, in the next step, the code for your badge is generated (Figure 8.17). Copy this code and place it anywhere you want in the body of your site's HTML code or as a sidebar widget on your WordPress blog.

## Figure 8.16. Creating a Flickr Badge, 4

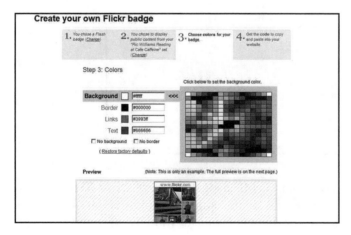

Placing the code from Figure 8.17 into a sidebar widget (see page 105) produces the Flickr badge on that WordPress site's sidebar as seen on Figure 8.12 on page 218.

## Figure 8.17. Copying Flickr Badge Code

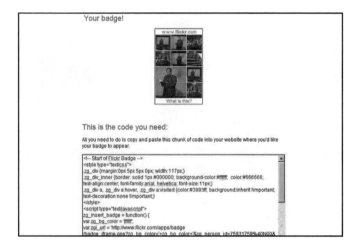

## Galleries and Adding Flickr Images to Blog Posts

One reason it is a good idea to organize your images in sets is that there are many plugins for WordPress and other applications that rely on sets to help you create galleries. Figure 8.12 on page 218 shows a gallery from a WordPress site that was created using the plugin called "Flickr Tag."[2] This plugin allows you to easily create galleries using your Flickr sets, as well as embed your Flickr images into your blog posts and pages.

Figure 8.18 shows the code that is used to create a gallery from Flickr sets using Flickr Tag. Each of your Flickr sets has a number, which are the numbers you see in the code. For instance, the "Ric Williams Reading at Cafe Caffeine" set we just created is shown in Figure 8.19. If you look at the address in the browser, you see the set's number, which is why the images for that set show up in the gallery as shown in Figure 8.12 on page 218.

---

[2]http://wordpress.org/extend/plugins/flickr-tag/

## Figure 8.18. Using the Flickr Tag Plugin for Galleries

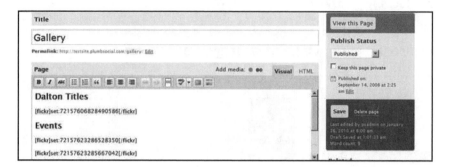

## Figure 8.19. Finding a Flickr Set Number Using Your Browser

Figure 8.20 shows how you can use the tool to embed images into blog posts or pages simply by clicking on the image (or set) you want to add.

Another good application for WordPress, as well as for a traditional Website, is Simple Viewer.[3] Once you have Simple Viewer installed, you can use an add-on called Flickr Viewer to import your Flickr images into a gallery on your Website.

## Figure 8.20. Using the Flickr Tag Plugin to Embed Images

---

[3] http://www.simpleviewer.net/simpleviewer/

# Image Sharing Strategy

- Get an account with the image community of your choice and fill out your profile completely (see Figure 8.21). Remember that this may be the only chance you get to make an impression on potential clients or readers.

## Figure 8.21. Using Key Terms in Flickr Profiles

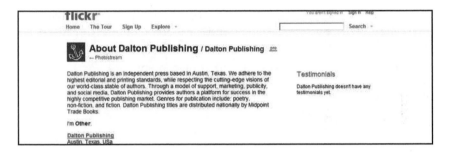

- Gather the images you can upload right away. This may include:
  › Logos
  › Head shots of company principals
  › Author photos
  › Book covers
  › Event photos
- Prepare a main key term list to use as tags for every image. This may be your company name, principal name, author name, book title, home city, etc.
- For each image you want to upload prepare:
  › A list of key terms to use as tags in addition to your main key term list.
  › A short title that uses at least two key terms.
  › A description that uses several key terms.
- Use a form like Figure 8.21.1 so you will be prepared when uploading images. A printable version of this form is available on the resource CD.
- Pull images from your account onto your blog and/or Website:
  › As a badge or widget
  › As an image gallery
- Connect with others by browsing images and commenting.

## Figure 8.21.1 Prep Form for Image Communities

| Image/Video/Document Community Upload Form | | | |
|---|---|---|---|
| Image Name | Title | Description | Tags |
| RicWilliamsCafe1 | Dalton Publishing author Ric Williams reading from his book, Woman in the Tower | Dalton Publishing author, Richard Lance Williams, reads from his book, Woman in the Tower at Cafe Caffeine in Austin, Texas. | ric williams, richard lance williams, woman in the tower, dalton publishing, cafe caffeine, austin texas |
| RicWilliamsCafe2 | Richard Lance Williams reading from his book, Woman in the Tower. | Dalton Publishing author, Richard Lance Williams, reads from his book, Woman in the Tower at Cafe Caffeine in Austin, Texas. | ric williams, richard lance williams, woman in the tower, dalton publishing, cafe caffeine, austin texas |

## Other Image Sharing Communities

While searching for a list of photo sharing sites, I came across an interesting chart by Chris Silver Smith called "Comparison of Image Sharing Sites for Potential SEO Benefit".[4] This chart lists a number of sites and how they can benefit your SEO placement.

# Video Sharing Sites

Many claim that video is the future of the Internet. That may be true, and if it is, YouTube and other video sharing sites are where you want to have a good presence when that future comes. Even if you do not have video of your own to upload, you can take advantage of these sites by building galleries from videos others have uploaded or by connecting to others by commenting on their videos.

## Using Video Sharing Sites

### Uploading and Optimizing Your Videos

Figure 8.22 shows the front page of YouTube.[5] From here you can search and watch videos or upload your own if you have an account. Clicking the "Upload" button in the upper area of this screen yields the Video Upload screen shown in Figure 8.23.

When uploading video clips, follow the same guidelines as you do for uploading images: Prepare a list of key terms and use them as tags and in the body of a video's title and description. YouTube also requires that you choose a category for your uploaded videos.

---

[4]http://silvery.com/PhotoSharingComparison.html
[5]http://www.youtube.com

## Figure 8.22. YouTube Home Page

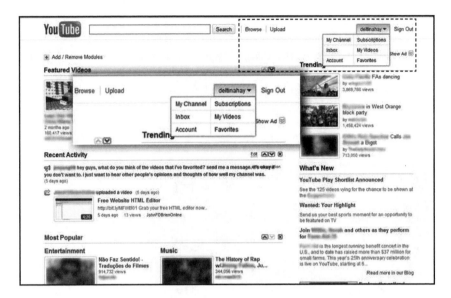

## Figure 8.23. YouTube Video Upload Screen

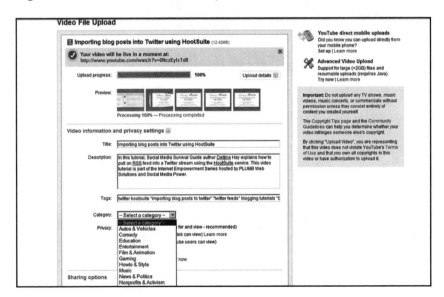

## Channels, Favorites, Queues, and Playlists

Your public page in YouTube is called your "channel." Figure 8.24 shows the Internet Empowerment Series channel. Get to this page by clicking on "My Channel" from the drop-down menu seen in Figure 8.22. You can edit your channel settings, including descriptions, colors, which videos or playlists to display, and more from this page as well. See Figure 8.25.

### Figure 8.24. YouTube Channel

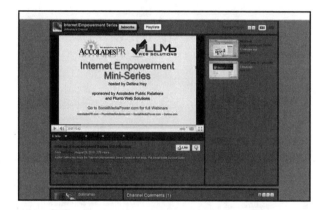

### Figure 8.25. YouTube Channel Options

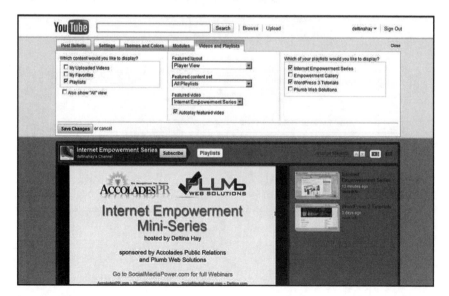

You don't have to upload your own videos to populate a channel on YouTube. You can add "Favorites" to your account as you browse the videos on YouTube. Others can browse your favorites on your channel page.

"Queues" are nice for saving groups of videos temporarily until you are ready to watch them or build a playlist with them.

"Playlists" are collections of videos that you can arrange in a specific order, share with others, or embed as galleries on your blog or Website.

You can add videos to your favorites, to a queue, or to a playlist by clicking on the little arrow under a video when you are browsing (see Figure 8.26).

## Figure 8.26. Adding Videos to YouTube Queue or Playlist

To edit your favorites, queues, and playlists, go to the "My Videos & Playlists" page (Figure 8.27). Reach this page by clicking "My Videos" from the pull-down menu seen in Figure 8.22.

## Figure 8.27. YouTube "My Videos & Playlists" Page

## Embedding Videos and Galleries

Each public video on YouTube has embed code that you can copy and paste into your Website or blog posts. See Figure 8.28. You can also copy links or share on other social sites by clicking the "share" button.

### Figure 8.28. YouTube Individual Video Detail

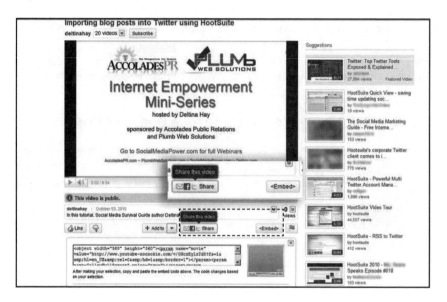

The easiest way to embed galleries is with playlists, since each YouTube playlist you create has its own embed code. To add a new playlist, click on playlists on your "My Videos & Playlists" page.

Figure 8.29 shows a playlist from our example called "Internet Empowerment Series." When you add playlists, use the same strategy as when adding individual videos. Use your best key terms as tags and in titles and descriptions.

You can add videos from your uploaded videos, your favorites, or from your queue to a playlist from this page (see Figure 8.30).

## Figure 8.29. YouTube Playlist Detail

## Figure 8.30. Adding Videos to YouTube Playlist

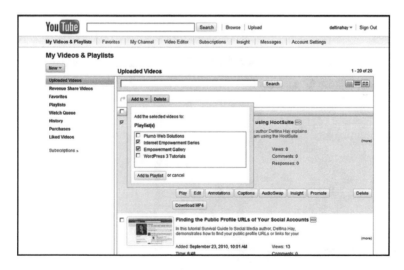

Once we add all the videos to our playlist, we again click on our playlist as seen in Figure 8.29. We copy the embed code for the playlist and embed it in a page on our WordPress site.

Figures 8.31 and 8.32 show the embedded code and the resulting video gallery on our WordPress powered Website.

YouTube has a nice handbook[6] with some good pointers on creating and uploading videos.

## Figure 8.31. YouTube Gallery Code Embedded

## Figure 8.32. Resulting Gallery from YouTube Embed Code

[6]http://www.youtube.com/t/yt_handbook_home

# Video Sharing Strategy

- Get an account with the video community of your choice and fill out your profile completely (see Figure 8.25 on Page 226). Remember that this may be the only chance you get to make an impression on potential clients or readers.
- Gather and prepare the video clips you plan to upload. YouTube accepts video files from most digital cameras, camcorders, and cell phones in the .AVI, .MOV, .WMV, and .MPG file formats.
  › Prepare a main list of key terms to use as tags for every clip. This may be your company name, principal name, author name, book title, home city, etc.
- For each video you want to upload prepare:
  › A list of key terms to use as tags in addition to your main key term list.
  › A short title that uses at least two key terms.
  › A description that uses several key terms.
  › A YouTube category.
- Use a form like Figure 8.33 so you will be prepared when uploading video clips. A printable version of this form is available on the resource CD.
  - Determine the organization of your account:
  › Decide which playlists to create in your account by person's name, by company, by authors, by book titles, by product, etc.
  › Create titles, descriptions, and key terms to use as tags for each playlist.
  › Browse YouTube videos to add to your playlists.
  › Create galleries on your Website or blog using the embed code from your playlists.

## Figure 8.33 Prep Form for Video Communities

| Image Name | Title | Description | Tags |
|---|---|---|---|
| RicWilliamsCafe1 | Dalton Publishing author Ric Williams reading from his book, Woman in the Tower | Dalton Publishing author, Richard Lance Williams, reads from his book, Woman in the Tower at Cafe Caffeine in Austin, Texas. | ric williams, richard lance williams, woman in the tower, dalton publishing, cafe caffeine, austin texas |
| RicWilliamsCafe2 | Richard Lance Williams reading from his book, Woman in the Tower. | Dalton Publishing author, Richard Lance Williams, reads from his book, Woman in the Tower at Cafe Caffeine in Austin, Texas. | ric williams, richard lance williams, woman in the tower, dalton publishing, cafe caffeine, austin texas |

Image/Video/Document Community Upload Form

# Document Sharing Sites

Document sharing sites present opportunities to reuse static Website information, white papers, presentations, and many other types of documents you may already have on hand, as well as new content.

## Document Sharing in Action

Scribd[1] is a good example of a feature-rich document sharing community. Figure 8.34 shows the Scribd home page. From this page users can search, discover, browse, read, and subscribe to others' documents. Users can create their own accounts and share documents publicly, privately, or even offer them for sale.

### Figure 8.34. Scribd Home Page

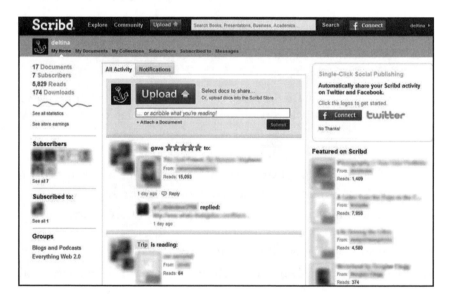

Figure 8.35 shows Dalton Publishing's Scribd home page. They have a number of documents that they have organized into collections. They presently have two collections, one of Dalton Publishing titles, and one containing social media documents and presentations.

---

[1] http://www.scribd.com

## Figure 8.35. Dalton Publishing's Scribd Page

Visitors can browse Dalton's documents, leave comments, download and embed the documents on their own sites, view documents on mobile devices, and share them on social sites like Facebook or Twitter. See Figure 8.36.

## Figure 8.36. Dalton Publishing on Scribd

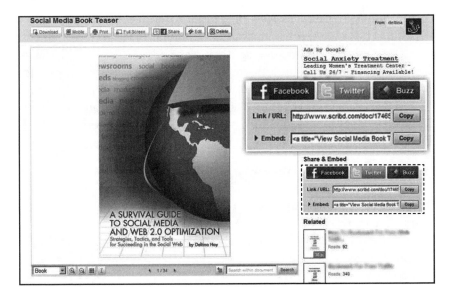

One nice feature, as seen in Figure 8.37, allows links to be embedded and subsequently followed from within the documents you share on Scribd. Not all document sharing sites offer this feature, and it is particularly handy if you are using your documents as sales tools and need to link back to landing pages.

**Figure 8.37. Embedded Links in Scribd Documents**

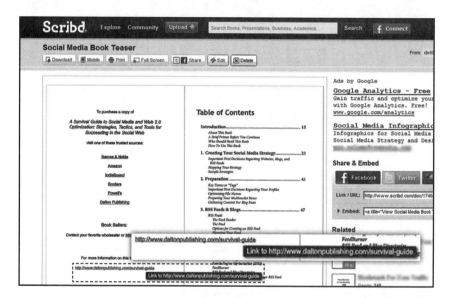

Dalton Publishing utilizes sites like Scribd in a number of ways. They place their book excerpts in a viral environment that can lead to direct sales from within the documents; they place advance review copies of their books in these communities in hopes of snagging a few reviews prior to the release of their books; and they use them to share presentations on social media and Web 2.0 sites on which they are thought leaders. Chances are that there are similar ways you or your business can utilize these sites.

## Using Document Sharing Sites

Once you have an account, fill out your profile completely and classify yourself properly. Figure 8.38 shows how you can classify your account (the community category) to help others easily find you. Sync your account with your Facebook, Twitter, and Google Buzz accounts where applicable. See Figure 8.39.

## Figure 8.38. Scribd Profile

## Figure 8.39. Sync a Scribd Profile

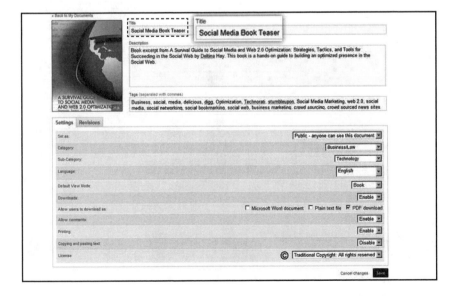

## Figure 8.40. Uploading Documents to Scribd

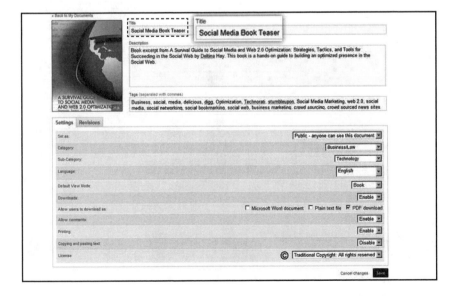

When uploading your documents, make sure your file names, descriptions, and tags contain relevant key terms. Figure 8.40 (on the previous page) shows additional Scribd settings you can apply to your uploaded documents. You can make a document public or private, choose from a number of default viewing options, and assign categories and subcategories. You may want to experiment with providing different categories and subcategories for certain documents. Figures 8.40 and 8.41 show a couple of different category options for the Social Media Book Teaser in our example.

You also have control over *how* others can access your documents, in what formats they can view them, whether they can print, download, or copy the content, etc. Pay special attention to how you attribute the copyright of your documents. See Figure 8.41. If you do not mind that your document is shared freely, but still want to get credit for creating it, choose the appropriate attribution option. If you know for certain that the content is in the public domain (or if you are the author and are placing it in the public domain), then choose the corresponding options. If the content of the document is from a copyrighted book or you want to copyright protect it, then choose the traditional copyright option. If you are unsure, check the copyright law[2].

## Figure 8.41. Scribd Settings

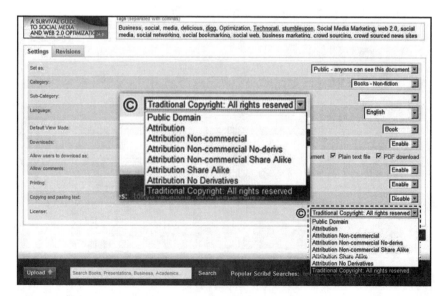

---

[2] http://www.copyright.gov/title17/

Figure 8.42 shows a Scribd document widget on a Website. To embed one of your uploaded documents, copy the embed code as seen in Figure 8.36 on page 233 and place the code where you want the widget to appear on your Website. (See Chapter 9: "Widgets and Badges" for more information on placing widget code.)

## Figure 8.42. Scribd Widget on Website

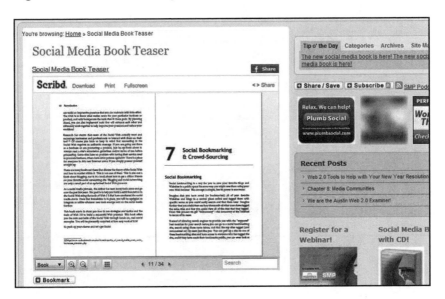

# Another Document Sharing Example

SlideShare[3] is a place to share and distribute presentations. Though you can use it for any type of document, it works particularly well for presentations and slide shows. Figure 8.43 shows a SlideShare home page. It is similar to Scribd, but is more focused on the presentations as opposed to the community.

Like Scribd, you can feature a collection of slides as a widget on your Website as shown in Figure 8.44. Another nice feature of SlideShare is its slidecasts, which are a combination of slides and audio.

---

[3] http://www.slideshare.net

## Figure 8.43. SlideShare Home Page

## Figure 8.44. SlideShare Widget

# Document Sharing Strategy

- Get an account with the document community of your choice and fill out your profile completely.
- Gather documents you can upload right away. These may include:
  - › Content from static Web pages
  - › Articles
  - › White papers
  - › Book excerpts
  - › Presentations
- Prepare document files as follows:
  - › Create a PDF or presentation of the document
  - › Make sure the links within the PDF are working
  - › Rename the file using at least one key term
  - › Note what type of copyright the document should have
  - › Note the limitations that should be set for use of the document (i.e., is it public or private, can it be downloaded, printed, etc.)
- Prepare a main key term list to use as tags for every document. This may be your company name, principal name, author name, book title, etc.
- For each document you want to upload prepare:
  - › A list of key terms to use as tags in addition to your main key term list
  - › A short title that uses at least two key terms
  - › A description that uses several key terms
- Use a form like Figure 8.45 so you will be prepared when uploading documents. A printable version of this form is available on the resource CD.
- Embed documents from your account onto your blog and/or Website:
  - › Individually
  - › As a collection
- Connect with others by browsing documents, subscribing to others' accounts, and commenting.

## Figure 8.45 Prep Form for Document Communities

| Document Community Name: Scribd | | | | | |
|---|---|---|---|---|---|
| Document Name | Title | Description | Tags | Notes | |
| WomanInTheTower.pdf | Woman in the Tower: Stories for the Wounded Child Excerpt | Woman in the Tower: Stories for the Wounded Child by Richard Lance Williams is a novel of fables told to a man in the throes of a life crisis... | Fiction, fables, story telling, dalton publishing, richard lance williams, jungian archetypes | Public, Traditional Copyright, disable download, disable copy and paste. | |
| SocialMediaTeaser.pdf | Social Media Book Teaser | Book excerpt from A Survival Guide to Social Media and Web 2.0 Optimization: Strategies, Tactics, and Tools for Succeeding in the Social Web by Deltina Hay... | Business, social, media, delicious, digg, Optimization, Technorati, stumbleupon, web 2.0, social bookmarking, social web, crowd sourcing | Public, Traditional Copyright, disable copy and paste. | |

# Searching and Search Engine Placement

You search images in Flickr, videos in YouTube, and documents in Scribd or SlideShare using search terms just as you do in a search engine like Google. Your search results return images, videos, or documents that have your search terms in their title or description.

Figure 8.46 shows a search in Flickr on the terms "publishing austin." In the results are a number of the images from Dalton Publishing's Flickr account, specifically, the ones with the terms "publishing" and "austin" in the images' file names.

Flickr displays details on each image that is returned in a search. The first image displayed from the search in Figure 8.46, for instance, shows:

## Figure 8.47. Exploring Tags in Flickr

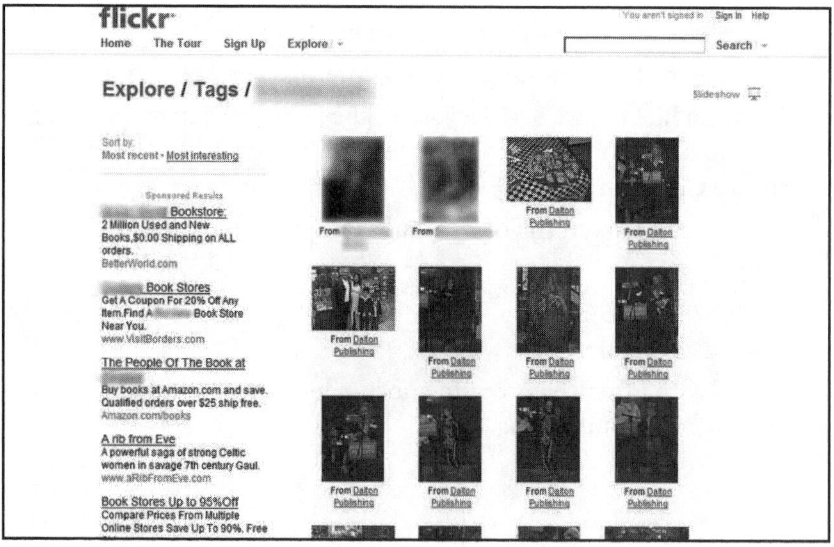

- The file name: "Dalton Publishing display at BookPeople in Austin, Texas"
- Who posted the image: by "Dalton Publishing"
- What tags it was assigned: Tagged with "austintexas, bookpeople, daltonpublishing"
- When it was taken and when it was uploaded
- Links to more photos by the poster of the image, or to their profile: "See Dalton Publishing's photos or profile"

## Figure 8.46. Search Results in Flickr

From here, you can further explore images by clicking on the tags that others have assigned to their uploaded images. By clicking on the "bookpeople" tag in our example, we get the results as shown in Figure 8.47. This shows all of the images in Flickr that are tagged with specific terms, not just the images of a particular user, thus further expanding and honing your search results.

It is during such a search that others may happen upon your profile. Figure 8.21 on page 223 shows Dalton Publishing's Flickr profile. Be sure and fill in your profile completely; it is how other users will ultimately find their way back to your blog, Website, or products.

An added perk to using Flickr is that your images also get good placement in the Yahoo! search engine. Searching Yahoo! Image search using the same terms we used in the previous example, we will see some of the same results. See Figure 8.48.

### Figure 8.48. Fickr Images in Yahoo!* Search Results

Figure 8.49 shows a search in YouTube using the term "deltina hay."

Like Flickr, YouTube displays details on each video that is returned in a search. These details include the name of the video, part of the description, when the video was added, who uploaded the video, how many times it has been viewed, how the video has been rated by others, and the video length.

From the search result's screen, one can watch a video, link to the profile of the person who added the video, and search under the same terms for channels and playlists that include the videos.

*All Yahoo! images reproduced with permission of Yahoo! Inc. ©2009 Yahoo! Inc. YAHOO! is a registered trademark of Yahoo! Inc.

## Figure 8.49. Search Results in YouTube

Figure 8.50 shows the playlists that are also part of the search results for our search terms. This is another way people can find you in a video community search, and why you want to optimize your playlists as well.

## Figure 8.50. Playlists in YouTube Search Results

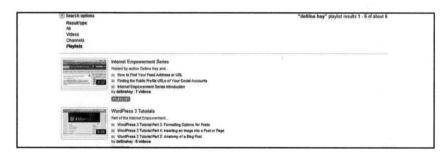

Figure 8.51 shows a search using the terms "les mcgehee" in Google video search. Just as with Flickr and Yahoo! Image search, one is most likely to see the videos from YouTube listed first in a Google video search.

## Figure 8.51. YouTube Videos in Google Search Results

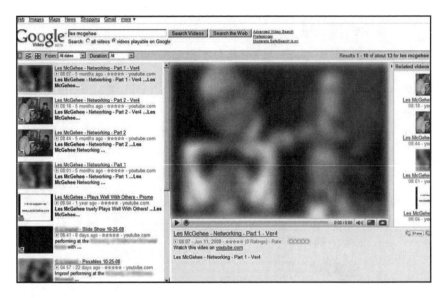

Since document sharing sites have the contents of the documents themselves to search, their search criteria does not have to be limited to a specific document's name, key terms, and descriptions. For instance, Figure 8.52 shows a search in SlideShare using the term "creating wordpress websites."

## Figure 8.52. A SlideShare Search

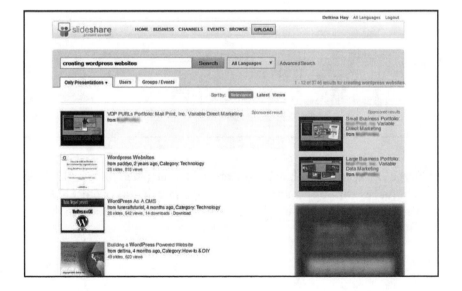

Even though that specific combination of terms is not used in the title, key terms, or description of the document entitled "Building a WordPress Powered Website," it still shows up on the first page of this search.

Figure 8.53 shows a Yahoo! search using "deltina hay" as the search term. As you can see, the corresponding SlideShare profile shows very nice placement.

**Figure 8.53. SlideShare in Yahoo! Search**

# Connecting with Others

Do not forget that the purpose of media sharing communities is for people to connect with each other through a shared medium like images and video. You can reach a lot of potential clients and readers by becoming a part of such communities, but you need to take the time to connect.

# This Chapter on the Resource CD

- Further Reading
- Linkable Resources
- Fillable Forms:
    > Image Sharing Strategy
    > Prep Form for Image Communities
    > Video Sharing Strategy
    > Prep Form for Video Communities
    > Document Sharing Strategy
    > Prep Form for Document Communities

# 9 Widgets & Badges

Figure 9.1 shows a sidebar from Dalton Publishing's social media Website. This Web page displays many widgets and badges. From the top down, they are:

- A widget from FeedBurner.com that helps visitors subscribe to the site's RSS feed via email
- A widget from AddtoAny.com that visitors can use to subscribe to Dalton's RSS feed in many different feed readers
- A widget from AddtoAny.com that visitors can use to share or bookmark Dalton's site in social bookmarking or crowd-sourcing sites
- A Facebook fan box widget that displays fans of Dalton's Facebook page and invites visitors to become a fan, too
- A number of badges—from MySpace to Shelfari—that lead a visitor to Dalton's profiles on their respective sites
- A widget from Flickr.com that imports and highlights images from Dalton's Flickr account
- A widget from Upcoming.org (not visible) that imports and lists Dalton's upcoming events

## Figure 9.1. Widgets on a Website

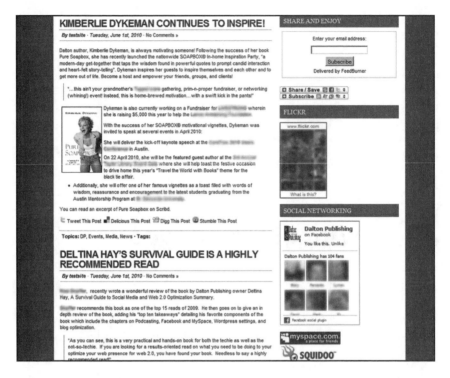

Widgets are snippets of code, usually displayed graphically, used to syndicate content, for example RSS feeds, or to add interactive features that users can drop onto their own blogs or Websites. Widgets are often customizable by the user and typically offer ways for users to pull information from the widget's originating site.

In the example above, each of the widgets demonstrated were created by going to a social site (like Flickr.com), finding where they offer widgets, customizing the widget to display specific images along with color and size options, copying the code, and placing the code within the Dalton Website via the WordPress widget panel (see page 122).

Though the terms widget and badge are often used interchangeably in the Web 2.0 community, a badge is typically just an icon or logo that has a link back to its source, which serves as a way of displaying one's membership or presence in a community on the Social Web. Widgets are also referred to as "Gadgets." You may have installed a gadget or two on your desktop if you use Windows Vista. To avoid confusion, we will refer to all of them as widgets, unless their source refers to them otherwise.

Widgets come in different styles and levels of complexity. Some are simple links back to their source, others are as complex as mini search engines you can implement on your own site. They also vary in user friendliness. Most widgets, though, are simple to install and set up. This is what makes them so successful.

Individual widget installation varies, but, generally, the process is as follows:

1. Discover where a site offers its widgets or badges.

2. Choose the type of widget you want to generate from the source site.

3. Set widget options, and, if applicable, customize the look and feel of the widget.

4. The source populates the widget with your profile information (if applicable) and your customizations.

5. The source then generates the code for your widget.

6. Copy the generated HTML, JavaScript, or Flash code.

7. Place the resulting code onto your Website or blog where you want the widget to appear.

The examples highlighted in the following sections of this chapter demonstrate the level of functionality of widgets, as well as real world examples of how to install and use them.

# Highlighting Your Social Web Presence

Some widgets help you show off all of the places you are in the Social Web. Some of these are just small icons that you download from a particular social site and place on your Website or blog with a link back to your profile or page. Other widgets pull information from your profile or from profiles you are connected to within a specific community.

# Social Networking

In Chapter 6: "Social Networking & Micro-Blogging," we showed you several examples of using badges and widgets to promote your social networking presence. See page 184 for one such example.

Here are a few, more specialized examples:

## Twitter

From the Twitter/Goodies/Widgets[1] menu, you can find a number of widgets to use on your Website, blog, or social networking sites.

Figure 9.2 shows the main Twitter widget options page. From here you can create widgets to display your Twitter updates or integrate Twitter into some of your other social networking sites.

### Figure 9.2. Twitter Widgets

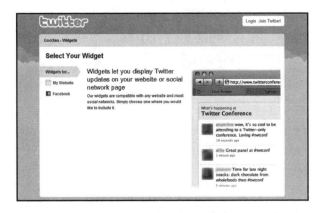

Figures 9.3 and 9.4 shows some of the screens used while integrating your Twitter account with your Facebook account. Figure 9.5 shows the resulting application page on Facebook.

Figures 9.6 and 9.7 show one way to create widget code to place on a Website or blog that displays your Twitter activity in a widget. You can change the settings, preferences, appearance, and dimensions of your

[1] http://twitter.com/goodies/widgets

## Figures 9.3 and 9.4. Creating a Twitter Widget for Facebook

## Figure 9.5. Twitter Widget on Facebook

widget from here, then test your settings and grab the code to place on your blog or Website. Figure 9.8 shows the result once the code is pasted onto the Social Media Power Website.

## Figures 9.6 & 9.7. Making a Twitter Widget

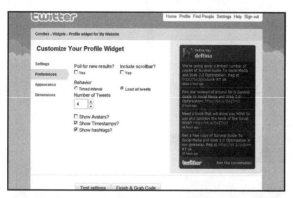

## Figure 9.8. Twitter Widget on a Website

## LinkedIn

LinkedIn offers a nice widget that displays your public profile as a sort of digital business card. Login to your LinkedIn account, go to "Developers" at the bottom of the page, and click on "LinkedIn Widgets." Figure 9.9 shows a few of the available widgets you can install on your Website.

### Figure 9.9. LinkedIn Widgets

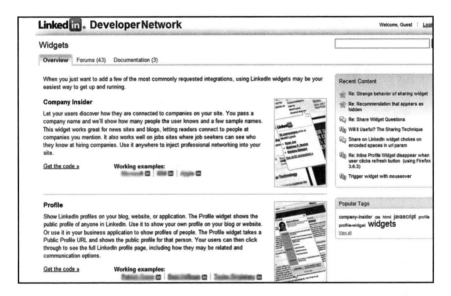

Figure 9.10 demonstrates the "Profile" widget. LinkedIn widgets are a little more involved than some of the others, but once they are set up, they work just fine. Follow the instructions carefully, and you should have no problem, or have your Webmaster help you.

Figure 9.11 shows an example of this widget on the "About Us" page on the Social Media Power Website.

## Figure 9.10. Creating LinkedIn Widgets

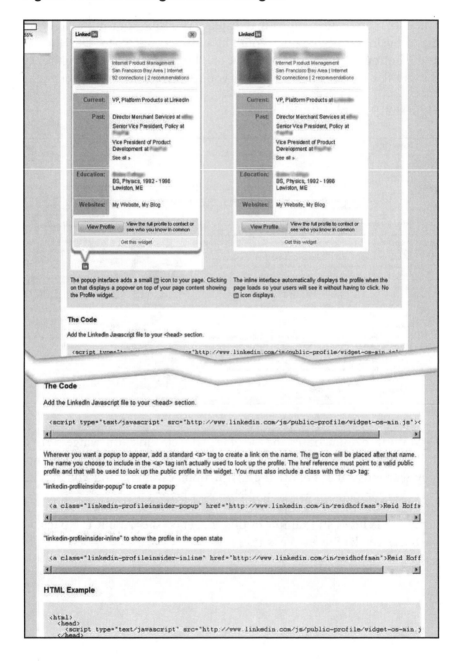

## Figure 9.11. LinkedIn Widget on a Website

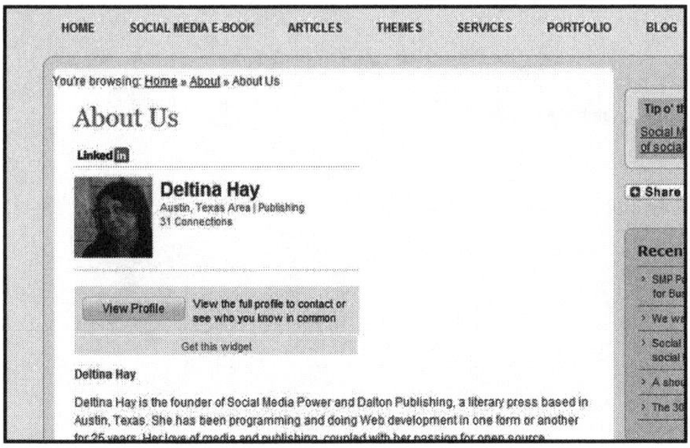

## Shelfari

This niche social networking site has a stylish widget that displays your favorite books on a graphic bookshelf. Log in to your Shelfari account and go to Profile/My Shelf/More/My Widgets. Figure 9.12 shows the first screen you see.

## Figure 9.12. Creating a Shelfari Widget

Figure 9.13 shows the next screen once you click "Get Started." If you are planning to place the widget on one of the social sites listed (Facebook, MySpace, etc.), then click on the corresponding icon.

We want to place the widget on a Website, so we choose the JavaScript option. Figure 9.14 shows a list of filtering options used to select the books you wish to display on your bookshelf widget.

## Figure 9.13. Creating a Shelfari Widget, 2

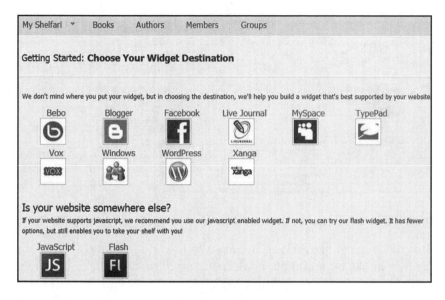

## Figure 9.14. Creating a Shelfari Widget, 3

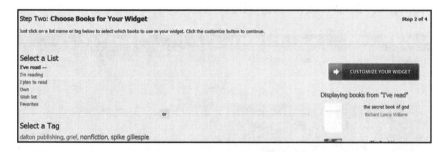

The next screen (Figure 9.15) shows ways you can further customize the widget. Once it is customized, copy the code and place it on the Website.

Figure 9.16 shows the resulting widget displayed on Dalton Publishing's social media Website.[2] Figure 9.17 shows the pop-up info box that shows when a visitor rolls over a book image.

---

[2] http://testsite.plumbsocial.com/about/

## Figure 9.15. Creating a Shelfari Widget, 4

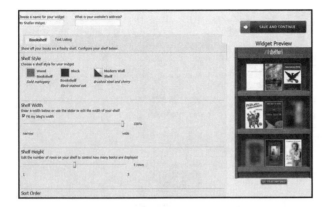

## Figure 9.16. Shelfari Widget on a Website

## Figure 9.17. Shelfari Widget on a Website, 2

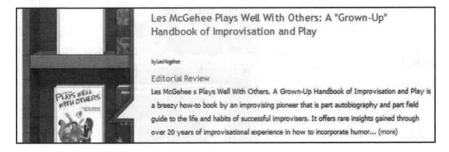

# Facebook Like Boxes

Formerly called "Fan Boxes," these widgets highlight a Facebook fan page and encourage site visitors to "like" the page, too. Figure 9.18 shows the process for creating this plugin. The right-hand sidebar of Figure 9.1 on page 248 shows this widget in action.

### Figures 9.18. Creating a Facebook Like Box

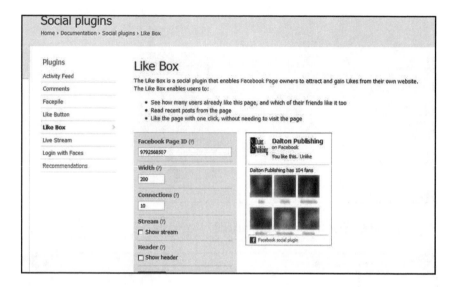

# Media Communities

Chapter 8: "Media Communities" shows you how to create and install a Flickr badge, which is a widget that pulls images from your Flickr sets onto your Website or blog. See page 218.

That chapter also shows you how to embed a YouTube gallery onto your Website. See page 228. You can make your own YouTube widget by creating an embedded player and simply adjusting the size of the player to fit your sidebar.

You can find more widgets for Flickr, YouTube, and other media communities in widget sharing communities (see the "Widget Communities" section on page 282) or as WordPress plugins (see the "Using Widgets in WordPress" section on page 278).

## Other Social Sites

You are likely to have many more sites that you want to highlight on your Website or blog. Some sites do not make their widgets or badges easy for users to find. To find available widgets for a site, first do a site-wide search using the search terms "widgets" or "badges." If that yields nothing, try searching the site's help area. If that still reveals nothing, try searching Google for "sitename widgets." If you were searching for YouTube widgets, for instance, you would search using the term "YouTube widgets."

# Sharing and Syndicating Your Content

In Chapter 7: "Social Bookmarking & Crowd-Sourcing," we discuss improving your Social Web presence by contributing to social bookmarking and crowd-sourcing sites. We also discuss the importance of integrating an RSS feed or blog into your Web presence in Chapter 3: "RSS Feeds & Blogs." In this section we look at some widgets that encourage others to subscribe to your RSS feed and to share your site on social bookmarking or crowd-sourcing sites.

## Feed Widgets

Chapter 3: "RSS Feeds & Blogs" shows you how to use feed widgets to promote your blog or RSS feed using FeedBurner chicklets and email widgets. See page 86. There are many more user-friendly ways to encourage people to subscribe to your feed. Some of them even give your feed some extra exposure in the Social Web.

Here are a couple of specific examples:

### Blidgets

The widget community Widgetbox[3] offers a feed widget called a "blidget." This blidget is a customizable widget that allows users to display your feed on their site. Read more about widget communities on page 282.

Get an account with Widgetbox, then click on the "Make a Blidget" button (see Figure 9.19).

On the next screen, enter your RSS feed or blog URL (see Figure 9.20). Refer to Chapter 3: "RSS Feeds & Blogs" on page 83 if you do not recall how to find your feed URL.

---

[3] http://www.widgetbox.com

## Figure 9.19. Creating a Widgetbox Blidget

## Figure 9.20. Creating a Widgetbox Blidget, 2

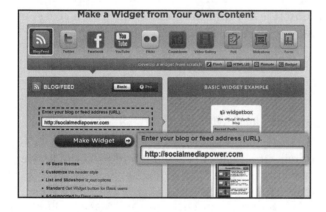

Figure 9.21 shows how you can customize your new feed widget, including adding an image, titles, tags, and a description. Use and reuse your best key terms whenever you can while creating your blidget.

Figure 9.22 on page 262 shows the finished blidget for Social Media Power. Widgetbox blidgets like the one we just created are free, but they also offer a pro version for around $30 a year that allows you to design custom themes for your blidget, among other features.

## Figure 9.21. Creating a Widgetbox Blidget, 3

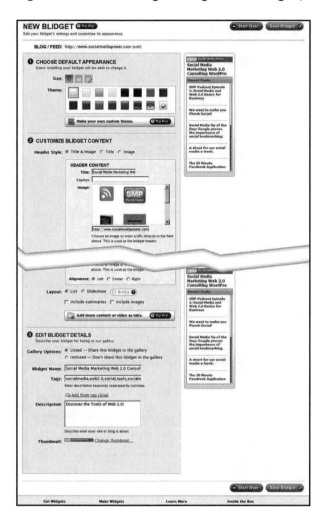

Once your blidget is complete, promote it on your Website or blog. Log in to Widgetbox and go to "My Widgetbox." Here you see all of your widgets, including the blidget you just created (see Figure 9.23). From this screen, make a note of your blidget's "permalink" (the URL that starts with http://widgetbox.com/widgets/).

Once you have your permalink, search the Widgetbox widgets for the "Blidget Promo Badge." Use this badge to create a widget that you can

### Figure 9.22. Creating a Widgetbox Blidget, 4

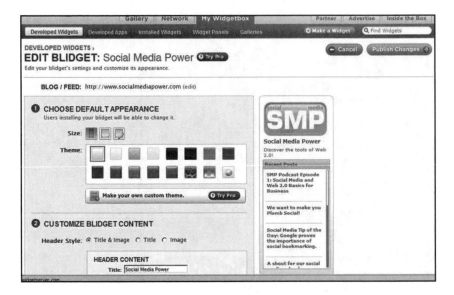

### Figure 9.23. Creating a Promo Widget for a Blidget

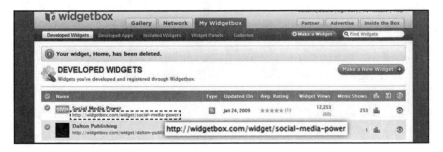

place on your site or other social sites that prompt people to get your feed as a customizable widget for their site.

Figure 9.24 shows how you can customize this widget for your site by changing the color and dimensions. Note that this is where you enter the permalink of your blidget.

Once it is ready, copy the code to place on your site or another social site just as you would any other widget (see Figure 9.25).

## Figure 9.24. Creating a Promo Widget for a Blidget, 2

## Figure 9.25. Creating a Promo Widget for a Blidget, 3

Figure 9.26 shows the respective widget on the Social Media Power Website. When a visitor clicks on this widget, they can subscribe to the feed and display it on their own site after customizing it.

Figure 9.27 shows where the visitor is taken when they click to get the widget.

Figure 9.28 shows the feed widget or blidget displayed on another site that has subscribed to it.

## Figure 9.26. Widgetbox Widgets in Action

## Figure 9.27. Widgetbox Widgets in Action, 2

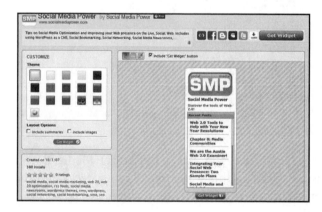

## AddtoAny

Figure 9.29 shows another convenient feed widget from AddtoAny[4] (see the button that says "Subscribe"). We saw this feed widget in action in Chapter 3: "RSS Feeds & Blogs." When a user clicks on this widget they can subscribe to your feed in many different feed readers.

---

[4] http://www.addtoany.com

## Figure 9.28. Widgetbox Widgets in Action, 3

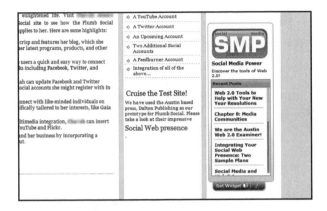

## Figure 9.29. AddtoAny Widget

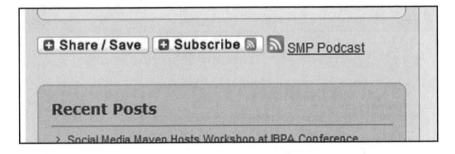

To create this feed widget, go to AddtoAny.com and click "Get the Share Button" (see Figure 9.30). You can get this button for many social sites, but we want it for a Website, so click on that option.

Figure 9.31 shows all of the options available to customize this feed widget. Enter a title for your feed and your feed URL, choose the look and feel of your widget, and click "Get Button Code" to generate the code for the widget.

A few other sites that offer feed widgets are AddThis,[5] netvibes,[6] and Google Gadgets.[7]

---

[5] http://addthis.com/

[6] http://eco.netvibes.com/submit/editor

[7] http://www.google.com/webmasters/gadgets/

## Figure 9.30. Creating an AddtoAny Subscribe Widget

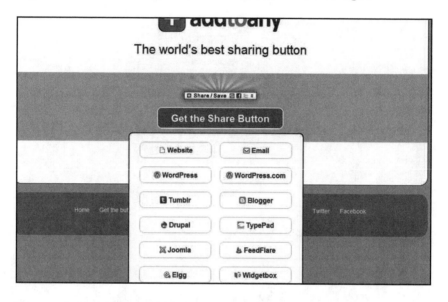

## Figure 9.31. Creating an AddtoAny Subscribe Widget, 2

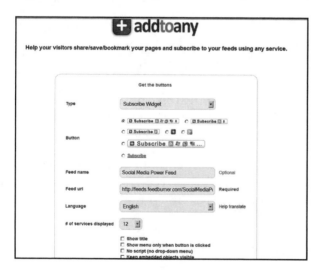

# Social Bookmarking and Crowd-Sourcing

In Chapter 7: "Social Bookmarking & Crowd-Sourcing," we mention the importance of making your site easy for others to add or share in these vital areas of the Social Web. Listed here are a few widgets that you can use on your Website or blog to accomplish this goal.

## AddtoAny

In addition to their feed widget, AddtoAny has a nice widget that helps visitors bookmark or share your site on their preferred social bookmarking or crowd-sourcing sites. Figure 9.29 on page 265 shows this widget in action (see the "Share/Save" button). Figure 9.32 shows another version of this widget, one that pops up when it is rolled over.

### Figure 9.32. AddtoAny Popup Sharing Widget

To create your share widget, go to AddtoAny.com and click "Get the Share Button" (see Figure 9.30 on page 266).

Figure 9.33 shows all of the options available to customize this widget. Enter your Website name and URL, choose the look and feel of your widget, and click "Get Button Code" to generate the code for the widget.

## ShareThis

ShareThis is more robust than some of the other share widgets. Figure 9.34 shows the options available for this widget. One of the things that distinguishes this widget is that, in addition to giving your visitors a way to share your site in the Social Web, it offers visitors a way to post your site to their social networking profiles or blog (see Figure 9.34).

## Figure 9.33. Creating an AddtoAny Sharing Widget

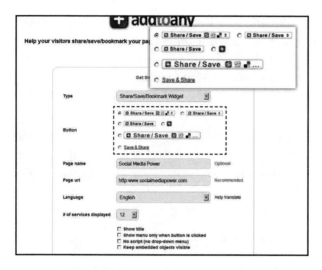

## Figure 9.34. ShareThis Widget

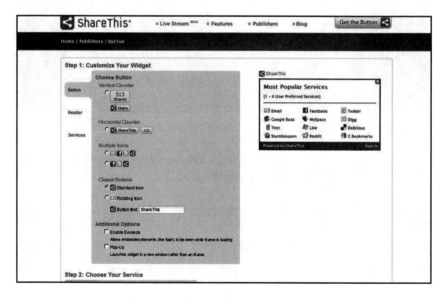

# Making Your Site More Interactive

Some widgets help optimize your Website or blog for Web 2.0 by making your site more interactive. These include widgets that help visitors find you in other places on the Social Web, suggest related content that your readers may find helpful, or offer customizable search tools. Following are some examples:

# Digg.com

You can display Digg[8] news stories on your site using Digg widgets. Figure 9.35 shows the screen for creating a Digg widget. You can filter stories for this widget by topic, author, or any number of other ways.

### Figure 9.35. Digg.com Widgets

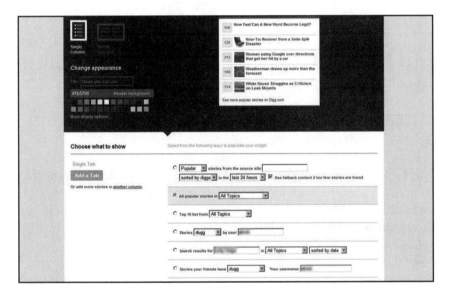

# Delicious.com

Figure 9.36 shows a widget offered by the social bookmarking site Delicious.com. This widget displays your Delicious bookmarks as a tag cloud. When one of the tags in the "cloud" is clicked, the visitor will be taken to all of your bookmarked sites on Delicious.com with that respective tag.

---

[8] http://about.digg.com/downloads/widgets

## Figure 9.36. Delicious.com Widget Example

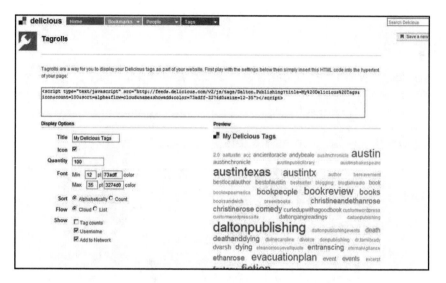

# Lijit

The Lijit[9] "wijit" is an approach to letting your readers search your content all over the Social Web, as well as your network's content. It is sort of like creating your own search engine for your readers, where you determine the sites that are included in the engine.

Figures 9.37 and 9.38 show this widget in action. When a user enters a search term into the widget on the Social Media Power Website (Figure 9.37), a resulting search screen pops up (see Figure 9.38). This search platform has a number of tabs that allow the user not only to search the Social Media Power Website, but to search every site in their "network" using the same search terms.

Once you have an account, you choose your content sources (what the search engine considers your "network") and input all of your profile information. You can then customize your search "wijit" and place it on your site for your readers to use.

---

[9] http://www.lijit.com

## Figure 9.37. Lijit Search Widget

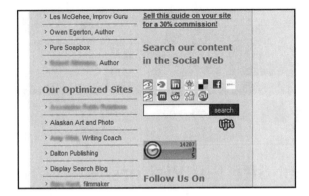

## Figure 9.38. Lijit Search Widgets Results

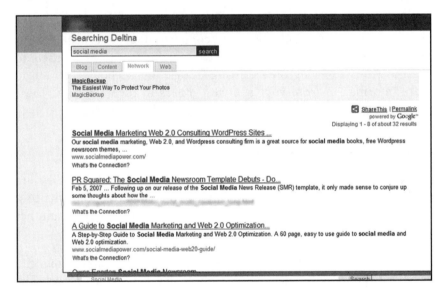

# Widgetbox Revisited

Widgetbox also offers widgets that can make your site more interactive for your visitors. See Figure 9.39. Widgets like polls, video galleries, and slideshows can help make your site "sticky" (keeping visitors on your site longer).

### Figure 9.39. Additional Widgetbox Widgets

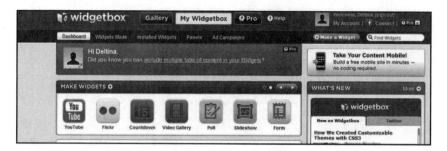

# Personalizing Your Site For Visitors

## Google and Facebook Connect

Distributed Social Networks (DSN), as these are called, allow Internet users to carry their social networking connections around with them as they surf the Web. These widgets offer ways for you to allow users to login to your site using their existing Google or Facebook IDs, and to share information from your site with others in their network. These tools are demonstrated in Chapter 12: "Pulling It All Together."

## Facebook Social Plugins

Though Facebook calls these tools "plugins," by definition, they are actually widgets. Plugins are typically add-ons or enhancements to a specific tool or site, not code that you place on your site from another source.

Regardless, these *widgets* offer ways for you to personalize your site visitor's experience similar to the DSN widgets discussed above. The main difference between these and an actual DSN is that a DSN is an opt-in tool—the user is *invited* to log in to your site and share their information via Facebook or Google. With Facebook's social plugins, however, a visitor just needs to be logged in to Facebook at the time they visit your site to be recognized.

(**Caveat:** There has been a lot of controversy over Facebook's privacy policies and the use of these particular "plugins" on sites external to Facebook. The Facebook team has made some improvements in how they notify its members and allow them to opt out of the plugins, but the solutions are less than ideal for many privacy advocates. I mention this so that you are aware that the issues exist, not to endorse nor oppose them.)

These widgets are designed to work well with sites that list products, reviews, movies, music, and so forth. Visitors can then "like" or "recommend" certain items and see which items their Facebook friends have "liked" as well.

As seen in Figure 9.40, Facebook offers several variations of these widgets, from the "Like Box" we already demonstrated previously in this chapter, to an "Activity" widget that shows a visitor what their friends have been doing on a site in the form of a feed displaying the things those friends have "liked" about a site or comments they may have left.

## Figure 9.40. Facebook's Social Plugins

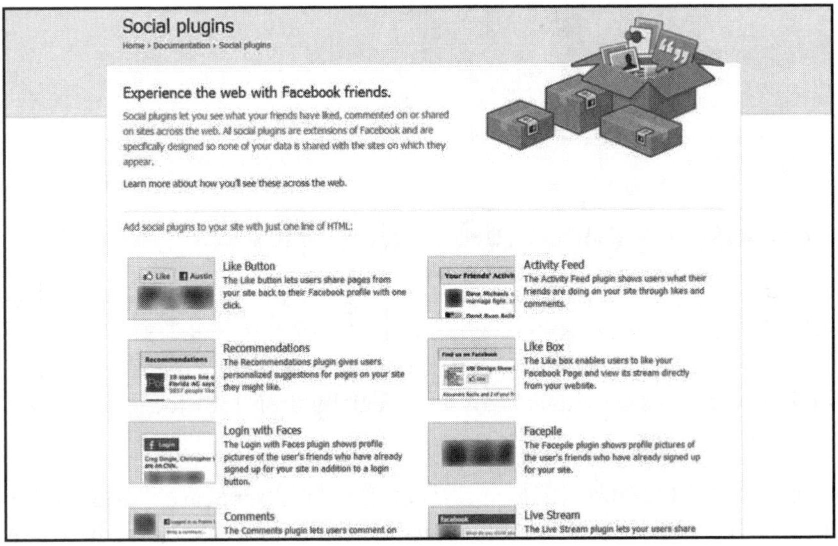

Figure 9.41 shows the process for making a "Like Button" for a Website. Once the code is copied and posted to a site, a visitor to that site is given the option to "Like" the site and that information is then published to their Facebook feed.

This is an oversimplified use of this widget, though. As I mentioned before, these widgets are ultimately designed to be used for individual products or listings. To get the full benefit of these widgets visit the Facebook developer page[10].

### Figure 9.41. Facebook's Social Plugins

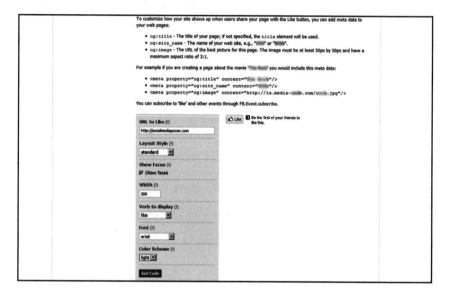

# Micro-Blogging and Geo-Tagging Widgets

We discussed the benefits of micro-blogging and geo-tagging services in Chapter 6: "Social Networking and Micro-Blogging." You can give your site a more personalized experience with real-time feeds from these sites. These types of widgets can be especially useful for local businesses or niche markets.

Figure 9.42 shows the process for creating a "Twitter Search" widget that displays a live feed for "Tweets" tagged with the term "social media." This type of widget can be handy for featuring the latest buzz on a product or business.

Figure 9.43 demonstrates a widget from Brightkite that displays a feed of text updates that users have "geo-tagged" from Austin, Texas. This feed can be further filtered to include a single address if desired.

---

[10] http://developers.facebook.com/plugins

## Figure 9.42. Twitter Search Widget

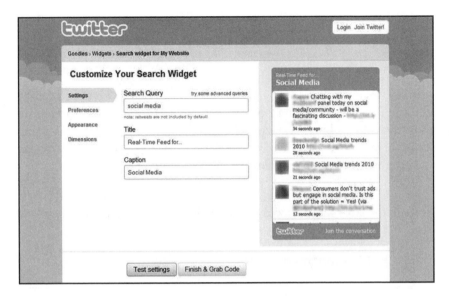

## Figure 9.43. Brightkite Geo-Tagging Widget

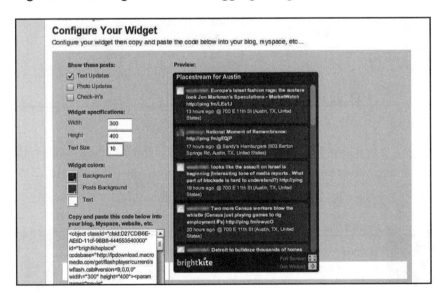

# Promoting Products and Making Money

Offering products for sale or placing ads on your site can be a simple process using widgets. Here are two examples:

## Amazon

You can feature your own or others' products using Amazon widgets on your Website or blog. Amazon offers referral fees for direct sales that result from your use of their widgets, too. Amazon widgets vary in size and complexity, but all of them are easy to set up and customize.

Figure 9.44 shows the range of widgets available at Amazon. The best strategy for choosing the widget that is best for your site is to pop one open and play around with it a bit.

### Figure 9.44. Amazon Widgets

You can offer simple, sidebar widgets for your products (Figure 9.45) or use widgets to create interactive features for your site (Figure 9.46).

### Figure 9.45. Amazon Widget Example

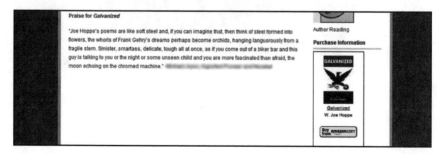

## Figure 9.46. Amazon Widget Example, 2

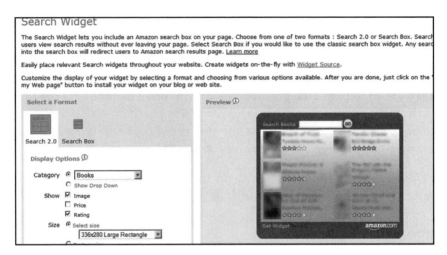

## Google Ads

No doubt you have seen Google ads on many sites you have visited. These ads can produce some decent income for sites with a lot of traffic. Figure 9.47 shows a couple of different options for Google AdSense members. In addition to the typical sidebar and header ad widgets that Google offers, you can install your own mini search engine on your site, and generate income from it.

## Figure 9.47. Google Adsense Widgets

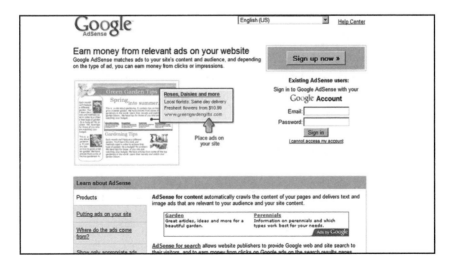

# Using Widgets in WordPress

In Chapter 4: "Building a WordPress Powered Website," we discuss that plugins are one of the features that give WordPress and other content management systems their tremendous power and flexibility. We also talk about plugins that can be used as "sidebar widgets" and how easy they are to set up and position on your WordPress site or blog. To activate a sidebar widget that is a WordPress plugin, install the plugin, then go to Appearance/Widgets and pull the widget onto your sidebar, as explained on page 122 of the aforementioned chapter.

Widgets in WordPress can exist on the sidebars, inside of pages, or directly in blog posts. We demonstrate each scenario below.

## Widgets in Sidebars

Having "widget-ready" sidebars is a huge convenience when it comes to placing widget code onto your site. Let's look at an example that demonstrates one of the widgets we created in a previous section and see how easy it is to place onto a WordPress sidebar.

From the WordPress dashboard, go to Appearance/Widgets. Figure 9.48 shows that the Social Media Power WordPress site has four sidebars to work with. We want to add a widget to Sidebar 2.

Refer back to the "Highlighting Your Social Web Presence/Social Networking" section on page 249 where we created a Twitter widget. Figure 9.7 in that section shows the step where we copy the Twitter widget code to place on our site. Continuing with that example, we copy the code onto our clipboard and return to WordPress.

We now need to add a "Text" widget to place our code into. Text widgets are empty widgets that you can populate with whatever code you like. We drag and drop a blank text widget onto the sidebar and paste the Twitter widget code in the body of the text box. We add the title "Follow Us On Twitter" and we are done, so we click "Save" to save the widget. See Figure 9.49.

Figure 9.50 shows the finished Twitter widget on our WordPress site.

## Figure 9.48. Creating a Sidebar Widget in WordPress

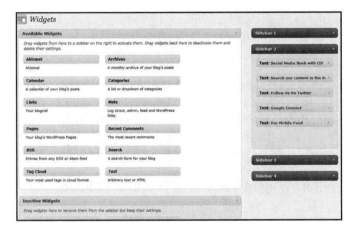

## Figure 9.49. Creating a Sidebar Widget in WordPress, 2

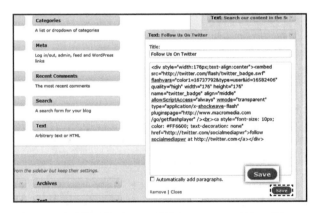

## Figure 9.50. Twitter Widget on a WordPress Site

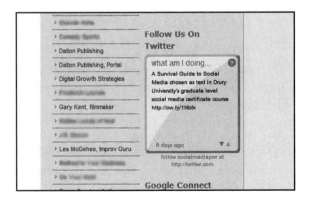

## Widgets in Pages

A good example of placing a widget inside a WordPress page is the Shelfari widget we demonstrated in the "Highlighting Your Social Web Presence/Social Networking" section on pages 249 and 250.

Once the code is copied (see Figure 9.15 on page 257), we place it on the page where we want the widget to appear. "Manage/Pages" brings us to the page editor, and clicking on the page title "About" takes us to the page where we want to add the widget code. Figure 9.51 shows where we added the code, and Figure 9.16 on page 257 shows the finished product.

**Figure 9.51. Shelfari Widget Code on a WordPress Page**

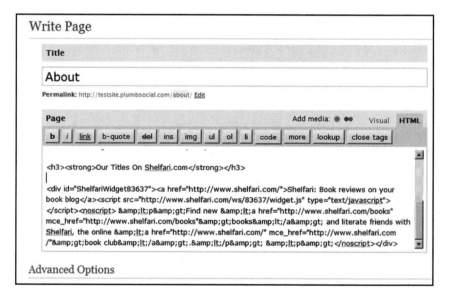

## Widgets in Posts

Some widgets live directly inside your blog posts so that readers can perform actions on individual posts, like sharing posts in social networking and crowd-sourcing sites.

As an example, the AddtoAny share widget, as demonstrated in previous sections, can also be added to individual blog posts so that readers can bookmark or share just a single post if they wish. This is accomplished by installing and activating the AddtoAny bookmark button plugin.[11] Once this plugin is installed and activated, the button appears in your posts automatically. Refer to Chapter 4: "Building a WordPress Powered Website" if you do not recall how to install and activate plugins.

Figure 9.52 shows the widget in action. When the "Bookmark" button is clicked within a particular post, the post can be saved or shared by the user to any number of social sites (see Figure 9.53).

### Figure 9.52. Adding a Widget to WordPress Posts

### Figure 9.53. Adding a Widget to WordPress Posts, 2

# Placing Widgets in Other Websites

Since there are countless ways of creating traditional Websites, it is impossible for us to cover all of the ways you might place widget code into your Website's code. If you maintain your own Website, you already have a good idea of how and where to place widget code so that a widget displays where you want it on your site.

[11] http://wordpress.org/extend/plugins/add-to-any/

If you have a developer who maintains your Website but who does not do your social media optimization, it is probably best for you to generate and copy the widget code yourself, send them the code, and tell them where you want the widget to appear on your site.

# Widget Communities and Directories

In the Feed Widgets section above, we demonstrated the "blidget." This feed widget is one of the features of the Widgetbox widget community.

Widget communities are sites where widget developers can highlight their widgets and others can install and use them. They usually have a user-friendly platform in which to create widgets of your own and a way for you to add them to the community. Other users can then install your widget on their sites, as seen in the blidget demonstration earlier in the chapter.

Some of these communities offer stats on how your widget is doing, as in the number of views and installs. See Appendix C for more information.

If you are searching for a widget to accomplish something specific, these communities are a good place to search. You can also find talented developers in these communities to create custom widgets for you.

You can also use widget directories to find widgets to place on your Website, blog, or personal page (like iGoogle or netvibes).

Here are a couple of widget directories to check out:

- netvibes ecosystem[12]
- Google Gadget directory[13]

# Creating Your Own Widgets

As we demonstrated with the Widgetbox blidget in the Feed Widgets section above, creating your own feed widget is not a difficult task. Of course, you need to have a blog or RSS feed in place to do so. A feed

---

[12] http://eco.netvibes.com/widgets
[13] http://www.google.com/ig/directory

widget is an easy way for you to become part of widget communities, and also offers your feed additional exposure.

You can create your own widgets to accomplish just about anything you want. Widgets can be valuable viral marketing tools if they become popular. If you have a good idea for a widget, there are a number of ways you can proceed.

As discussed in the previous section, most widget communities have user-friendly platforms for creating widgets. Or, if you do not have the skills to create one yourself, you are likely to find a good widget developer in one of these communities to do it for you.

Some platforms (Widgetbox for instance) let you create "Remote" widgets that do nothing more than display an existing Web page. This is a quick and easy way for you to create a widget of your own.

Google Gadgets[14] is also a good platform for creating widgets. Many of the other platforms import and convert Google Gadgets for you, so you can get more mileage out of your widget. Google even provides examples of popular gadgets[15] that you can freely use as templates for your own. You can also search the Google Gadget directory for ideas.[16]

You can create widgets (or "Applications," as they are usually called) specific to particular platforms, like Facebook.[17]

There are some specialized skills involved for creating anything but the most basic widget. A basic knowledge of XML (see Appendix B), HTML, and JavaScript are typically required.

If you want to take the plunge, see Appendix C for a demonstration of how to build a widget of your own.

---

[14] http://www.google.com/webmasters/gadgets/
[15] http://code.google.com/apis/gadgets/docs/legacy/gs.html#GGE
[16] http://www.google.com/ig/directory?synd=open
[17] http://developers.facebook.com

# Working Widgets into Your Strategy

Chapter 12: "Pulling It All Together," discusses the importance of integrating and streamlining your Social Web presence as much as possible. Widgets are an integral part of this process. By utilizing the types of widgets discussed in this chapter, especially the ones that help social tools work together, you will be well on your way.

## A Good Plan to Follow

- Use widgets and badges to highlight your Social Web presence
- Use widgets that pull images, video, events, books, and other information from media or other communities you are a part of onto your site
- Add widgets to your site that can add interactivity—but only if it makes sense to do so
- Place widgets on your site to personalize your visitors experience
- Implement widgets to highlight your products offered for sale on other sites like Amazon
- Add RSS feed widgets to help visitors subscribe to your content
- Use widgets to help visitors share your site on social bookmarking and crowd-sourcing sites
- Place social bookmarking and crowd-sourcing widgets at the end of your blog posts to make each individual post easy for others to share
- Create your own widget if it makes sense to do so
- For security reasons, only install widgets from trusted sources

This plan is recreated on the resource CD.

## Do Not Clutter Your Site

Only add widgets to your site that you believe will benefit your visitors or are essential to your presence; don't place them just for the sake of placing them. Sites can start looking cluttered and disorganized when they have too much on their sidebars.

If you have a substantial Social Web presence that you want to highlight, consider creating a separate social media portal just for that purpose. See PLUMB Web Solutions[18] for ideas.

# This Chapter on the Resource CD

- Further Reading
- Linkable Resources
- Fillable Forms:
    - › Working Widgets into Your Strategy Worksheet

---

[18] http://plumbwebsolutions.com

# 10 Social Media Newsrooms

## What Is a Social Media Newsroom?

Imagine having just one place where you can tell the media, prospective clients, book reviewers, or anyone who wants to know all about you, your business, or your book, exactly what they need to know—a place where they can:

- View all your major media coverage
- See all of your past and present news releases
- Look up all of your past and future events
- Read and link to all of your book reviews
- See and link to all of the places where you have a presence in the Social Web, including any widgets or badges you may have available
- Download multimedia material like photos, company logos, podcasts, vidcasts, etc.
- View bios on each key person in the company, along with links to their social or business networking profiles like LinkedIn, Facebook, Twitter, etc.

- Check out your own purpose-built Delicious page linking to other sites relevant to your business.

- Subscribe through RSS feeds to any portion of information on the site.

- Share any content on the site with their friends or colleagues via email or by posting to social bookmarking indexes like Delicious or Digg with one click

- Send you an instant message using AIM, Yahoo Messaging, MSN, Skype, etc.

- Link directly to your latest blog posts

- Search the site or the entire Web using either Google or Technorati

- Link to other blogs or Websites that are relevant to your message

- See all Technorati tags related to your content

- Comment directly on your media coverage, news releases, and events.

That marvelous place is a Social Media Newsroom (SMNR). Similar to a traditional online newsroom, it lists media coverage, news releases, events, media contact information, and so forth, but it also includes social media and Web 2.0 elements that allow visitors to share and interact with its content.

The SMNR fulfills the traditional purpose of a newsroom while taking advantage of the tremendous indexing opportunities social bookmarking and RSS feed services like Technorati, Delicious.com, Digg, and FeedBurner provide. Imagine that every entry made in your newsroom (*all* of your media coverage, news releases, bios, photos, vidcasts, podcasts, events, etc.) was not only indexed in Google and all of the other search engines, but also in popular bookmarking and RSS feed services, making your content accessible to millions of Social Web users. This is the true power of the SMNR for entrepreneurs, small businesses, authors, and small presses—it offers unprecedented exposure at next to no cost.

This fantastic exposure is a byproduct of the original reason the SMNR was created, but it has grown beyond a mere electronic repository. Originally designed by Todd Defren of SHIFT Communications,[1] the social media newsroom has become the blueprint for the new media—a media that understands multimedia and wants a one-stop shop for every

---

[1] http://www.shiftcom.com

bit of material they will need for their coverage. This new media wants something that is fully downloadable and print ready, easily shared with their colleagues, with links and searches that will lead them directly to more relevant information. More important, though, they want a place that welcomes their comments and invites interactivity. They want to be able to talk back, to create a true media exchange.

# Do You Need a Social Media Newsroom?

A social media newsroom is for individuals or businesses who tend to get or want to get a lot of media coverage, or who put out news releases on a regular basis. Even if you or your business do not fit into either of these categories, but you are building an impressive presence on the Social Web, you may consider building a newsroom just to highlight that fact and show off your presence. However, I do not recommend building a newsroom unless you have the resources to keep it up-to-date.

If you already have a Website with most of these features, you might wonder why you need a newsroom. First, a newsroom tells the members of the media and prospective clients that you are making a *serious* effort to make their jobs easier. A social media newsroom is akin to a news release in that standardization is essential to allow for easy navigation and content extraction by the media.

Second, as mentioned earlier, a social media newsroom (if built using a platform such as WordPress) means that each entry in your newsroom, from a news release to a simple image, can be automatically indexed in search engines, RSS feed indexes, and social bookmarking services, since each entry is added as a separate entry that can be given its own key terms. This means someone can find your site by running into your company logo image, by searching for a blog on the subject of your business expertise, by looking up relevant sites tagged in Technorati or Delicious.com, or by searching for RSS feeds.

But a social media newsroom should not replace your existing Website. You still want a place for blogging and to have a more traditional place to present other information. Do all of your "selling" on your Website. Your SMNR is not a sales tool. Your newsroom is meant to be a neutral place to present all of your media materials.

# Building Your Social Media Newsroom

It is best to build your newsroom separate from your primary site (perhaps as a subdirectory of the main site). Use a blogging or CMS platform such as WordPress, Typepad, Joomla!, or Drupal. Doing so means your newsroom will have built-in RSS feed support and be widgetized (widgets and badges from other social sites are easy to place on the site). I prefer to use WordPress.

## Install WordPress (or other CMS) and Your Theme

It is recommended that you read Chapter 4: "Building a WordPress Powered Website" before continuing. You may also want to refer to the newsroom examples depicted at the end of the chapter as you proceed.

The first step is to install WordPress (see Appendix A) and choose a theme. You can use any suitable theme, but using a theme that is specifically designed for newsrooms can save you a lot of work. Go to the resource CD for a list of recommended WordPress newsroom themes.

Next, install and prepare your theme. See Chapter 4: "Building a WordPress Powered Website," on page 114.

## Design the Functionality of the Theme

When designing the layout of your newsroom, keep in mind that the site needs to stay "flat." That means there is no navigation within or off the main page. One purpose of the page is to truly make all of your media available in one place, at a glance. Note that in most of the examples featured in this chapter the main sections of the newsroom are scrollable content boxes. This allows any number of items to be placed in these sections without needing to incorporate navigation. This rule does not apply to the "Social Media" section or if you build your own social media news releases (see page 299).

The best way to control which entry appears in which respective content box is to use WordPress categories. In other words, each entry in the newsroom is actually a blog entry or "post," and assigning this post to a specific category will determine which content box the post will appear in.

If you are comfortable altering cascading style sheets and changing a modest amount of PHP code, then you can learn how to create your own scrollable, category-driven content boxes in WordPress A theme designed specifically for newsrooms, however, should already have this functionality, or something similar, built-in.

Create the following categories in WordPress (depending on which sections you choose to maintain):

- Media (for media coverage you have received)
- News (for news releases)
- Reviews (for book reviews)
- Events
- Team (for team members or authors)
- Multimedia (for multimedia gallery items)
- Social Media (for social badges, widgets, etc.)

Make sure that your multimedia items, such as audio and video, do not take the visitor away from the newsroom, unless it is from a badge or widget within your "Social Media" section. You can install plugins that will allow them to watch or listen on the spot, or only offer a download option.

Something to keep in mind when choosing or designing your theme is to keep it clean. Use a simple theme with no built-in images save for your logo or book cover image in the header. And keep the colors as neutral as possible. The *content* is what you want your visitors to notice.

## Set Up Your Newsroom Sections

Next, set up, but do not yet populate, the following main sections in your newsroom (each of these sections should have respective categories as described above):

- Media Coverage: a section offering direct links to online sources or to PDFs of media coverage your company or book has received.
- News Releases: a section listing links to traditional or Social Media News Releases (see page 299).
- Events: a section to list events your company is hosting such as book signings, etc.
- Book Reviews (or another industry-specific section): a section offering direct links to online sources or to PDFs of reviews your company or book has received.

- Social Media: a section with links to all of the other places where you have a presence on the Social Web. This section should also list badges or widgets from other social sites such as a Flickr badge, an Upcoming. org widget, a Facebook widget, Twitter widget, etc.
- Multimedia: a section to hold images, audio/video clips, PDF documents, slides, etc. This section contains your company logo, book cover, author/CEO photos, sales sheets, flyers, brochures, etc.
- Team or Author: a section containing biographies on each key person in the company, along with links to their social or business networking profiles like Facebook, LinkedIn, Twitter, etc.
- Add other main sections as your industry demands. There may even be sections here that do not apply to your industry. The main thing is to make certain you have a WordPress category created for any main section you require.

In addition to the main sections, include:

- A section to list RSS feeds that allow visitors to subscribe to individual sections of the room, like media coverage, news releases, or book reviews—or to all of the items in the newsroom
- A way for readers to share the content of the site, using:
  - › email
  - › social bookmarking sites like Delicious.com, Technorati, StumbleUpon, etc.
  - › crowd-sourced news sites like Digg, Mixx, Propeller, etc.
- A small section for instant message indicators for key media contacts using AIM, Yahoo Messaging, MSN, Skype, etc. The "IM Online" WordPress plugin is useful for this.
- The ability for visitors to search the site or the Web using either Google or Technorati
- Links to other blogs or Websites that are relevant to your message
- A section of links to blogs or RSS feeds of key company personnel or of major clients
- Technorati tag cloud. There are a number of good plugins for this. Search the plugin section on WordPress.org.
- If you have video clips that are relevant to your message, you may want to feature them toward the top of the newsroom.

# Preparing to Populate Your Newsroom

Use the following list to gather all of the information you need to populate your newsroom and to complete any preparatory tasks. There is also a worksheet on the resource CD.

## Folders

To make it easy to reference your items, create the following applicable folders to hold the items for the "main" sections of your newsroom (add a folder for any additional "main" sections you add to your newsroom), as well as a general folder for miscellaneous images:

- yoursite.com/newsroom/media
- yoursite.com/newsroom/news
- yoursite.com/newsroom/multimedia
- yoursite.com/newsroom/events
- yoursite.com/newsroom/reviews
- yoursite.com/newsroom/socialmedia
- yoursite.com/newsroom/images

This will help keep your content organized and you will always know where to upload and link to the items you need.

## Icon Set

Choose a multimedia icon set and upload it to your "image" directory. This set should include icons to represent news items, podcasts, video clips, PDFs, DOCs, etc. They will look something like the icons in Figure 10.1. The best way to get a complete set is to purchase one from a royalty-free photo stock site like istockphoto.com. The prices are quite reasonable.

## Preparing Documents, Images, and Other Multimedia Items for Your Newsroom

For each image you plan to place in your newsroom:

- Create a print-ready PDF version:

## Figure 10.1. Internet Icon Set from istockphoto.com

> › Large jpg files often give errors when opening in browsers, so to guarantee you have good, printable versions of your images, save them as PDF files.

- Create a small, thumbnail version:
  - › These are the images that will be visible on your newsroom. You want your newsroom to load quickly, so do not place large image files on it. Always place small, thumbnail images that can be clicked on if there is a need to download a larger image.
  - › Thumbnail images should be jpg or gif, and be no more than 200 pixels wide and 72 dpi. The easiest way to create these in PhotoShop is to resize and use the "Save for Web" option.
- Upload each version to its respective directory.

For each video clip or podcast you plan to place on your newsroom:

- Try to keep the file size under 10 megabytes.
- Even if you have a thumbnail image to represent a specific podcast or video, use an image from your icon set to represent the item. This helps to keep multimedia items distinct and consistent for your users.
- Upload each file to its respective directory.

For each document you plan to place on your newsroom:

- If possible, convert all documents, presentations, etc. to PDF documents.

- Use images from your icon set to appropriately represent your documents (whether PDF, Word Doc, etc.).
- Upload each file to its respective directory.

**A note on file names:** Develop a naming convention for the files you create that uses only alpha characters. Instead of john_doe_headshot. jpg, you might consider JohnDoeHeadshot.jpg. This can save you a lot of grief later on. It is also a good idea to use at least one good key term in each file name.

## Gather the Following Images, Documents, Links, or HTML Code for the Main Sections of Your Newsroom

For each team member or author you want under the "Team" or "Author" section:

- Headshot image
- Brief bio (PDF version)
- Link to blog
- Links to networking profiles in LinkedIn, Facebook, Twitter, etc.

For the social media section gather widgets, badges, or links to:

- Facebook pages
- MySpace pages
- Squidoo lenses
- Twitter accounts
- Media accounts like Flickr and YouTube
- Document sharing accounts like Scribd and SlideShare
- Social calendar accounts like Upcoming or Eventbrite
- Social bookmarking accounts like Delicious, Technorati, etc.
- Purpose-built Delicious pages (see page 199)
- Second Life locations
- Other social sites you have a presence in

Multimedia:

- Logos
- Book cover art
- Executive or author photos
- Press kits and sales sheets (as PDFs)
- Podcasts (downloadable only)
- Video clips (downloadable only)
- Book trailers
- White papers you would like to permanently feature (as PDFs)
- PowerPoint presentations (converted to PDFs)
- Brochures (as PDFs)
- Other promotional or relevant multimedia items

For each item that will be featured in the "Media Coverage" section of your newsroom:

- A small logo from the media source cited (or one from your icon set)
- A short lead-in to the story featured
- A link to original story or PDF version of the story cited

For each item that will be featured in the "News Releases" section of your newsroom:

- The main title and date of the news release
- Create a social media news release (see the "Social Media News Releases" section on page 299)
- A link to the full news release if hosted on a third-party site like PRWeb

For each item that will be featured in the "Reviews" section of your newsroom:

- A small logo from the review source cited (or one from your icon set)
- A short lead-in to the featured review
- A link to or a PDF version of the review cited

For each item that will be featured in the "Events" section of your newsroom:

- A short lead-in to the event
- A link to more information or map to the event

Repeat for any other "main" sections you create for your newsroom.

Gather the following additional information:

- Media contact information: name, telephone number, and email address
- RSS feeds for blogs belonging to key team members or authors
- Links to blogs/sites you regularly read or reference related to your industry

# Complete the Following Preparatory Tasks

## FeedBurner

Get a FeedBurner account for your newsroom and follow the instructions on page 82 to "burn" the main feed to your newsroom.

Once you have a FeedBurner feed for the main newsroom, burn a feed for each main section. This will mean that users can subscribe only to posts that you place in specific sections of the newsroom. As an example, a publishing company might have a separate feed for an author's reviews that the author can then display on his or her own Website. Similarly, if a member of the press is only interested in your current news releases, he could subscribe only to that category. Refer to the "Burning More Than One Feed" section on page 87.

Optimize each of these feeds by following the guidelines in Chapter 3, "RSS Feeds & Blogs."

## Purpose-Built Delicious Pages

We discussed purpose-built Delicious pages in Chapter 7: "Social Bookmarking & Crowd-Sourcing," on page 199. A social media newsroom is the perfect venue for this application of social bookmarking.

List your most relevant Delicious pages on your social media newsroom. If you have not created them yet, here are some tags to consider:

- delicious.com/your.account (link to main page)
- del.icious.com/your.account/public.relations
- del.icious.com/your.account/client.name
- del.icious.com/your.account/competition
- del.icious.com/your.account/book.title
- del.icious.com/your.account/author.name
- del.icious.com/your.account/business.name
- del.icious.com/your.account/product.name
- del.icious.com/your.account/principal.name

### Technorati

Create a Technorati account and "Claim" your newsroom when it is ready. It is a good idea to do the same thing in some of the other top social bookmarking sites as well. See Chapter 7: "Social Bookmarking & Crowd-Sourcing." Start saving favorite blogs in Technorati, limiting them to blogs that are relevant to your newsroom.

### Instant Messaging Services

Establish an account with at least one instant messaging (IM) service from the following: AIM, ICQ, IRC, Jabber, MSN, Skype, Yahoo!. I recommend using Yahoo! Messenger in WordPress, as it leads to fewer errors than some of the other services.

# Populating the Newsroom

Once all of the preparation is complete, you can begin populating your newsroom. Many of the smaller sections and lists contain static information that you can input once into the sidebars, such as the contact information, the links to blogs, links within the social media section, etc. Use the examples at the end of this chapter as a guide.

The items within the main sections, however, need to be entered as individual blog posts or entries, with the proper categories assigned to each so that they appear only in their proper sections.

Refer to the "Optimizing and Promoting Your Blog and RSS Feed" section on page 78, and apply the same principles to your newsroom entries. This ensures that each entry gets maximum exposure in the Social Web, as well as in the search engines.

# Social Media News Releases

A social media news release is essentially a traditional news release that is social media and Web 2.0 optimized. In short, the release encourages interactivity, is easily shared in the Social Web, and contains other Web 2.0 elements.

Generally, these elements include:

- Multimedia items such as downloadable images, audio/video files, or PDF/DOC files
- A way for readers to comment directly on the news release content
- An obvious and easy way for readers to bookmark the news release in social bookmarking sites or to share it via email
- Technorati tags and links to purpose-built Delicious pages (see page 295)

## Creating Social Media News Releases

You can create your own social media releases or use a service like PR Web[2] (see the resource CD for a list of additional services).

As mentioned earlier, a social media news release is just a traditional release with added elements. You do not need to change your present format except to insert some additional sections. Figure 10.2 shows an example.

---

[2] http://www.prweb.com/

As you can see, this release contains all of the traditional sections of a news release, but also includes the following sections:

## Figure 10.2. Social Media News Release

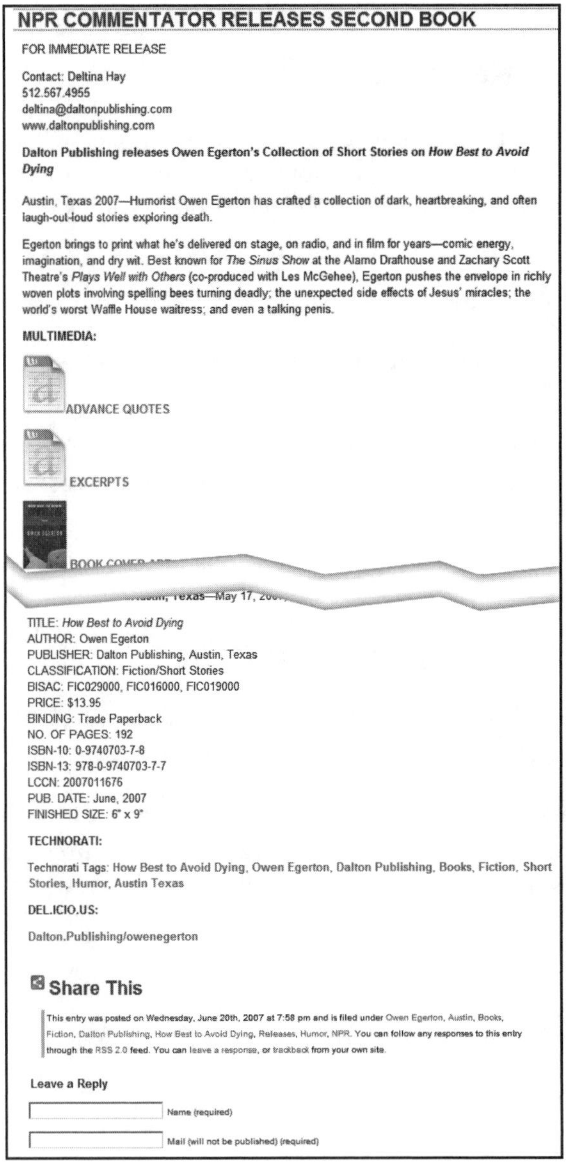

**NPR COMMENTATOR RELEASES SECOND BOOK**

FOR IMMEDIATE RELEASE

Contact: Deltina Hay
512.567.4955
deltina@daltonpublishing.com
www.daltonpublishing.com

**Dalton Publishing releases Owen Egerton's Collection of Short Stories on** *How Best to Avoid Dying*

Austin, Texas 2007—Humorist Owen Egerton has crafted a collection of dark, heartbreaking, and often laugh-out-loud stories exploring death.

Egerton brings to print what he's delivered on stage, on radio, and in film for years—comic energy, imagination, and dry wit. Best known for *The Sinus Show* at the Alamo Drafthouse and Zachary Scott Theatre's *Plays Well with Others* (co-produced with Les McGehee), Egerton pushes the envelope in richly woven plots involving spelling bees turning deadly; the unexpected side effects of Jesus' miracles; the world's worst Waffle House waitress; and even a talking penis.

**MULTIMEDIA:**

ADVANCE QUOTES

EXCERPTS

BOOK COVER ART

...stin, Texas—May 17, 200...

TITLE: *How Best to Avoid Dying*
AUTHOR: Owen Egerton
PUBLISHER: Dalton Publishing, Austin, Texas
CLASSIFICATION: Fiction/Short Stories
BISAC: FIC029000, FIC016000, FIC019000
PRICE: $13.95
BINDING: Trade Paperback
NO. OF PAGES: 192
ISBN-10: 0-9740703-7-8
ISBN-13: 978-0-9740703-7-7
LCCN: 2007011676
PUB. DATE: June, 2007
FINISHED SIZE: 6" x 9"

**TECHNORATI:**

Technorati Tags: How Best to Avoid Dying, Owen Egerton, Dalton Publishing, Books, Fiction, Short Stories, Humor, Austin Texas

**DEL.ICIO.US:**

Dalton.Publishing/owenegerton

**Share This**

This entry was posted on Wednesday, June 20th, 2007 at 7:58 pm and is filed under Owen Egerton, Austin, Books, Fiction, Dalton Publishing, How Best to Avoid Dying, Releases, Humor, NPR. You can follow any responses to this entry through the RSS 2.0 feed. You can leave a response, or trackback from your own site.

**Leave a Reply**

Name (required)

Mail (will not be published) (required)

## Multimedia Section

Figure 10.3 shows an example of a multimedia section. You want to offer the following downloadable items, prepared as explained beginning on page 294:

- PDF or Word documents:
  - › Book excerpts
  - › White papers
  - › Advanced reviews
  - › Brochures
  - › Any document that will enhance or expand on the subject matter contained within the release
- Images:
  - › Author photos
  - › Company executive photos
  - › Book cover art
  - › Company logos
- Podcasts and video clips

## Figure 10.3. News Release Multimedia Section

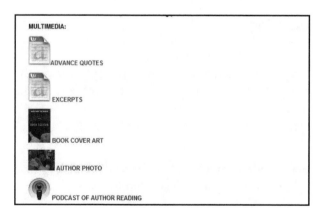

## Technorati Tag Section

Use this section to list links to Technorati pages that are tagged with a list of key terms relevant to your release (see Figure 10.4). Read more about Technorati in Chapter 7: "Social Bookmarking & Crowd-Sourcing," page 200.

### Figure 10.4. News Release Multimedia Section

## Social Bookmarking Section

In this section, provide links to any relevant Delicious pages. Though not depicted in Figure 10.4, you could also provide links to relevant pages on Digg.com or any other social bookmarking or crowd-sourced news site. See Chapter 7: "Social Bookmarking & Crowd-Sourcing."

## Sharing and Commenting

Make it easy for the reader to share or bookmark your release in any number of ways. This is accomplished in our example by utilizing the ShareThis widget (see page 267). Allowing visitors to comment on the release makes it truly interactive.

## Social Media Section

If you do not have a social media newsroom to refer readers back to, you should consider adding a section to your release that lists where you are in the Social Web.

This should include links to your profiles or pages on:

- Facebook
- LinkedIn

- Twitter
- Squidoo
- Flickr
- YouTube, etc.

Using a blogging platform such as WordPress to create your releases makes it easy to add these additional social media optimizing features. Commenting is already built in, and there are a number of good plugins for adding Technorati tags to WordPress posts and for social bookmarking. See Chapter 4: "Building a WordPress Powered Website."

If you already have a social media newsroom created in WordPress, create each of your social media releases as a post of your newsroom and optimize accordingly (see Figure 10.10 on page 309).

# Social Media Newsroom Examples

The social media newsroom in Figure 10.5 is from social media newsroom pioneer SHIFT Communications and is the template we use in this book. I am always pleased to drop by their newsroom and find that nothing much has changed, save for the content—which is how it should be.

## Figure 10.5. SHIFT Communications Newsroom
### http://www.shiftcomm.com/newsroom/

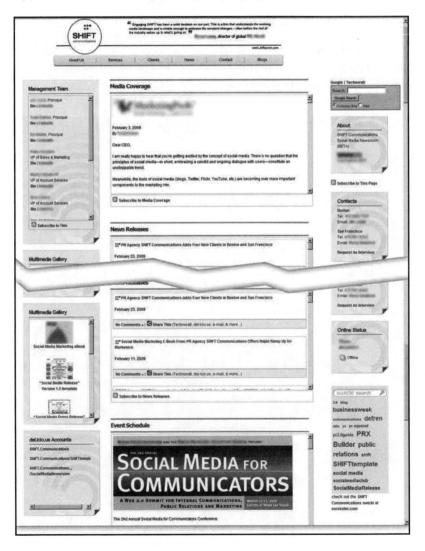

Most of the newsroom sections mentioned above are depicted in the newsroom example in Figure 10.6. I like to point out to clients, especially authors and publishers, that the breakdown of the RSS feeds in a newsroom can be a valuable tool. For instance, the following author features a feed to all of her latest media coverage on her own Website, and the publisher feeds in all of her book reviews onto her author page on their site.

## Figure 10.6. Pure Soapbox Social Media Newsroom
## http://www.puresoapboxnewsroom.com

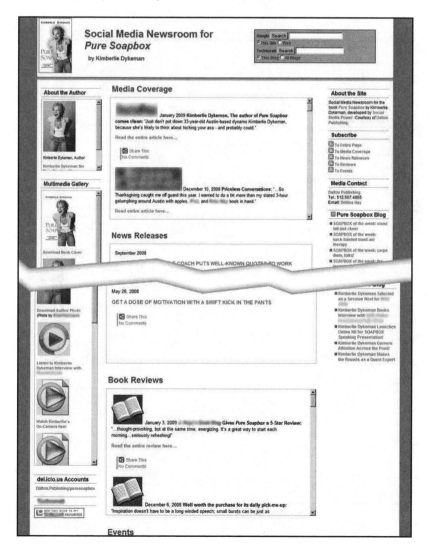

The PR firm in Figure 10.7 uses their newsroom a little differently. They list the latest media coverage and releases of their clients in the main area of the newsroom. They also create social media newsrooms for most of their clients, and link to them in the sidebars as shown. The lower half of their newsroom follows the more standard format.

## Figure 10.7. Accolades Public Relation's Newsroom
## http://www.accoladespr.com/newsroom

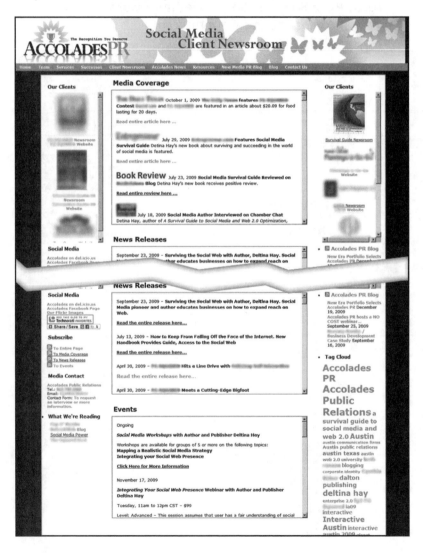

The newsroom in Figure 10.8 is an example of a simple, corporate social media newsroom.

## Figure 10.8. Fathom SEO's Social Media Newsroom
## http://www.fathomseo.com/pressroom/

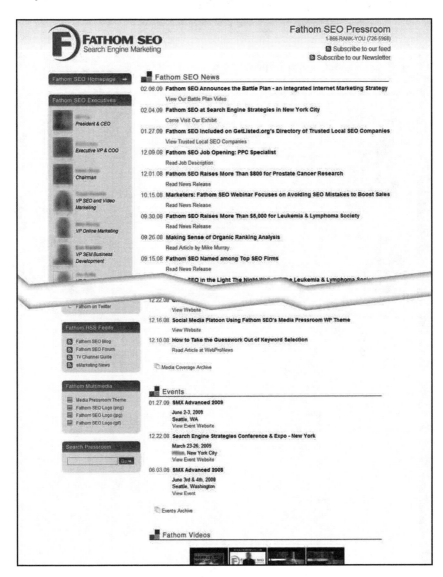

The following performer also includes a section that hosts his latest newsletters, so he won't have to recreate the information from the newsletter in his newsroom every month.

## Figure 10.9. Social Media Newsroom of Les McGehee
## http://www.lesmcgehee.com/newsroom

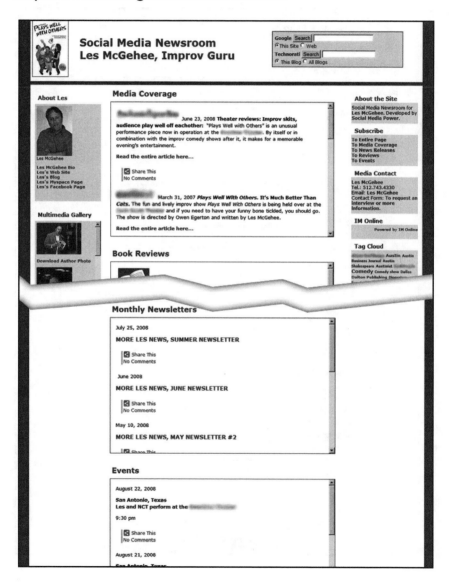

Figure 10.10 shows the top of a social media news release (see page 299) for this newsroom. This release is created as a post in the WordPress platform that the newsroom was created in. Notice that the release has the same right sidebar as the newsroom, and a link to return to the newsroom on the left. This is the only place where a newsroom should not be "flat," as discussed on page 290.

## Figure 10.10. Social Media News Release

# This Chapter on the Resource CD

- Linkable Resources
- Fillable Forms:
  › Social Media Newsroom Prep Sheet

# 11 More Social Tools

We certainly cannot cover all the tools available on the Social Web in this book, especially since new tools pop up almost daily. However, there are a few more tools we would like to mention in this chapter, ones that can benefit most social media strategies.

## Social Calendars and Event Tools

Posting your events in social calendars and event tools is a great way to get extra exposure. They offer a convenient way for you to post your events in one place and highlight them in many ways on many different platforms.

Upcoming[1] is a good example. Users can search Upcoming for events in their region, confirm their attendance at events, share events with others, and more. Figure 11.1 shows the main page of Upcoming for Dalton Publishing.

[1] http://www.upcoming.org

## Figure 11.1. Upcoming.org*

All of Dalton's events are posted to their Upcoming account. They then post an Upcoming badge on their Website (Figure 11.2), their Facebook profile, and other places in their Social Web presence that have applications or plugins that let them import their Upcoming events.

## Figure 11.2. Upcoming Badge on a Website

*All Upcoming.org images reproduced with permission of Yahoo! Inc. ©2009 Yahoo! Inc. Upcoming is a registered trademark of Yahoo! Inc.

Eventbrite[2] is an event tool that is more robust than Upcoming. Figure 11.3 shows an Eventbrite widget on a Website. Visitors to your site can register for events using this widget and see all of your upcoming events in a calendar form. Eventbrite offers features for free and paid events, is easily customized, and integrates well with Facebook and other social sites.

30 boxes[3] is another excellent calendar, to-do list, event organizer, and more that integrates nicely with other social accounts.

## Figure 11.3. Eventbrite Widget on a Website

# Geo-Tagging or Location Tools

We discussed the concept of geo-tagging or location sharing earlier in the book as it relates to social networking and for using as widgets. Geo-tagging is a way for users to tag their location so that others can find them, or to engage in conversation about or around a location. It has great potential as a marketing tool, especially for local businesses.

[2] http://www.eventbrite.com/
[3] http://www.30boxes.com

For an idea of how you might use these tools, Gowalla[4] offers local businesses a way to offer patrons special deals when patrons "check-in" from the business location or add the business as a favorite spot. See Figure 11.4. This has the potential to drive a lot of traffic to a business.

Different tools offer different types of features. For instance, we saw how to create a Brightkite[5] widget in Chapter 9: "Widgets & Badges."

## Figure 11.4. Gowalla Options

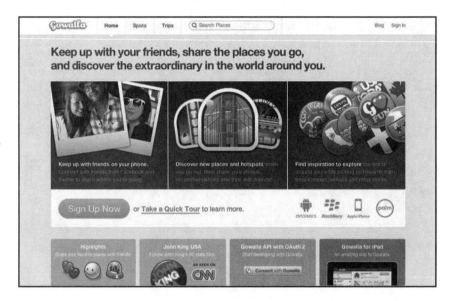

Foursquare[6] in another popular geo-tagging tool worth checking out.

# Hybrid Social Tools

There are a number of social tools that are difficult to classify because they fit in a variety of categories. Some of these tools pull feeds from other social tools into them, others feed content out to other tools, and still others are stand-alone pages or sites that have social characteristics.

[4] http://gowalla.com/
[5] http://brightkite.com/
[6] http://foursquare.com/

One thing they all have in common is that they offer some means of interactivity and sharing.

## FriendFeed

FriendFeed[7] is a lifestreaming tool. A lifestream is similar to a blog in that it is a chronologically ordered collection of information, but its content consists mostly of feeds or "streams" of information from other social sites—like WordPress, Facebook, Flickr, Delicious, Twitter, etc.

A lifestream is a running list of your activity within the social sites that you choose to import into it, consisting of anything from imported blog posts to bookmarked Websites, to comments on videos, and so forth. In addition, people can interact with and subscribe to your lifestream. You can also include your friend's updates in your FriendFeed.

Figure 11.5 shows a FriendFeed stream, and Figure 11.6 shows the screen where all of the different accounts are fed into the stream.

### Figure 11.5. FriendFeed Stream

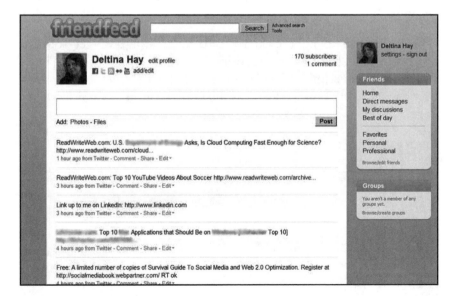

---

[7] http://friendfeed.com/

## Figure 11.6. FriendFeed Options

Note that you are not limited by one of any type of account. This example feeds in three blogs, a Facebook account, two Flickr accounts, an Intense Debate account, a SlideShare account, a Twitter account, and a YouTube account.

A lifestream like FriendFeed can be useful for creating a widget—or even a Website—that features updates from all of your social accounts. Figure 11.7 shows the FriendFeed widgets available (you can get to this screen by clicking "Tools and Widgets" at the bottom of the main FriendFeed page).

## Figure 11.7. FriendFeed Widgets

These widgets can be customized for a number of uses. Figure 11.8 shows a Website whose entire home page is a FriendFeed widget. There is also a smaller widget at the top of the right sidebar that invites visitors to subscribe to the feed. This is an ideal solution for someone who has a lot of accounts in the Social Web and needs a central place to feature them all.

## Figure 11.8. FriendFeed Widgets on a Website

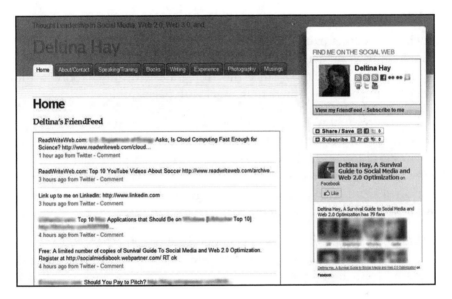

## Posterous

Posterous[8] is an integration tool, a blogging tool, and another way to connect to people. By integration tool, we mean that you can send the entries posted on a Posterous account to several of your other social accounts. So, where FriendFeed imports updates from your other accounts, Posterous exports your updates to your other accounts. We discuss this feature of Posterous in Chapter 12: "Pulling It All Together."

One unique feature of Posterous is that you can email all of your updates (images, links, posts, etc.) right from your email.

---

[8] http://posterous.com/

# Tumblr

Tumblr[9] is a combination blogging, micro-blogging, and social networking tool that integrates well with other social tools and that can even serve as a Website. Tumblr has a very healthy community of users, which makes it a desirable site to build a presence "off the beaten path."

# Social Pages

Social pages differ from the hybrid tools we discuss above in that they are stand-alone Web "pages," as opposed to blogging tools or lifestreams. They are still social tools since they integrate with other tools in the Social Web and allow others to interact with page authors.

The pages created with these tools are sites where, instead of creating a page about yourself, your book, or your business, you create pages about a particular topic. Visitors can search for pages on particular topics or ones authored by specific people. Pages that do well on such sites are usually instructional pages: "how to" pages and lists like "top 10" pages. Ad proceeds can be donated to charity or paid to the author.

Squidoo[10] is a good example. "Squidoo is about finding people when you care what they know instead of who they know." This is how the Squidoo team describes their service. On Squidoo, a page is called a "lens." Squidoo lenses can be especially successful for consultants or nonfiction authors who have a lot to say about their topics.

You can create as many lenses as you like on Squidoo. A good strategy is to create one for each major topic you write about or type of service you offer. Make each page as rich with helpful information as you can. Don't use your lens only to promote your book or service; use it to demonstrate your expertise in your respective field or book topic.

Figure 11.9 shows one of Social Media Power's lenses. As you can see, there are a lot of ways to integrate your Social Web presence and other social tools into a Squidoo lens, including importing RSS feeds, Delicious. com bookmarks, blogs from Google blog search, Lijit widgets, Amazon products, and more.

---

[9] http://www.tumblr.com/
[10] http://www.squidoo.com/

## Figure 11.9. Social Media Power's Squidoo Lens

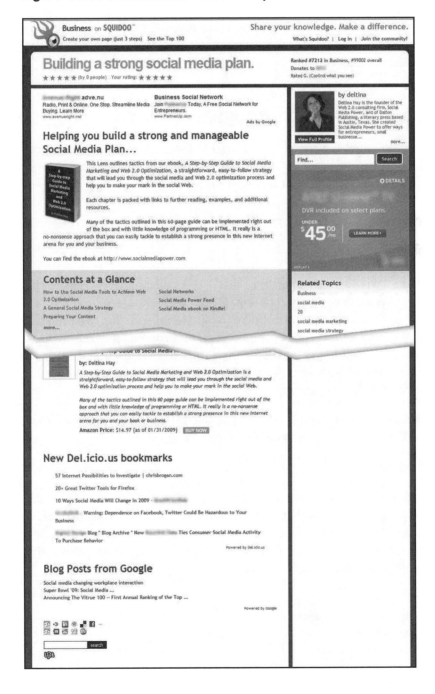

Hubpages[11] is another social page site worth a close look. Their pages are search engine optimized and they offer a 60-40 split for Google Adsense, Amazon Affiliate, and other ad revenue generated by authors' pages. They also integrate well with YouTube, Flickr, and other social tools that can help enhance your pages.

# Collaborative Technologies

Other tools that have emerged alongside the Social Web are enhanced collaborative and learning tools. These tools can be synchronous or asynchronous (real-time or face-to-face versus not).

## Asynchronous Environments

### Wikis

A Wiki ("wiki" is Hawaiian for "fast") is a collaborative Website that allows anyone to update its content. Once established, a Wiki essentially becomes an ever-changing online database of information. Maintaining a Wiki can be a time-consuming process, requiring a lot of moderation, but can be worth it if you have a community of contributors who have a lot to say about your topic. Wikis can also serve as powerful collaboration tools for project management and enterprise teams.

There are a number of platforms available for creating your own Wiki, including MediaWiki,[12] WikiDot,[13] and WikiSpaces.[14]

### Cloud Tools

Cloud or Web-based tools like Google Docs[15] or Google Wave[16] can greatly improve productivity for virtual teams or for small businesses that would rather not invest in expensive software. These tools are especially convenient for those who work wirelessly. We discuss cloud computing in more detail in Chapter 13: "Looking to the Future."

---

[11] http://www.hubpages.com
[12] http://www.mediawiki.org
[13] http://www.wikidot.com
[14] http://www.wikispaces.com
[15] http://docs.google.com/
[16] http://wave.google.com/

# Synchronous Environments

## Conferencing Tools

Conferencing and e-learning tools like Dimdim[17] and GoToMeeting[18] have become much more affordable over the past few years. These sites can be the perfect solution for offering Webinars or training for companies or individuals who could otherwise not afford such services. Skype[19] is also a good conferencing option.

## Immersive Environments (Virtual Worlds)

These sites are virtual 3-D worlds created by the participants. Environments like SecondLife[20] are proving to be particularly successful training tools for colleges, businesses, and other organizations.

This is one social media tool you should experience first-hand before deciding to add it to your strategy. Once you have a feel for a virtual world, you can begin to see other possibilities that might apply to you, like building a virtual book club or opening a virtual presentation area for your business.

# This Chapter on the Resource CD

- Further Reading
- Linkable Resources

---

[17] http://www.dimdim.com/
[18] http://www.gotomeeting.com/
[19] http://www.skype.com/
[20] http://secondlife.com/

# 12 Pulling It All Together

In this chapter we focus on the big picture: using your social media tools to optimize your existing Website and making them all work together to minimize the efforts of maintaining your presence.

Items that are most commonly integrated include:

- Blogs/RSS Feeds
- Images/Videos
- Social Bookmarks
- Events
- Slideshows/Documents
- Short status updates

## Integration Methods

The items mentioned above can be integrated using specific methods—all of which we have already seen demonstrated throughout the book. These methods include:

# Internal Settings

Figure 12.1 shows Friendfeed's internal settings that allow you to import feeds from many different social sites.

### Figure 12.1. Friendfeed Settings for Importing Feeds

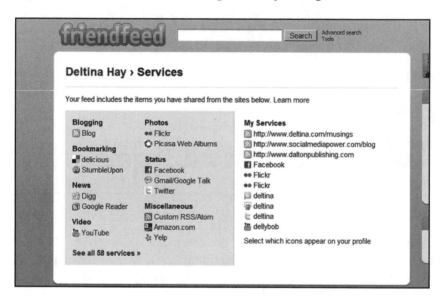

# Plugins

Figure 12.2 shows an example of a WordPress plugin that integrates with a Flickr account to import images into blog posts. We saw this plugin in action in Chapter 8: "Media Communities."

### Figure 12.2. Flickr Tag Plugin in WordPress

## Embedded Code

Figure 12.3 shows how video galleries can be added to any Website or blog by using embedded code from YouTube. We saw this example first in Chapter 8: "Media Communities."

**Figure 12.3. Video Gallery from YouTube Embed Code**

## Applications

Figure 12.4 is the result of a LinkedIn application that imports SlideShare presentations into a LinkedIn profile. We first saw this application in Chapter 6: "Social Networking & Micro-Blogging."

## APIs

Integrating through a tool's API means that you place specific code on your own site that accesses the tool's programming interface. You almost always need an API key to do this.

### Figure 12.4. LinkedIn Application Importing SlideShare

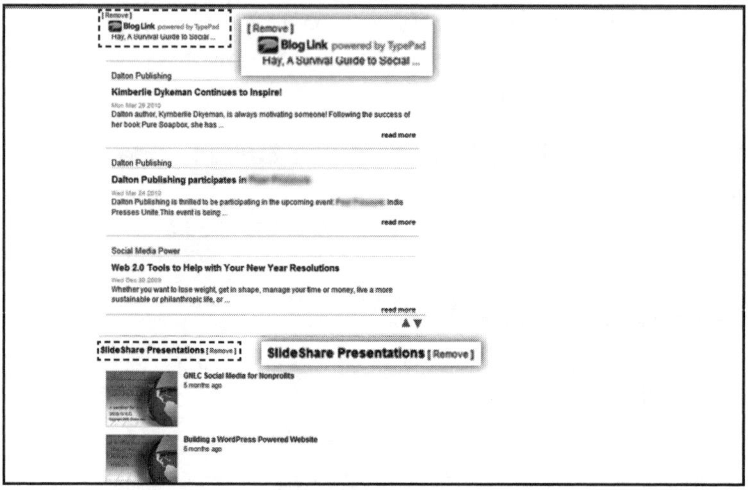

# Integration Tools

## Distributed Social Networking

Using distributed social networking means that users can carry their ID and/or their social network around with them on the Web. They would be able to connect their profile, friends, and other content seamlessly across many sites. For instance, if a visitor to a Website has a Google account, and that Website offers Google Friend Connect (see the example below), then the visitor could access the site without having to create a new account—they could use their Google account to login to the site.

### Google Friend Connect

The general idea is that you add your site to the Google Friend Connect platform, upload a couple of Google-provided HTML files to your site, then use the platform to create widgets and other applications that you can then place on your site for your visitors to use. Figure 12.5 shows the set-up screen.

Figure 12.6 shows a Google Friend Connect widget in action on SocialMediaPower.com that allows their visitors to sign on to their site with their Google ID. They can even change their profile settings or share your site with their friends in other networks.

## Figure 12.5. Google Friend Connect in Action

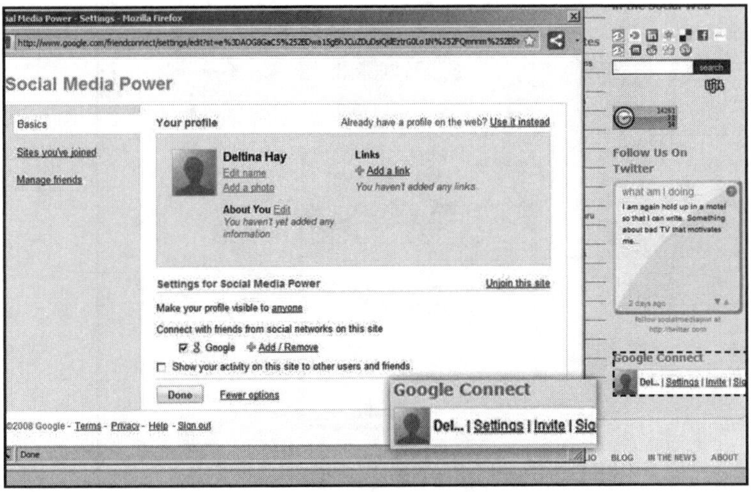

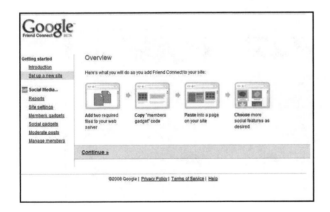

## Figure 12.6. Google Friend Connect Set-Up

# Facebook Connect

Facebook Connect works similarly to its Google counterpart. Figures 12.7 and 12.8 shows a demonstration offered by the Facebook Connect platform.

## Figures 12.7 & 12.8. Facebook Connect Demonstration

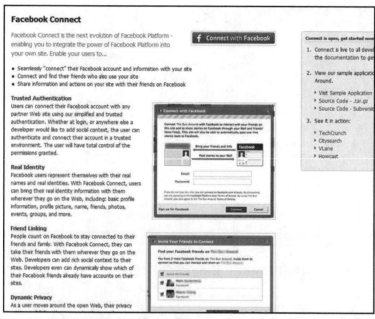

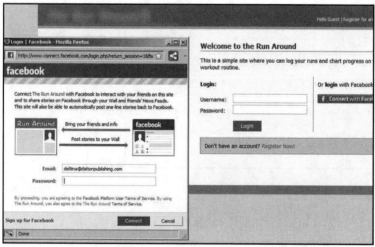

# Streamlining Tools

There are a number of tools available to help you integrate and manage your social accounts. Integration tools use APIs to help you update many accounts at once. Lifestreaming tools offer a platform for highlighting your social accounts in one place.

## Ping.fm

Ping.fm[1] allows you to make status updates to many accounts at once from one central location. With one entry, you can update your Facebook news feed, your LinkedIn status, the wall of your Facebook Page, your Twitter account, and much more.

Figure 12.9 displays some of the social sites you can feed status updates and other entries into using Ping.fm.

## Figure 12.9. Ping.fm

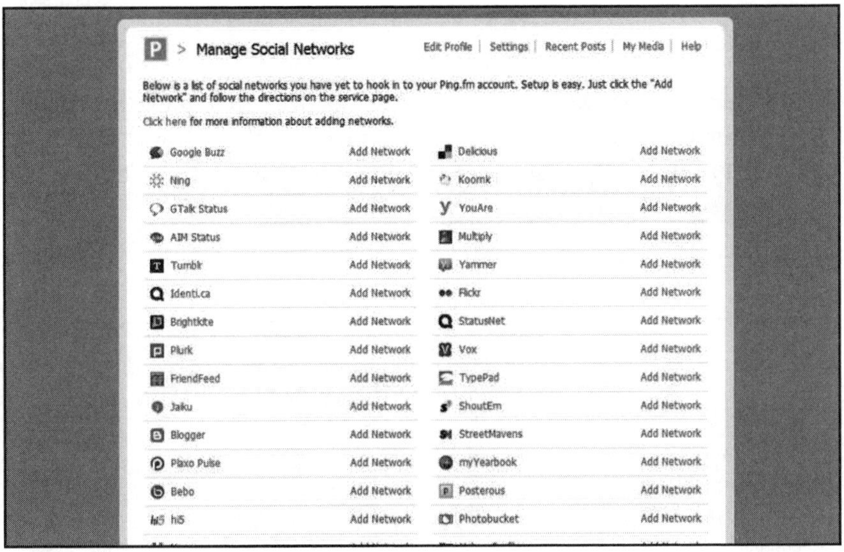

You can post to all of the accounts you add to this service, or just one. You can even create custom posting groups using any combination of your accounts. See Figure 12.10.

---

[1] http://ping.fm

## Figure 12.10. Ping.fm Custom Posting Groups

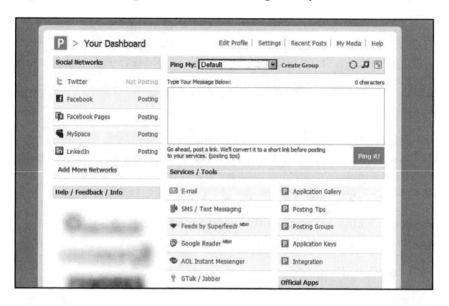

## HootSuite

HootSuite is another integration tool that is ideal if you have more than one Twitter account to manage. This is a nice tool that allows you to post updates at a later date, attach links, shrink your URLs automatically, and much more. See Figure 12.11.

## Figure 12.11. HootSuite

You can also update many of your other social accounts using this tool. You can classify individual "streams" by type of update such as regular tweets, retweets, or mentions, and even manage lists. See Figure 12.12.

## Figure 12.12. HootSuite Features

One of the accounts that HootSuite updates is Ping.fm. Take special care not to duplicate updates to your accounts by adding them to more than one integration tool. See the "Mapping Your Own Integration Plan" section on page 342 to help avoid these problems.

HootSuite is a robust tool with a lot of features. It has statistics tools for tracking Twitter accounts or individual tweets (Figure 12.13), a feature for importing RSS feeds and blogs to automatically post to your accounts

## Figure 12.13. HootSuite Features, 2

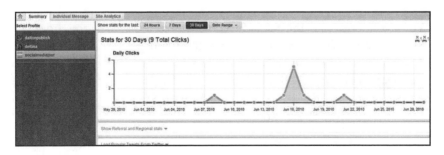

(Figure 12.14), and plugins for mobile devices and desktop use of the tool (Figure 12.15), just to mention a few.

## Figure 12.14. HootSuite Features, 3

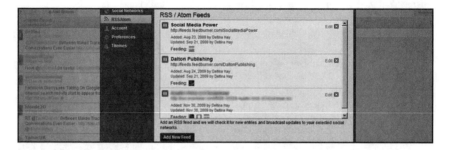

## Figure 12.15. HootSuite Features, 4

# FriendFeed

We have mentioned the FriendFeed tool several times throughout the book as a place where you can stream all of your accounts to one place. This tool pulls all of the activity from the accounts you choose to add to it, and streams it in real time—hence the term "lifestream." Figure 12.16 shows a FriendFeed stream. FriendFeed is discussed in more detail in Chapter 11: "More Social Tools."

## Figure 12.16. FriendFeed Stream

## Posterous

Posterous[2] is a bit of a hybrid. It is an integration tool and a blogging tool all in one. You post entries via your email account to Posterous, and the tool will post it to your Posterous blog as well as any number of other social accounts. See Figure 12.17.

## Caveats

Integration tools should be used *in addition to* regular updates to your social accounts. They are a great way to make updates across the board, but should not replace interacting within each of your chosen communities individually.

Ping.fm gives you the option to populate your blog as well as status updates, but to get the most from your blog posts they should originate at the source. If you optimize your blog entries (see Chapter 3: "RSS Feeds & Blogs") with SEO plugins and proper tagging and categorization, then feeding from a service like this will undercut those efforts. However, there is no harm in using this tool *in addition to* regular, full length, optimized blog posts.

---

[2] http://posterous.com/

## Figure 12.17. Posterous

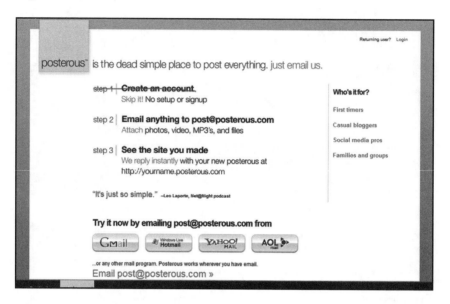

# Optimizing Your Website

Remember that social media and Web 2.0 optimization mean optimizing for interactivity, sharing, and collaboration. With that in mind, determine if your existing Website is optimized by asking yourself a few questions about it:

- Can users interact with the content?
- Can visitors share the content easily with others?
- Does the site encourage collaboration?

Social media and Web 2.0 optimized Websites use technologies such as blogs, RSS feeds, widgets, and social bookmarking to allow visitors to interact with and share the site's content, thus creating an environment of collaboration. We have talked at length about these tools and technologies throughout this book, and now is your chance to apply them.

## A Website Optimization Plan

Outlined below is a Website optimization plan. Each item listed refers to the chapter or chapters where you can learn about applying a specific tool, if applicable.

## Essential Tactics

- Add a blog or RSS feed to your Website and optimize it.
  - › Chapter 3: "RSS Feeds & Blogs"
- Offer several ways for others to subscribe to your RSS feed or blog.
  - › Chapter 3: "RSS Feeds & Blogs"
  - › Chapter 9: "Widgets & Badges"
- If your blog or social media portal is external to your Website, add a prominent link to it on your Website and show the link on every page.
  - › Chapter 9: "Widgets & Badges"
- Add badges or widgets that link to your profiles and pages on social networking sites.
  - › Chapter 6: "Social Networking & Micro-Blogging"
  - › Chapter 9: "Widgets & Badges"
- Use widgets that let visitors share your Website on social bookmarking and crowd-sourcing sites.
  - › Chapter 7: "Social Bookmarking & Crowd-Sourcing"
  - › Chapter 9: "Widgets & Badges"
- Feature your shared images, videos, and documents from media communities on your Website using widgets or badges.
  - › Chapter 8: "Media Communities"
  - › Chapter 9: "Widgets & Badges"
- Use widgets or badges to highlight the other tools you utilize on the Social Web, like Eventbrite or Squidoo.
  - › Chapter 11: "Other Social Tools"
  - › Chapter 9: "Widgets & Badges"

## Additional Tactics

- Add distributed social networking, Facebook "Like" buttons, and other personalization features to improve your visitor experience.
  - › Chapter 9: "Widgets & Badges"
  - › Chapter 6: "Social Networking & Micro-Blogging"
- Add RSS feeds from other sources to your Website.
  - › Chapter 3: "RSS Feeds & Blogs"

336 The Social Media Survival Guide

- Start a Podcast, Vidcast, or Webcast and feed it from your Website.
  > Chapter 5: "Podcasting, Vidcasting, & Webcasting"
- Add image galleries, video galleries, or slide shows using your media community accounts.
  > Chapter 8: "Media Communities"
- Start a social media newsroom.
  > Chapter 10: "Social Media Newsrooms"

# Streamlining Your Social Web Presence

With a bit of planning you can streamline the process to keep all of your Social Web accounts fresh and engaging without breaking your back or breaking the bank. The trick is to make your social accounts work together. Most social sites use open source to make it easy for developers to write applications that enhance the features of the site—we saw this concept in action in many of the previous chapters.

This section demonstrates a sample integration plan, showing examples of streamlining specific items like RSS feeds, images, videos, etc. It then shows you how to map your own integration plan that can help avoid some of the pitfalls.

## Integrating Social Accounts

Below is an integration plan with examples that you can use to streamline your Social Web presence. Each section refers to the chapter or chapters where you can learn more about implementing the tactic.

### Feed Your Feeds

Feed your RSS feed or blog into each of your social accounts that have the option or applications available. Figures 12.18 and 12.19 shows Dalton Publishing's blog (the first entry of which is "TONIGHT: The World's Most Dangerous Improv") feeding into their Facebook and Ning accounts respectively. Figure 12.20 shows Social Media Power's blog as it is fed into their Twitter account via HootSuite.

## Figure 12.18. Feeding Blogs and Images into Facebook

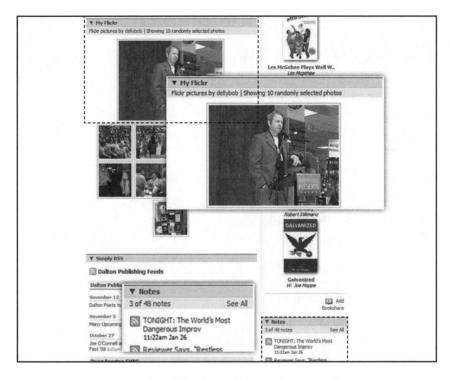

## Figure 12.19. Feeding Blogs and Images into Ning

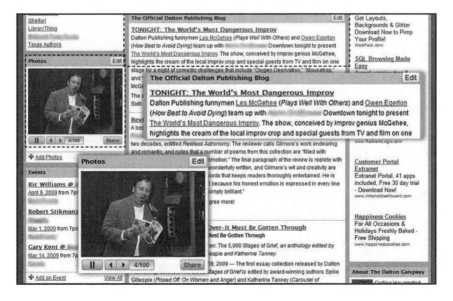

### Figure 12.20. Feeding a Blog into Twitter via HootSuite

Refer to the following chapters for more information:

- Chapter 6: "Social Networking & Micro-Blogging"
- Chapter 3: "RSS Feeds & Blogs"
- Chapter 11: "More Social Tools"
- Chapter 9: "Widgets & Badges"

## Integrate Your Images

Feed your images from Flickr or other image sharing sites into your social accounts that have the option or applications available. Figures 12.18 and 12.19 show Dalton Publishing's Flickr images imported onto their Facebook and Ning accounts respectively.

Refer to the following chapters for more information:

- Chapter 8: "Media Communities"
- Chapter 6: "Social Networking & Micro-Blogging"
- Chapter 9: "Widgets & Badges"

## Integrate Your Video

Feed your video clips from YouTube or other video sharing sites into your social accounts that have the option available. Figures 12.21 and 12.22 show some of the "Internet Empowerment Series" YouTube videos imported into Facebook and Twitter accounts, respectively.

Refer to the following chapters for more information:

- Chapter 8: "Media Communities"
- Chapter 6: "Social Networking & Micro-Blogging"
- Chapter 9: "Widgets & Badges"

## Figure 12.21. Imported YouTube Videos into Facebook

## Figure 12.22. Imported YouTube Videos into Twitter

## Integrating Other Social Tools

The tactics you use here will depend on which social tools and sites are part of your social media strategy. Investigate each of the social tools and sites you use to finds ways to integrate other tools. Listed below are a few specific examples to give you a taste of how you might integrate some of your other social tools into your Social Web presence.

Figure 12.23 shows a portion of Social Media Power's Squidoo lens. This lens imports Social Media Power's Delicious.com bookmarks using a Squidoo application. It also features Social Media Power's Lijit search portal widget.

Figure 12.24 shows an example of importing Upcoming.org events into a Facebook profile. This is accomplished by implementing a Facebook application.

Figure 12.25 shows an example of SlideShare presentations and blog posts importing into a LinkedIn account using LinkedIn applications.

## Figure 12.23. Lijit and Delicious Imported into Squidoo

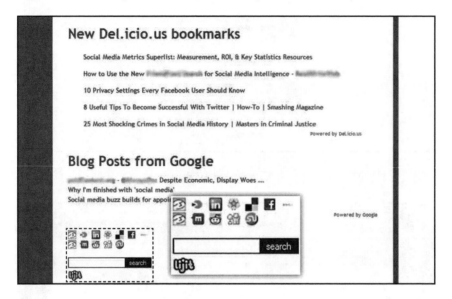

## Figure 12.24. Importing Upcoming Events into Facebook

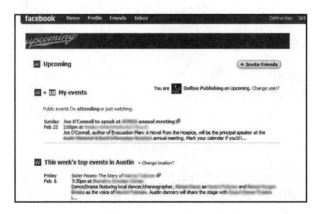

Refer to the following chapters for more information:

- Chapter 7: "Social Bookmarking & Crowd-Sourcing"
- Chapter 11: "More Social Tools"
- Chapter 6: "Social Networking & Micro-Blogging"
- Chapter 9: "Widgets & Badges"

## Figure 12.25. LinkedIn Application Importing SlideShare

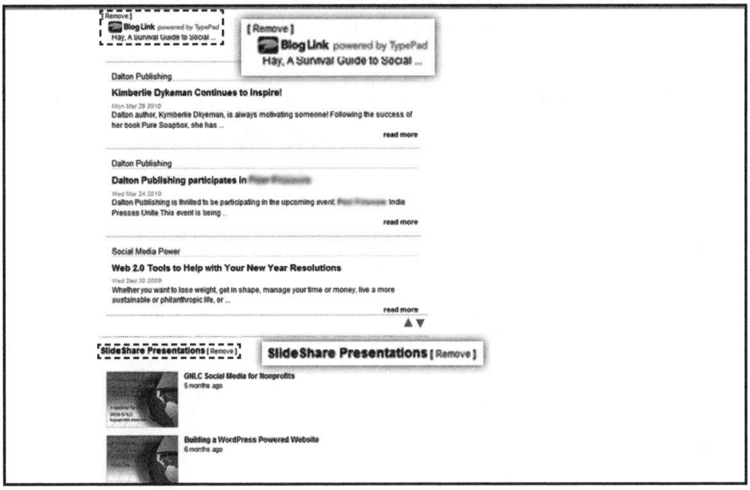

## Investigate and Repeat

The very nature of the Social Web is to connect people through social platforms and applications. So, when deciding whether to invest the time and resources into a new social tool or site, you should investigate how well it accommodates other popular social tools.

Ask these questions of each tool or site you consider, where applicable:

- Does it let you feed in and display your own blog posts?
- Does it allow you to pipe in images from your image sharing site?
- Does it allow you to embed your videos from your favorite video sharing tool?
- Has it been added to the repertoire of social sites used by streamlining tools like Ping.fm yet?
- Is the site listed as an option by sharing-widgets like AddtoAny?
- Do your existing social tools or sites have applications that integrate the new tool?
- Do blogging platforms like WordPress have plugins that allow you to integrate the tools into your blog?

For the tools and sites you do decide to use, integrate them as best you can by repeating the applicable steps above.

# Mapping Your Own Integration Plan

The first step to successful integration is to have a plan. If you just start feeding sites into each other without a plan, you can end up with duplicated content, run into dead ends, or worse. In this section, we will use two realistic scenarios to demonstrate how to map a plan for successful social media integration.

## The Process

Given a typical social media strategy, the following are some general areas that can almost always be integrated or streamlined:

- Distributing your blog or RSS feed
- Updating social networking status updates and Twitter posts
- Distributing Images and Video

We begin by determining how each of these general areas can be streamlined by, or integrated with, the other tools in our strategy, and create maps to visualize these relationships. Creating visual maps can help us see potential problems easier.

We use the maps to break the plan down into tasks. We can then implement the plan by completing individual tasks.

Once these general areas are integrated and streamlined, we move on to integrating the other tools in our strategy.

Finally, we test the plan.

## Example Plan One

For this scenario, imagine we have the following accounts:

- A Blog/RSS feed
- A Facebook Profile
- A Facebook Page
- A LinkedIn Account
- A Twitter Account
- A Flickr Account
- A YouTube Account

We want to create a plan that will streamline the following tasks:

- Distributing our RSS feed
- Updating our short status updates
- Distributing our images
- Distributing our video clips

We visually map each area individually For this plan we utilize the integration tool Ping.fm (see page 329).

## Distributing Our Blog/RSS Feed

We investigate each of the tools in our strategy and conclude that we can feed our blog or RSS feed entries according to the map in Figure 12.26.

### Figure 12.26. Distributing Blog/RSS Feed Entries Map

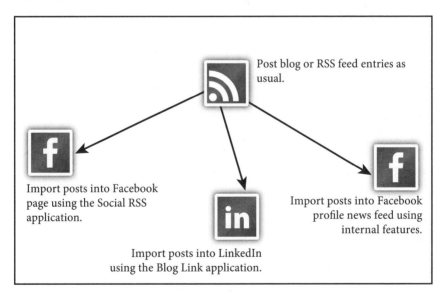

Post blog or RSS feed entries as usual.

Import posts into Facebook page using the Social RSS application.

Import posts into Facebook profile news feed using internal features.

Import posts into LinkedIn using the Blog Link application.

## Updating Status Updates and Twitter Posts

This is an area where we need to be particularly careful not to duplicate our efforts. There are many options available to us, since most social tools import entries from each other. For instance, we can import Twitter entries to Facebook, and Facebook entries to Twitter. If we decide to do both, we have a mess. That is why it is best to use an integration tool to manage all of the updates. But remember that the updates you send to *all* of these accounts should be *in addition to* regular entries you make to them individually.

We decide to use the Ping.fm tool to streamline all of our status updates, and map that portion of the plan accordingly. See Figure 12.27.

## Figure 12.27. Updating Statuses/Twitter with Ping.fm Map

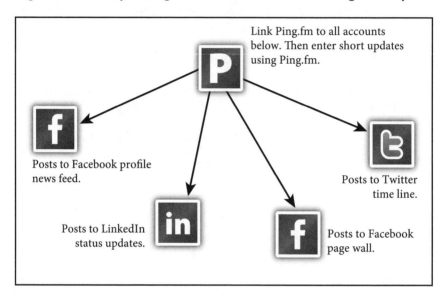

## Distributing Images

We research each of the tools in our strategy to discover which will integrate with our Flickr account, and map that portion of the plan. See Figure 12.28.

## Distributing Video

We investigate the tools in our strategy to find out how we can integrate them with our YouTube account, and map that into the plan. See Figure 12.29.

## Implement and Test

Now that our general areas are mapped into tasks, we can implement each task individually. Then, we test using the guidelines outlined at the end of this section.

## Figure 12.28. Distributing Images Map

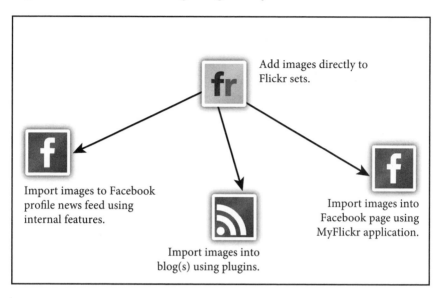

## Figure 12.29. Distributing Video Map

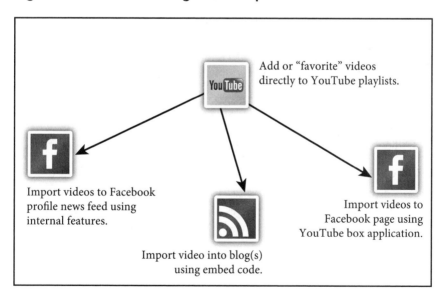

# Example Plan Two

For this scenario, imagine we have the following accounts:

- Two Blogs/RSS feeds
- A Facebook Profile
- A Facebook Page
- A LinkedIn Account
- Two Twitter Accounts
- A Flickr Account
- A YouTube Account

And that we plan to add the following accounts at a later date:

- A SlideShare Account
- A Google Buzz Account

First, we map each of these general areas:

- Distributing our RSS feeds
- Updating our short status updates (including both Twitter accounts)
- Distributing our images
- Distributing our video clips

This scenario has two different Twitter accounts, so we add HootSuite to the plan. HootSuite is a tool that helps us manage more than one Twitter account (see page 330). From HootSuite, we can post entries to one or both Twitter accounts as well as export them as updates to Ping.fm.

Because implementing this plan has potential for duplicating entries, we need to be very careful. While HootSuite updates Ping.fm and both Twitter accounts, Ping.fm updates the statuses of our other accounts. We need to make sure that:

1. We don't set HootSuite to update any other statuses.

2. We don't update the Twitter accounts using Ping.fm.

This plan allows us the convenience of the HootSuite platform, and the flexibility of using Ping.fm to integrate just about any other tool we choose to add later.

We can also export blog/RSS feed entries as status updates to specific Twitter accounts using HootSuite, so we add that tactic to our plan as well.

## Distributing Our Blogs/RSS feeds

In addition to Facebook and LinkedIn, we feed our blog/RSS feed entries into HootSuite to take advantage of that tool's ability to import our blog posts into our Twitter accounts.

HootSuite will allow us to import the feeds to Ping.fm as well, but we will have duplicate entries if we do that. We choose not to use Ping.fm to import blog posts since we limit the length of Ping.fm entries.

Note that, except for the Facebook news feed, we have the option of importing one or both blogs to any of the other tools. Figure 12.30 shows the resulting map for this portion of the plan.

## Figure 12.30. Distributing Blog/RSS Feed Entries Map

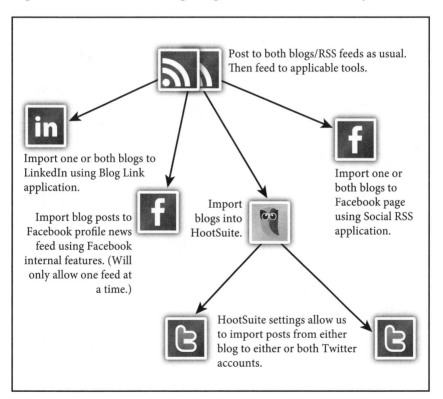

## Updating our Status Updates and Twitter Accounts

Here is where the plan has potential for getting sticky. We need to be careful that we don't duplicate updates by posting to the same accounts from both Ping.fm and HootSuite as mentioned earlier.

Figure 12.31 shows our map for this portion of the plan, and visual inspection does not reveal any duplication.

Note that we can decide on a post-by-post basis which accounts we want to update: any combination of the two Twitter accounts and Ping.fm.

## Figure 12.31. Updating Statuses with HootSuite/Ping.fm Map

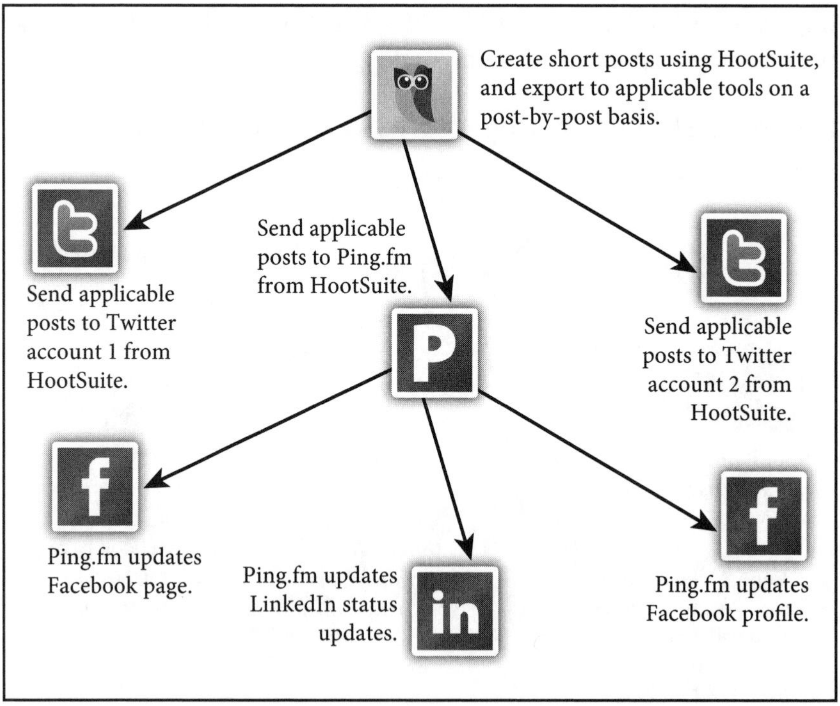

Create short posts using HootSuite, and export to applicable tools on a post-by-post basis.

Send applicable posts to Ping.fm from HootSuite.

Send applicable posts to Twitter account 1 from HootSuite.

Send applicable posts to Twitter account 2 from HootSuite.

Ping.fm updates Facebook page.

Ping.fm updates LinkedIn status updates.

Ping.fm updates Facebook profile.

## Distributing Images

This portion of the plan is the same as in the plan one example. See Figure 12.28 on page 345.

## Distributing Video

This portion of the plan is the same as in the plan one example. See Figure 12.29 on page 345.

## Adding Remaining Tools

Now that our main areas are mapped, we move on to mapping the remaining tools in our strategy.

### SlideShare

By searching applications and built-in features within the tools in our strategy, we discover that SlideShare presentations can be imported into our LinkedIn account, Facebook profile, and Facebook page. So we add the map in Figure 12.32 to our plan.

### Figure 12.32. Integrating SlideShare

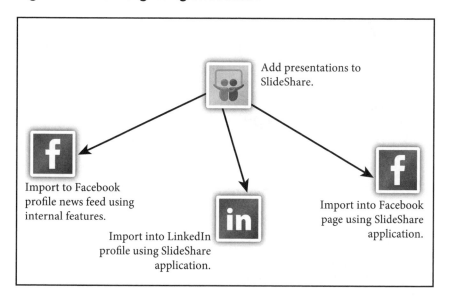

### Google Buzz

Since we have a Ping.fm account, the first thing we do when we add a social networking, micro-blogging, or similar tool, is check to see if we can update that tool using Ping.fm. We discover that Google Buzz is, indeed, one of the tools that Ping.fm updates, so we add Google Buzz to the status update map we created earlier. See Figure 12.33, and refer back to Figure 12.31 on page 348.

### Figure 12.33. Integrating Google Buzz

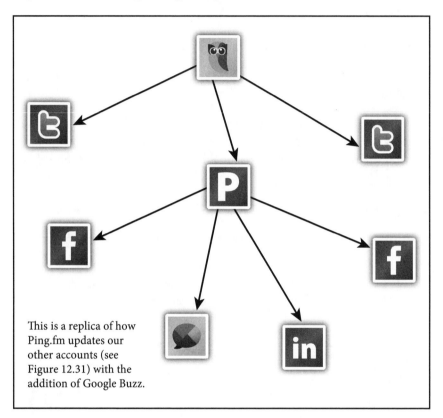

This is a replica of how Ping.fm updates our other accounts (see Figure 12.31) with the addition of Google Buzz.

### Implement and Test

Now that our general areas and our additional tools are mapped into tasks, we can implement each task individually. Then we test using the guidelines outlined below.

## Testing an Integration Plan

- Warn your readers that you are testing a new plan, and apologize ahead of time for possible duplicate entries

- Keep all of your tools open in tabs on your browser; you may be able to delete unwanted updates to tools like Facebook, Twitter, or LinkedIn if you catch them in time
- Post an entry to your blog or RSS feed
- Post an image to your Flickr account
- Post a video to your YouTube account
- Post status updates from your tool of choice
- Post entries or multimedia to the other integrated tools in your strategy
- Repeat the test three times. This may seem excessive, but sometimes discrepancies will not reveal themselves the first couple of times out.

The ability to integrate so many of the tools in your strategy is one of the things that makes the Social Web so powerful. However, you *can* have too much of a good thing. Planning ahead, mapping your plan, and continuing to directly interact within the communities in your strategy, though, will keep your efforts in check.

# This Chapter on the Resource CD

- Linkable Resources
- Fillable Forms:
    › Website Optimization Plan
    › Integration Plan

# 13 Looking to the Future

We are rapidly moving toward a phase of the Internet that will ultimately result in a new era of micro-computing. The initial steps of Web 3.0 have already been taken. They are about making online content easier for machines to understand and interpret and opening up and linking large sets of data in consistent ways. This movement has paved the way for cloud computing, which gives everyone affordable access to more sophisticated technology, and opens the door for even novice developers to build robust applications for the Internet. Cloud computing, coupled with easily implemented Web-based applications have, in turn, made mobile computing less of a pastime, and more of a full-fledged computing solution.

In this chapter, we will discuss each of the fundamental elements that are moving us toward this application-driven, Web-based, mobile computing era. We only give an overview here, but keep your eyes peeled for a future "Survival Guide" that will cover these topics in much more detail.

## Web 3.0

Finding a definition for Web 3.0 is no easy task when most people are still trying to grasp Web 2.0. However, it is a necessary task since Web

3.0 technologies are encroaching on the Internet quickly. Perhaps the best way is to start at the proverbial beginning.

# Web 1.0: The Internet in One Dimension

In the beginning, the Internet was flat. Think of it as a collection of documents (Websites) lined up side by side. Though many of the sites may have linked to each other, those links simply took a user straight to the linked site, and *maybe* back again.

Each Website was classified using metadata composed of meta-keywords, meta-descriptions, and meta-titles that described what the content of the Website was about. At their simplest, search engines used established search algorithms to comb through all of the Websites' metadata to return what it considered relevant results based on your choice of key words.

Internet inventor Timothy Berners-Lee refers to this phase of the Internet as a "Web of Documents." See Figure 13.1.

**Figure 13.1. Web 1.0**

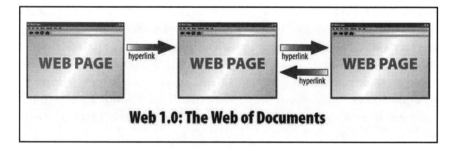

# Web 2.0: A Two Dimensional Internet

This next generation of the Internet added another dimension: Collaboration.

This added dimension means that Websites are linked in a more collaborative way. Instead of sending a visitor away from a site to view related content, the content is actually drawn into the visited site from the related site using RSS feeds or widgets. It becomes important, then, that we make our content available to be shared easily with other sites.

But it isn't only the Websites that are more collaborative, it is also the users of the Websites' content. Internet users tag and comment on content to the point of creating what has been coined "folksonomy"—the taxonomy of the Internet by its users. Furthermore, users themselves are collaborating and interacting throughout the entire Internet.

Search engines and other search-related sites have a whole new layer to consider in their searches: user-tagged Web content and the relevant connections between the users themselves.

Berners-Lee named this Internet phase the "Web of Content." See Figure 13.2.

### Figure 13.2. Web 2.0

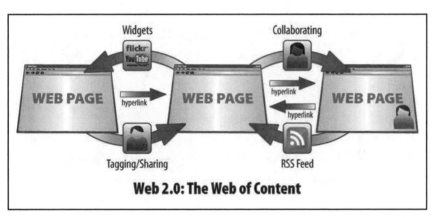

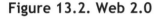

## Web 3.0: The Third Dimension

Even with the rich metadata, collaboration between Websites and users, and user-generated relationships to draw from, machines are still machines, and they still find it difficult to discern actual meaning from human-generated content. The third evolutionary step of the Internet aims to fix that by adding the dimension of "semantics."

The goal of this phase is to make the content of the Web more easily interpreted by machines. Web content is typically written for humans, which means that it is produced with aesthetics in mind—little attention is paid to consistency or relevancy of the content itself. This change to relevancy of content is a major aim of Web 3.0.

Tim Berners-Lee calls this phase (rather passionately) the "Web of Data." See Figure 13.3.

**Figure 13.3. Web 3.0**

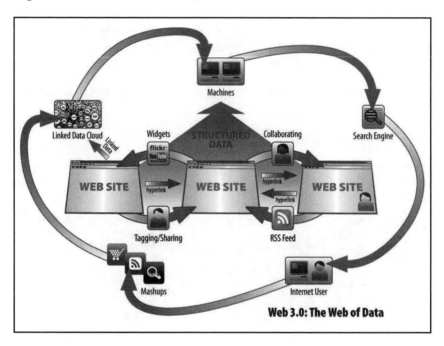

## The Semantic Web

The Semantic Web is a huge step toward Web 3.0, where the ultimate goal is to make Web content more machine-friendly. Most Websites are produced using HTML, which is a general syntax used to make a Website "look" a certain way. The Semantic Web, on the other hand, is based on markup languages that focus on tagging the content by what it "means." So, where HTML is about syntax (order), the Semantic Web is about meaning. A more "semantic" Internet will allow search engines to produce more relevant results because the searched content will be "marked up" in such a way that the engines (machines) can make more sense of it.

The Semantic Web is *not* AI (artificial intelligence), as some people seem to think. It is about making the content easier for machines to interpret, not about making the machines themselves smarter. Two ways in which this is accomplished is through structured data and linked data.

# Structured Data

You can prepare your content now in a way that will help search engines include it in very relevant search results, or offer additional information about your content directly in search result listings.

For instance, you can offer ways for your contact information, products, or reviews to show up directly in a Google or Yahoo search result by adding a few tags and attributes to your content that will transform it into what is called "structured data."

Contact and location information, events, friend lists, products, reviews, and tags (as they apply to blogs and other social tools) are all perfect types of structured data, and can be tagged in standard formats called "markup formats" to make it easy for search engines to recognize them as such. And it won't even affect the way your content displays on your own Website.

Structured data is not a new concept. It has been around for some time, waiting in the wings for the search engines to take it seriously. Its wait is over. In 2009, Google introduced "Rich Snippets"[1], a feature that recognizes markup formats and displays the content in your search listing accordingly. Here is an example from their site (refer to Figure 13.4):

## Figure 13.4. Rich Snippets Example

---

[1]     http://googlewebmastercentral.blogspot.com/2009/05/introducing-rich-snippets.html

In reference to Figure 13.4, Google states that:

*Rich Snippets give users convenient summary information about their search results at a glance. We are currently supporting data about reviews and people. When searching for a product or service, users can easily see reviews and ratings, and when searching for a person, they'll get help distinguishing between people with the same name. It's a simple change to the display of search results, yet our experiments have shown that users find the new data valuable—if they see useful and relevant information from the page, they are more likely to click through...*

Google is supporting the two most standard markup formats: "Microformats" and "RDFa." Both of these standard formats are very straightforward. Anyone with experience building a Website can easily use them to mark up their existing Web content as structured data.

If you have a WordPress blog, or if your Website is powered by a CMS like WordPress, then there are plugins available that will help you structure your content easily. Search the plugin directories for "microformats" or "RDFa."

Refer to Appendix D: "Preparing Your Content for the Semantic Web" for an introduction to structuring your content using microformats and RDFa.

## Linked Data

Linked Data also refers to a way of structuring data, but it does so by using the Web to create links between data from many different datasets and classifies it using an established data commons. By using a common reference to represent a piece of data, that data can be linked easily to and from other sources of data, creating what is referred to as a "Web of Data."

The most impressive of these Webs of Data is the Linked Open Data (LOD) cloud. Pictured in Figure 13.5, as of July 2009, this "cloud" is growing at a tremendous rate. In the center of this cloud (only a small part of it) is "Dbpedia," which is the dataset that feeds Wikipedia. This should give you an idea of the size of this data cloud.

The basic idea is that Linked Data is published to the Web using a very specific model called the "RDF data model." The interlinking data from

## Figure 13.5. Linking Open Data cloud diagram
(by Richard Cyganiak and Anja Jentzsch. http://lod-cloud.net)

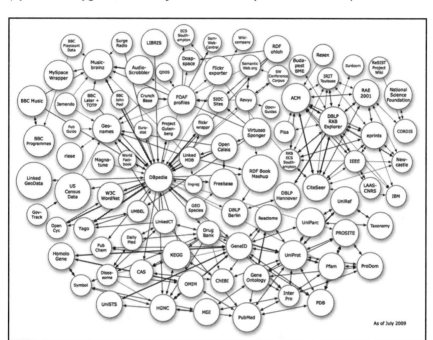

different data sources adheres to a special linking structure known as "RDF links."

The resulting "Web of Data" can be accessed by semantic Web browsers that navigate between different data sources, similar to how traditional Web browsers navigate between HTML pages. A semantic browser, however, is following RDF links to related data as opposed to hyperlinks to other Web pages.

For example, if someone is reading data about you, they may discover a link to data about your book and follow it to a source that has information about reviews of your book or product information about your book. So, by discovering *you* they discover your book perhaps in the Amazon database, which then leads them to more information in the Google Book Search database, and further, to a review located in a data source located somewhere else. What is important to understand is that the user is surfing through data sources, not popping around on Websites, so their surfing is much more relevant and meaningful, and, of course, much less distracting.

Refer to Appendix D: "Preparing Your Content for the Semantic Web" for an introduction to using RDF to add your content to the LOD.

The Web of Data is not just a bunch of interlinked databases that can be surfed conveniently, though. One of the things that makes Linked Data so powerful is *what* one can do with the data once it is linked in a consistent way. Given the right tools and know-how, anyone can draw from this tremendous resource to create powerful applications. Remember, that this is the Linked *Open* Data cloud, so the data is available for all developers to access, and given the types of tools we have seen emerge from Web 2.0, imagine what will come from developers tapping into this vast resource.

Refer to the "RDF Book Mashup" example in Appendix D: "Preparing Your Content for the Semantic Web" for a good example of what we mean by this.

# Cloud Computing

In addition to opening up and linking their data, many Internet service companies are also offering their software and hardware infrastructures on a pay-per-use basis. This is a component of the trend know as "cloud computing," where "cloud" refers to the Internet itself. Cloud-based applications and services, then, exist "in the cloud," or more accurately, on a server that is not your own, with capabilities you likely could not access otherwise.

This trend creates a way for all of us to increase our hardware capacity or add software capabilities without investing in new infrastructure, training new personnel, or licensing new software. It gives everyone affordable access to more sophisticated technology, and opens the door for even novice developers to build robust applications for the Internet.

Generally, cloud computing refers to services that are Web-based (offered on the Internet), and are sold on demand. Consumers pay for cloud services by units, i.e. by the hour or by the gigabyte, and can use as much or as little as they want. Many cloud services even offer a basic, free version.

Cloud computing services fall into three general categories: Infrastructure-as-a-Service (IaaS), Platform-as-a-Service (PaaS), and Software-as-a-Service (SaaS).

# Infrastructure-as-a-Service

IaaS is a model in which the customer outsources their equipment needs for storage, hardware, and servers (infrastructure). The cloud vendor owns the equipment and is responsible for maintaining it. The customer typically pays on a per-use basis. This model allows the client to pay only for the capacity they need, with the ability to add more, as necessary.

The attractiveness of this model lies not in the equipment itself, but in the features that reside on the equipment and the way it is managed. For instance, Amazon Web Services[2] (AWS) offers an infrastructure that allows anyone to utilize the same reliable technology that powers Amazon.com, complete with database capabilities, payment processing, content delivery, and more. Other IaaS providers like RackSpace[3] offer pay-per-use Website hosting services that include a plethora of tools to help develop robust and optimized Websites.

Another advantage of cloud infrastructures is that they utilize what is called "load management" or "clustering" over the cloud (i.e., over many different machines). This results in faster and more reliable Web applications and Websites.

# Platform-as-a-Service

PaaS are software and product development tools hosted by the provider and accessed online by the customer. Even novice developers can build Web applications without the need to install any special software or programming tools, and can deploy their applications right from a Web browser. In many cases, a developer doesn't even need to write code, since the provider typically has an archive of code one can copy and alter as needed.

Pricing for PaaS is usually based on how many clicks an application receives, or how many users access the application over a specific period

---

[2] http://aws.amazon.com/
[3] http://www.rackspacecloud.com/

of time, though Google App Engine is free for up to 5 million page views per month.

Examples include Force.com[4] and Google App Engine[5]. Force.com offers a business development platform that can be used to manage customer relations and similar types of business applications. Google App Engine is used for anything from custom social networking services, to mobile applications, to Twitter tools, to entire Web communities.

You are not likely to run out and start building applications today if you are not a developer, but be aware that PaaS cloud services are becoming more user-friendly all the time. WaveMaker[6] is an example of a cloud service that offers a "drag and drop" platform for building Web 2.0 applications.

## Software-as-a-Service

In this model, the cloud vendor hosts the hardware (infrastructure), the software, and the data so that users can access the service from anywhere, on any computer. SaaS alleviates the need for the consumer to purchase software or even install anything on their own computer. Growing Internet accessibility has made this type of service more and more appealing, especially to small businesses.

You are probably familiar with many services that fall into this category already. These include Web-based email services like Google's gmail, file sharing services like Dropbox, and Web 2.0 development tools like Kickapps[7]. One of the most useful of these services is Google Apps[8]. Applications offered through Google Apps include Gmail for business, Google Calendar, Google Docs, Google Groups, Google Sites, and Google Video.

The pricing structure for SaaS is usually based on storage space and charged by blocks of gigabytes, though some may use a pay-per-click or pay-per-user pricing models.

[4] http://www.salesforce.com/platform/
[5] http://code.google.com/appengine/
[6] http://www.wavemaker.com/
[7] http://www.kickapps.com/
[8] http://www.google.com/apps/

## Choosing Cloud Vendors

Choose your cloud vendors wisely. Since a cloud service provider is bearing responsibility for your data and personal information, make sure they are an established company with good references. Even a new service can be a good choice if you look into who the developers are and what others are saying about the service. Read the terms of use, terms of service, and privacy terms, and note what kind of responsibility they are willing to take if something should happen to your data.

# The Mobile Web

The Mobile Web is more than just mobile phones. We have already witnessed the popularity of the application-driven iPad, and Google is teaming up with Verizon to create an iPad-like tablet using Android.

But the tablets are not necessarily going to satisfy those of us who need more enterprise functionality. To that end, Google's Chrome OS[9] is an operating system that is geared toward "the cloud" and designed for use on netbooks. The idea is to have a "born connected" operating system that is built for "born connected" computers.

Imagine an operating system that only needs to load your Internet browser and your protected identity, and does it in seconds. The need for installing software, storing gigabytes of data, and having to protect it all from viruses is coming to an end. We are headed for a Web-based, application-driven computing era that will change everything.

## Preparing for the Mobile Web

There are things you can do now to make certain your existing Web presence is properly formatted for the mobile Web. There are also some tools that can help you create a mobile site using your existing Web presence.

---

[9] http://googleblog.blogspot.com/2009/07/introducing-google-chrome-os.html

## Optimizing Your Existing Presence

Your first step should be to see how your existing site measures up on mobile devices. Ready.mobi[10] is a tool that can help you do that.

Next, look for a service or tool that can help you improve how your site performs on mobile devices. If your site is powered by WordPress or another CMS, there are a number of plugins and themes that can optimize your site for mobile visitors. The best plan is to test a few of these plugins with different devices and choose the one you like the best (search the plugins directory for "mobile").

If you have a traditional Website, Mobify.me[11] is a tool that can help you optimize any Website for the Mobile Web. They have free and premium options.

## Creating a New Mobile Site or Application

There are some tools and services that can quickly and easily help you create a mobile site or application. Wapple[12] can help you build and host a mobile site, and Grapple Mobile[13] can help you build your own mobile application.

Widgetbox[14] has a particularly nice mobile tool. Figure 13.6 shows a mobile site created with the Widgetbox Mobile Sites tool. You can create a site like this in minutes by importing content from your existing social accounts, including blog posts, Twitter updates, Facebook pages, etc. You can then add a script to your Website that will redirect mobile visitors to your mobile site.

Widgetbox also has a new Mobile Web App[15] tool that uses the same process to create mobile applications for iPhone or Android. AppMakr[16] is another mobile application service worth checking out.

---

[10] http://ready.mobi
[11] http://www.mobify.me
[12] http://wapple.net/
[13] http://www.grapplemobile.com
[14] http://www.widgetbox.com/mobile/make/
[15] http://www.widgetbox.com/mobile/builder/
[16] http://www.appmakr.com

## Figure 13.6. Widgetbox Mobile Sites

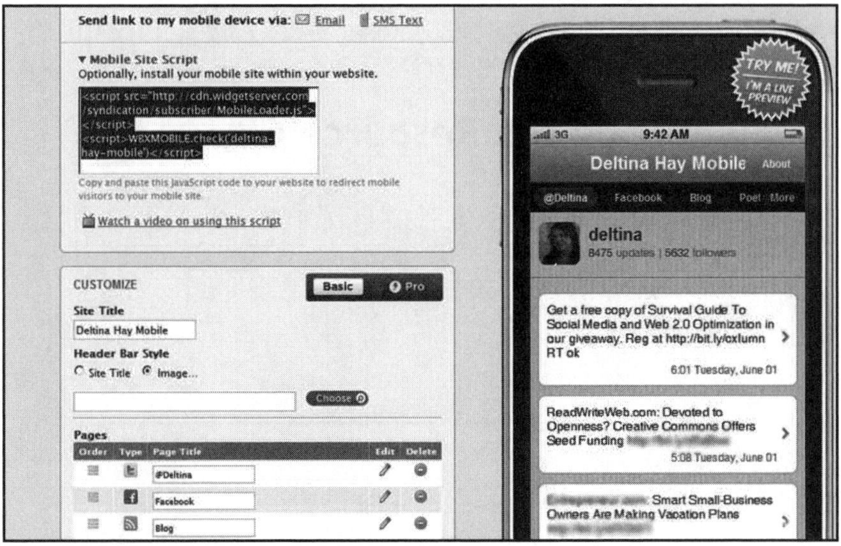

## Mobile Analytics and Directories

There are services available to analyze your mobile site traffic. PercentMobile[17] is one that also has a WordPress plugin. Once you have your site or blog optimized for the Mobile Web, register it with mobile site directories like Mpexo[18].

# Keeping Your Eye on the Social Media Pie

To keep on top of the latest trends in social media, subscribe to the feeds of some of the leaders in social media news and trends.

These include, but are not limited to:

• ReadWriteWeb[19]
• Mashable[20]
• SocialMedia.biz[21]

---

[17] http://percentmobile.com/
[18] http://www.mpexo.com/
[19] http://www.readwriteweb.com/
[20] http://mashable.com/
[21] http://www.socialmedia.biz

Staying on top of the latest trends will keep your social media strategy fresh and effective and will clue you in to which tactics are still working and which ones are fading out.

# This Chapter on the Resource CD

- Further Reading
- Linkable Resources

# 14 Measuring Your Success

Unfortunately, there is no easy, one-click solution to measuring your success in the Social Web. If you are mostly interested in how your efforts have improved your Website rankings or traffic, then you can use traditional Web statistics tools like Google Analytics. There are even ways you can measure how well your efforts have paid off in social bookmarking, crowd-sourcing, and social networking sites. However, measuring the more qualitative elements like conversations, brand awareness, and relationship building can be more of a challenge. There are a number of tools that have surfaced recently, though, that can help.

## Know Your Goals

Knowing what it is you want your social media strategy to accomplish will help you measure its success. Define your goals clearly as you plan your strategy so you will have a way to measure your return on investment (ROI) easily. Some of these goals may include:

- Increasing Website traffic
- Driving sales or new business
- Monitoring brand awareness

- Improving customer relations
- Managing reputation
- Establishing credibility
- Creating buzz
- Improving public relations

Obviously, each of these goals requires a different measurement approach, but each still falls into one of two classic metric categories: qualitative or quantitative.

# A Qualitative Framework

There are many schools of thought on how to establish a framework for *qualitative* measurement of social media. Reproduced here are two that I feel have merit:

Peter Kim of BeingPeterKim.com[1] defines the following framework for measuring social media engagement based on user interactions with different social media channels:

1. **Attention.** The amount of traffic to your content for a given period of time. Similar to the standard Web metrics of site visits and page/video views.

2. **Participation.** The extent to which users engage with your content in a channel. Think blog comments, Facebook wall posts, YouTube ratings, or widget interactions.

3. **Authority.** Ala Technorati, the inbound links to your content—like trackbacks and inbound links to a blog post or sites linking to a YouTube video.

4. **Influence.** The size of the user base subscribed to your content. For blogs, [it is] feed or email subscribers; [it is] followers on Twitter or Friendfeed; or [it is] fans of your Facebook page.

Kim also suggests taking into account an x-factor that he calls sentiment, since "the spirit driving user participation matters."

---

[1] http://www.beingpeterkim.com/2008/09/a-framework-for.html

Aaron Uhrmacher of Mashable.com[2] offers this advice for measuring qualitative social media ROI:

> First, determine what you want to measure, whether it's corporate reputation, conversations, or customer relationships. These objectives require a more qualitative measurement approach, so let's start by asking some questions. For example, if the objective is to measure ROI for conversations, we start by benchmarking ourselves with questions like:

> - Are we currently part of conversations about our product or industry?
> - How are we currently talked about versus our competitors?

> Then to measure success, we ask whether we were able to:

> - Build better relationships with our key audiences?
> - Participate in conversations where we hadn't previously had a voice?
> - Move from a running monologue to a meaningful dialogue with customers?

> There are companies that offer services to assist with this kind of measurement, which requires a great deal of human analysis on top of the automated results to appropriately assess the tonality and brand positioning across various social media platforms.

## A Quantitative Framework

Measuring site traffic, sales, and other more quantitative effects of your social media plan may be an easier task, but you still need to have baseline numbers and specific goals in place to accurately measure your ROI.

A basic framework may start by measuring the following:

- Placement in search engines (see the "Search Optimization" section below):
  › Traditional Search Engines
  › Social Search Engines

---

[2] http://mashable.com/2008/07/31/measuring-social-media-roi-for-business/

> › Blog Search Engines
> › Real-Time Search Engines
> › Semantic Search Engines

- Rankings in blog search engines:
  - › Technorati
  - › BlogPulse
- Placement of social networking pages in searches:
  - › Facebook pages
  - › Squidoo pages
- Ranking in social bookmarking sites:
  - › Delicious.com
  - › StumbleUpon
- Popularity in crowd-sourcing sites:
  - › Digg.com
  - › Reddit.com
- Popularity of shared multimedia within media communities:
  - › Flickr.com
  - › YouTube.com

In addition to monitoring your own progress in these channels, you should frequently run searches to see how your competitors are doing.

# Search Optimization

By search optimization we mean optimizing for any place on the Internet someone might use to search for you, your products, or your services. This includes the following search engines, that we demonstrate using similar search terms:

## Traditional Search Engines

These include the usual suspects: Google, Yahoo!, Bing, etc. As seen in Figures 14.1 and 14.2, traditional search engines are now incorporating social, real-time, semantic, and blogs directly or in addition to their search results.

## Figure 14.1. Google Search Results

## Figure 14.2. Yahoo! Search Results

## Social Search Engines

These search engines return results from the Social Web, including video, images, social bookmarking sites, social networks, etc. Figure 14.3 shows our search results in the social search engine Surchur[3].

### Figure 14.3. Surchur Search Results

## Real-Time Search Engines

Real-time search engines like OneRiot[4] return results from the Social Web in "real time." Results show current conversations and Tweets. Figure 14.4 shows our search results as returned by OneRiot. (Note: OneRiot is now more of an ad platform for the real-time Web.)

## Semantic Search Engines

As we learned in Chapter 13, semantic implies "meaning." A semantic search engine like Hakia[5], then, will attempt to return results that are based more on meaning or relevancy than popularity. See Figure 14.5.

---

[3] http://www.surchur.com
[4] http://www.oneriot.com
[5] http://www.hakia.com

## Figure 14.4. OneRiot Search Results

## Figure 14.5. Hakia Search Results

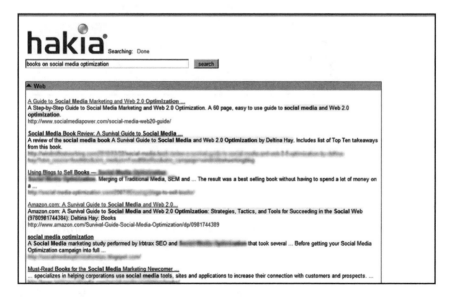

## Blog Search Engines

These engines search blogs and RSS feeds as opposed to traditional Websites. Technorati is probably the most popular. We show Google Blog Search[6] in Figure 14.6, however, to show the "real time" search features shown in the left sidebar, which again demonstrates how the traditional search engines are now returning real-time search results.

### Figure 14.6. Google Blog Search Results

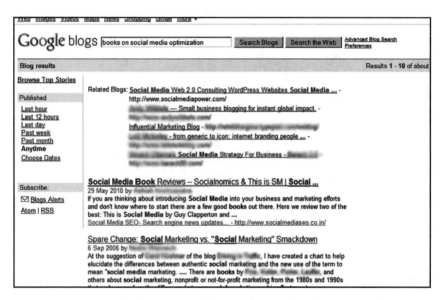

## Optimizing for All "Engines"

There is a lot of hype and theory out there about these different types of search engines and how you need to optimize separately for each one. But when you get right down to it, most search optimization tactics apply to all of the engines described above in one way or another. With that in mind, we want to follow a framework that encompasses the best overall search optimization plan.

Such a framework should focus on the following general areas regarding all of your Web content optimization:

---

[6] http://blogsearch.google.com

## Relevancy

This area includes the relevancy of your Web content to your meta keywords, titles, and descriptions, as well as the relevancy of your outgoing links, the "friends" you keep, the topics you blog about, etc.

## Accuracy

In addition to giving you more credibility, keeping your content and outgoing links accurate will help with your search results and site popularity.

## Meaning

As we discussed in Chapter 13, applying microformats and maintaining an RDF file will optimize your content for semantic search engines, helping them derive meaning from your content.

But optimizing your content is not enough if you want it to place well in social and real-time search results. We need to add two additional tactics to our framework that apply to our overall Web presence:

## Frequency

Regularly blogging, bookmarking, micro-blogging, and contributing to other social sites will keep your content optimized for the social and real-time engines.

## Diversity

Don't spread yourself *too* thin, but maintaining a blog, contributing to at least one social networking and micro-blogging site, and sharing images/video/documents in media communities will help keep your presence diverse enough to place you in all of the current engines.

Your ideal optimization plan, then, is to follow the social media optimization strategies, tactics, and tools discussed throughout this book, as well as some traditional search optimization tactics[7]. What you will find is that many of the tactics overlap.

---

[7]http://www.searchenginejournal.com/55-quick-seo-tips-even-your-mother-would-love/6760/

The framework discussed here is the basis of the author's next book. In that book, she further develops the framework, and uses her signature down-to-earth, real-world, approach to help you create a search optimization plan that will get you the best overall placement for your entire Web presence in the most relevant search venues.

# Tracking Tactics

You can track your social media efforts using some simple tactics. The suggestions here are a few you can incorporate easily with accessible tools.

## URL Shortening

In Chapter 6: "Social Networking & Micro-Blogging," we talked about using URL shortening services to save room in your Twitter and Facebook posts. Not all services are created equal, though. When choosing a service, make sure they offer a way for you to track the short URLs you create—bit.ly[8] is one such service.

There are also plugins for WordPress and other CMSs that help you create and track your own short URLs. Pretty Links[9] is one.

## Landing Pages

If the goal of a campaign is to direct visitors to specific information or product on your site, you should create landing pages specifically for that campaign. You can then track the activity on that page separate from the rest of your site.

If you are looking to increase a mailing list, be sure to add a form on your landing page to capture names and emails. There are many plugins to choose from if you are using WordPress, such as WP Email Capture[10].

---

[8] http://bit.ly/
[9] http://blairwilliams.com/pretty-link/
[10] http://wordpress.org/extend/plugins/wp-email-capture/

## Email Addresses

If you are tracking a major campaign, it is a good idea to create an email address specific to the campaign. If you have an email address posted somewhere as a link, you can track it like this: deltina+test@deltina.com where "test" will show up in the subject of an email sent to deltina@deltina.com.

# Tools to Help You Measure

Listed below is a selection of time-honored and new tools that can help you get additional insight into how well your social media plan is contributing to your overall Web presence.

## Internal Tools

Take advantage of the tools within the sites where you already have a presence, or within your blogging platform. In Chapter 6: "Social Networking & Micro-Blogging," we saw how to view analytics on Facebook pages using Facebook Insights.

In Chapter 12: "Pulling It All Together," we looked at HootSuite which is a tool for managing and tracking your Twitter accounts. This is a great tool to use to view analytics on your Twitter activity.

Take advantage of the analysis tools for your RSS feed or blog offered by FeedBurner. See Chapter 3: "RSS Feeds & Blogs" page 77 for details.

There are also plugins you can add to your WordPress site that help track visitor statistics. WordPress Stats[11] is a popular one.

## Google Analytics[12]

Google Analytics is a must-have tool to measure and analyze traffic on a Website. Figures 14.7, 14.8, and 14.9 show some of the many features of Google Analytics.

---

[11] http://wordpress.org/extend/plugins/stats/
[12] http://www.google.com/analytics

## Figure 14.7. Google Analytics

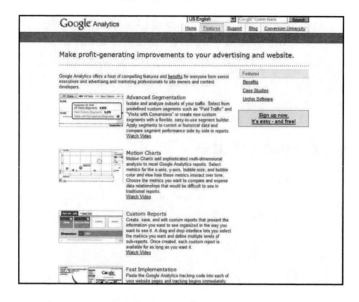

## Figure 14.8. Google Analytics, 2

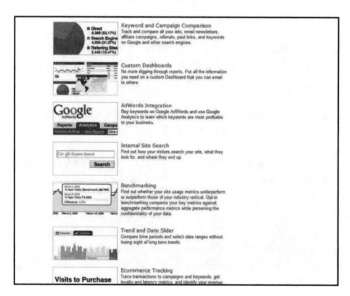

## Figure 14.9. Google Analytics, 3

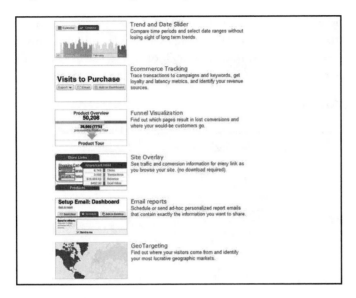

# Google Alerts[13]

Google Alerts (see Figure 14.10) are email updates of results based on a specific topic. As an example, you can create a Google Alert for a specific blog post using the title of the post. You can request results from the Web, from blogs, from news stories, or from all of these sources.

## Figure 14.10. Google Alerts

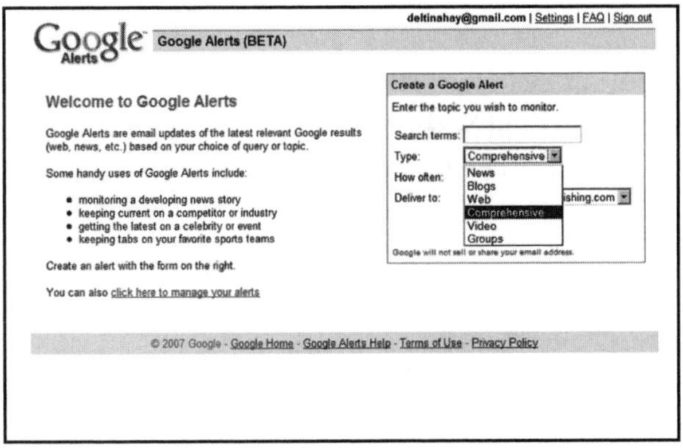

![Google Alerts interface screenshot]

---

[13] http://www.google.com/alerts

## Google Trends[14]

You can use Google Trends (Figure 14.11) to get an idea of Web search trends around certain key terms or other topics. Google Trends also shows how frequently your topics have appeared in Google News stories, and in which geographic regions people have searched for them the most.

### Figure 14.11. Google Trends

## Technorati[15]

In addition to being a blog search engine, Technorati also has some ratings features. Technorati Authority is one of those features; it is the number of blogs linking to a Website in the last six months. The higher the number, the more Technorati authority the blog has.

## BlogPulse[16]

BlogPulse is also more than just a blog search engine. As shown in Figure 14.12, this site offers many tools to help track blog trends, conversations, statistics, and more.

---

[14] http://www.google.com/trends

[15] http://www.technorati.com

[16] http://www.blogpulse.com

## Figure 14.12. BlogPulse

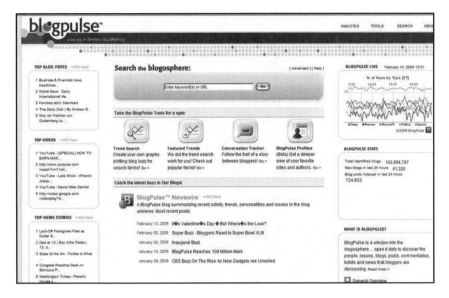

# Klout[17]

Klout uses an algorithmic approach to measure Twitter influence and reach. Klout's algorithmic approach to rating influence has merit, but it is best to wait until you have been "out there" for some time before checking your "influence." See Figure 14.13.

## Figure 14.13. Klout

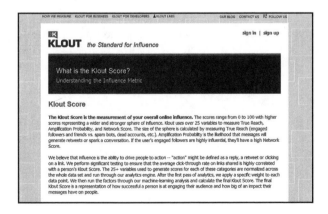

[17] http://klout.com/

# Twitter Search[18]

Use this tool to track real-time Twitter conversations on a given key term. Figure 14.14 shows a search on the term "survival guide to social media," which can give the author some insight into what others are saying about her book.

## Figure 14.14. Twitter Search

# Tweet Reach[19]

This tool returns analytics on specific tweets based on key terms. Figure 14.15 shows an example.

# PostRank[20]

PostRank is a scoring system that ranks online content, such as RSS feed items, blog posts, articles, or news stories. According to their site, "PostRank is based on social engagement, which refers to how interesting

[18] http://search.twitter.com

[19] http://tweetreach.com/

[20] http://www.postrank.com

## Figure 14.15. Tweet Reach

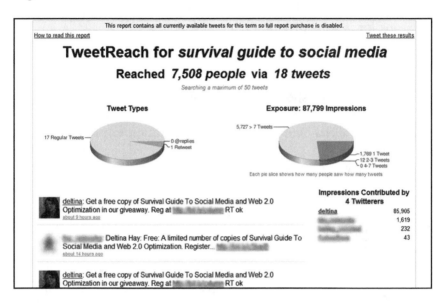

or relevant people have found an item or category to be. Examples of engagement include writing a blog post in response to someone else, bookmarking an article, leaving a comment on a blog, or clicking a link to read a news item."

## Figure 14.16. PostRank 5 Cs

The PostRank system uses what it calls the 5 Cs to rank content (see Figure 14.16). This can help you get an idea of what these types of ranking sites look for in what they call "relevant content."

# Xinu[21]

Xinu is a service that shows not only how well your site or blog is doing in traditional search engines, but also in blog search engine, crowd-sourcing, and social bookmarking sites. In addition to page rank, Xinu also shows backlinks, syndication stats, and indexed pages. Figure 14.17 shows this service in action.

### Figure 14.17. XinuReturns.com

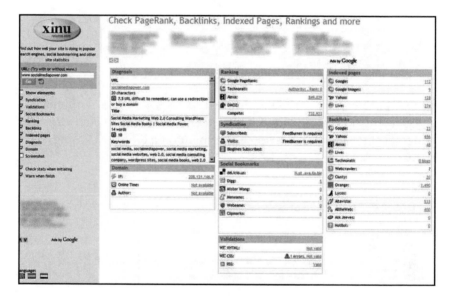

# Social Analytics Services

Radian6[22] and JitterJam[23] (Figures 14.18 and 14.19) are paid services that can help you manage individual campaigns, brand and reputation, even your entire Social Web presence. JitterJam is a "Social CRM"

[21] http://www.xinureturns.com/

[22] http://www.radian6.com/

[23] http://www.jitterjam.com/

## Figure 14.18. Radian6

## Figure 14.19. JitterJam

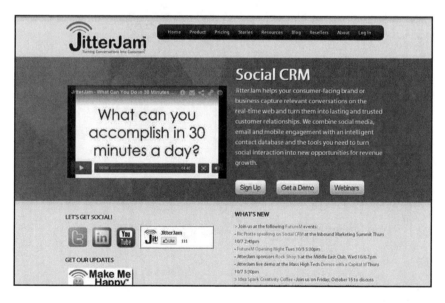

combining social media monitoring and analytics with powerful CRM services. PostRank, discussed above, also has pro services.

# Come to Your Own Conclusions

Each person or business has their own definition of what success means for a social media strategy. Be careful not to fall for the advice given by many "analysts" out there. You may read about how your feed should have so many subscriptions, your blog posts so many comments, your social networks so many friends, etc., but these numbers are subjective. Only you know how your reputation or customer relations are improving, how your sales are increasing, how your credibility it is rising, and so forth.

I am not saying you shouldn't keep on top of changes, just find a few reliable sources and stick with them. My recommendations for informative sites focusing on changes in the world of social media:

- Mashable[24]
- ReadWriteWeb[25]
- SocialMedia.biz[26]
- SocialMediaToday[27]

# This Chapter on the Resource CD

- Further Reading
- Linkable Resources

---

[24] http://mashable.com/
[25] http://www.readwriteweb.com/
[26] http://www.socialmedia.biz/
[27] http://www.socialmediatoday.com/

# 15 Conclusion

**A few concluding points...**

## Marketing in the Social Web

When marketing in the Social Web, many businesses make the mistake of applying old methods to the new tools. The Social Web is not a place for the old hard pitch. People on the Social Web want to be listened to; they want to interact. They do not want to hear praises by the branders; they want to read what others have to say about a product or service. And they do not want to be inundated with offers and event announcements. If they find your message appealing, they will want to learn more about what you have to offer. Reference the resource CD for some recommended books and sites about social media marketing.

## Practicing Good "Netiquette"

Before establishing your presence on any social site, read the site's submission guidelines or terms of use. Do not assume that just because others are engaging in questionable behavior that it is *acceptable* behavior.

Refraining from any sort of "spamming" should go without saying, but the types of things that are considered spam in the Social Web might surprise you. For instance, only bookmarking your own posts or pages and only contributing self-promoting items to social networks are typically unacceptable behaviors that can get you blacklisted or just plain ignored.

If you find you are using plugins or applications created by independent developers, consider sending them a donation—even a few dollars can mean a lot to them.

Never delete links embedded in open source software, such as the "Powered by WordPress" reference in the footer of a WordPress powered Website.

If you use other people's material, always give them credit—even if the information seems generalized. This will accomplish a couple things for you: It will establish you as a courteous user and it will give you links back to more places in the Web.

Be kind and courteous—even when others are not.

# Getting Help

Do not forget that there are many good forums and wikis out there to help you. Open source applications and many of the social tools discussed throughout this book were built through collaboration, so it is natural that others are more than willing to share their knowledge with you to help you succeed. And, once you become skilled, you may want to choose a forum in which to share your own knowledge.

# Maintaining and Expanding Your Foundation

Remember, you first want to create a foundation in the Social Web that you can build upon and expand using new tools that you have researched for usefulness and their ability to integrate with your existing Social Web presence.

You also want to occasionally evaluate the tools that are working and not working for you, and perhaps weed some out or ramp them up. Just because it seemed like a good idea initially does not mean that a tool will benefit your presence indefinitely.

Finally, you want to keep abreast of each tool's latest features and keep any open source platforms and installed plugins you are using up-to-date with the latest versions.

# My Final Word on Key Terms

Imagine for a moment that there were no "traditional" Websites as we know them. That instead, all you had was your presence in social networking, social bookmarking, crowd-sourcing, media communities, and other social sites. Further, imagine that there were tools similar to "traditional" search engines that helped Internet users find other people, products, or services that matched a specific criteria. How do you think such a tool would work?

They would likely accomplish this task by searching profiles, conversations, connections, and other activity in the Social Web for relevancy to the users' search criteria, and return the results accordingly. (We touched on this concept briefly in Chapter 14: "Measuring Your Success" when we discussed search optimization.)

Now imagine that you have used and reused, and used and reused again, your best key terms throughout your entire Social Web presence in a natural way. I imagine such consistent use of key terms would yield the kind of great search results that anyone might seek in the Social Web.

So, I finally rest my case on the use of good key terms. And there was much rejoicing!

**Here's to your success in the Social Web...**

# Appendix A: Installing WordPress

## Preliminary Tasks

First, you need to install the software that keeps WordPress running properly: specifically, PHP[1], MySQL[2], and phpMyAdmin[3]. PHP is the scripting language used to create WordPress. MySQL is the database WordPress uses to store your posts, pages, and most everything else associated with your WordPress site. phpMyAdmin is a convenient interface used to access and manage your MySQL database. Provided you don't run into major problems with WordPress in the future, you only need to access MySQL this once to create your database and database admin account.

Before you proceed, you need to have FTP access. Refer back to the "FTP Access" section on page 109, and follow the instructions for getting FTP access, if you do not already have it.

---

[1] http://www.php.net/
[2] http://www.mysql.com/
[3] http://www.phpmyadmin.net

# Installing Preliminary Software

Install the latest versions of these applications that your host allows. I use Westhost.com, and they have generously offered to let me demonstrate this process using their site manager. If you have a hosting account with Westhost, follow these instructions precisely, otherwise, your chosen host has similar tools and screens available for you to accomplish the same tasks.

Go to your site manager (or control panel, as it is often called). This is the URL yoursitename.com/manager (remember that these instructions are for Westhost hosted accounts only). See Figure A.1. Enter the username and password that Westhost emailed to you when you created your account, and click "login." You see a screen similar to Figure A.2. Click on "Install & Manage" under the Site Applications heading in the left sidebar.

### Figures A.1 & A.2. Preliminary Tasks to Perform

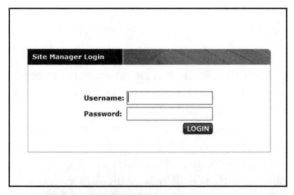

From this screen (see Figure A.3), click on "PHP 5.2.6" (or whatever is the latest version) under the Development heading. Check the box to agree to the terms on the next screen you see. A screen like Figure A.4 displays. Leave the check boxes as they are and click "Finish."

From the main Install & Manage screen again (Figure A.3), click on "MySQL 5.0.27" (or whatever is the latest version). Click on the check box to agree to the terms on the next screen.

## Figure A.3. Preliminary Tasks

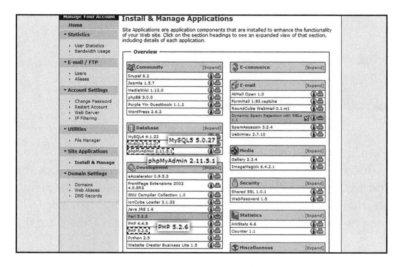

## Figure A.4. Preliminary Tasks: Installing PHP

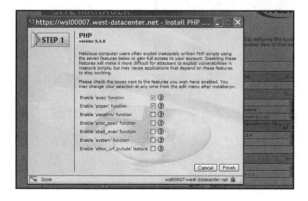

The next screen you see is Figure A.5, which asks for a password. For convenience, you may want to make this the same password as you use to access your site manager. Once you enter the password, be sure to make note of it and click "Finish."

## Figure A.5. Preliminary Tasks: Installing MySQL

Again, from the main Install & Manage screen (Figure A.3), click on "phpMyAdmin 2.11.5.1" (or whatever is the latest version). Click the agree to terms check box on the next screen. On the next screen (Figure A.6), note that your username and password for phpMyAdmin will be the same as the username and password you use to access your site manager.

## Figure A.6. Preliminary Tasks: Installing phpMyAdmin

**Important:** Before you continue, create a text file (Wordpad or Notepad file) and keep it open on your desktop. For future reference you want to save all of the configuration information you create from here on out in this file.

## Creating the Database

Now, create the database and database admin user that WordPress needs to run. To access your phpMyAdmin panel, go to the URL http:// yoursite.com/pma. (Remember, this applies only to a Westhost hosted account. If you are with another host, you should check with them as to how to access phpMyAdmin.)

Figure A.6 shows the phpMyAdmin panel. Create a database as shown, but for security reasons do not name it "wordpress." I suggest naming it something like "XYZwordpress," where "XYZ" is a three letter code you can easily associate with your site. Enter the database name and click "Create."

**Figure A.6. Creating the Database**

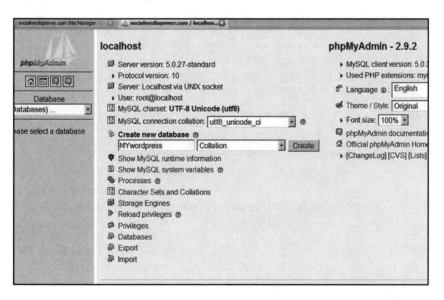

Return to the home panel of phpMyAdmin and click on "Privileges." Choose "Add a new user." Refer to Figure A.7 and do the following:

- Enter the admin username (do not make this name obvious). Use a name like XYZadmin as opposed to just admin. (Again, "XYZ" is a three letter code you can easily associate with your site.)
- Choose "Local" for host. (This may be different for some hosting sites—Godaddy.com, for example.)
- Click the "Generate" key to generate a big, ugly password. (For security reasons, you want a big and ugly password.)

## Figure A.7. Creating the Database User

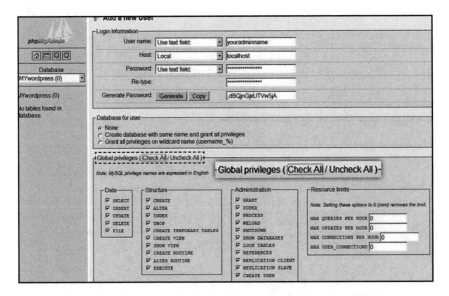

- Click "Copy" to copy the big, ugly password into the password fields.
- Click "Check All" for Global privileges.
- Before you click "go," put the database name, admin user name, and the big, ugly password in your text file so you will not lose it.
- Select "Go" at the bottom of the screen.

You are now armed with the information you need to configure and install WordPress.

# Downloading and Installing WordPress

Follow these steps to download WordPress and prepare the wp-config file:

- Go to WordPress.org and download the latest version of WordPress. Be sure and download the .zip file and not the tar.gz file. Unzip the folder (extract all files) onto your desktop.
- Open the wordpress folder and find the file named "wp-config-sample. php." Right click on the file and rename it "wp-config.php".
- Open wp-config.php in a text editor (use Wordpad or Notepad, NOT Word). The file will look similar to the file depicted in Figure A.8.
- Change the code that is highlighted in Figure A.8 as follows:
  › "XYZwordpress" is the name you gave your database.

## Figure A.8. WordPress Configuration File

```php
<?php
// ** MySQL settings ** //
define('DB_NAME', 'XYZwordpress');    // The name of the database
define('DB_USER', 'XYZadmin');     // Your MySQL username
define('DB_PASSWORD', 'dBQjnGjxUTw5jA'); // ...and password
define('DB_HOST', 'localhost');    // 99% chance you won't need to change this value
define('DB_CHARSET', 'utf8');
define('DB_COLLATE', '');

// Change each KEY to a different unique phrase.  You won't have to remember the phrases later,
// so make them long and complicated.  You can visit http://api.wordpress.org/secret-key/1.1/
// to get keys generated for you, or just make something up.  Each key should have a different phrase

define('AUTH_KEY', 'first unique key'); // Change this to a unique phrase.
define('SECURE_AUTH_KEY', 'second unique key'); // Change this to a unique phrase.
define('LOGGED_IN_KEY', 'third unique key'); // Change this to a unique phrase.

// You can have multiple installations in one database if you give each a unique prefix
$table_prefix  = 'wp_';  // Only numbers, letters, and underscores please!

// Change this to localize WordPress.  A corresponding MO file for the
// chosen language must be installed to wp-content/languages.
// For example, install de.mo to wp-content/languages and set WPLANG to 'de'
// to enable German language support.
define ('WPLANG', '');

/* That's all, stop editing! Happy blogging. */

if ( !defined('ABSPATH') )
       define('ABSPATH', dirname(__FILE__) . '/');
require_once(ABSPATH . 'wp-settings.php');
?>
```

› "XYZadmin" is the database admin user you created.

› The password is the big, ugly password you generated as your database admin password.

› Use the URL (http://api.wordpress.org/secret-key/1.1/) as suggested in Figure A.8 to generate your secret keys. Note: Your version will likely have more keys than are shown here.

› Change the table prefix "wp" to any different two letter code.

• Once these changes are made, save your new wp-config.php file by clicking File/Save.

## Uploading the WordPress Files to Your Hosting Account

Using FTP access, upload all of the WordPress files and folders onto the root directory of your hosting account. **IMPORTANT:** You want to upload the files and folders INSIDE the "wordpress" folder, not just the folder itself—read on for clarification.

The following demonstrates the process using the FTP browser WS-FTP and a Westhost hosted account. Note that the process will be similar using any FTP browser or hosting account.

Figure A.9 shows what you should see when you first connect to your Westhost account via FTP. What this shows are the files on the remote computer (your hosted account) on the right, and the files of the local computer (your computer) on the left. To transfer files, either highlight them and click the appropriate arrow, or drag and drop them.

To get to the host's root directory, double-click on "www" (see Figure A.9). Next, double-click on the name of your domain (see Figure A.10). In this example, the domain name is "bookpublishingpower." You will now be in your hosted account's root directory.

Next, in the left, or local, area of the FTP browser, find the directory on your computer that has the WordPress files you downloaded and unzipped earlier. Figure A.11 shows what you should see now: your wordpress files to the left and your hosted account's root directory on the right. Be careful NOT to upload only the wordpress folder. Instead, you want to open that folder and upload the files and folders that are inside of it.

## Figures A.9 & A.10. Uploading WordPress via FTP

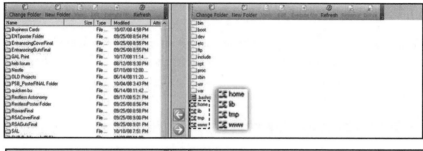

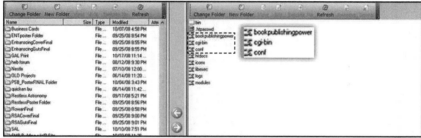

## Figure A.11. Uploading WordPress via FTP

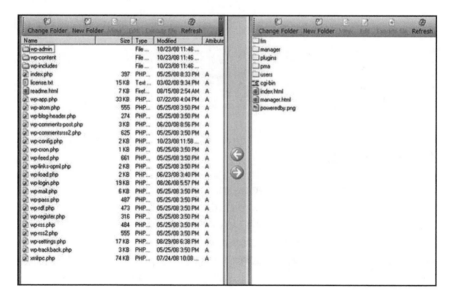

Now, highlight all of the WordPress files and folders and copy them over to the hosting account. You will also need to change the name of the index.html (or index.htm) file, if one exists. Many hosts place a temporary index file in your root directory that you can replace once the site is developed. In our example, we changed the name of the index. html file to index-old.html.

Figure A.12 shows you what the files in your hosting account's root directory should look like once you are finished. Please note that this may vary with different hosts, but the WordPress files and folders will be the same for the most part (they may vary slightly in newer versions).

**Figure A.12. Uploading WordPress via FTP**

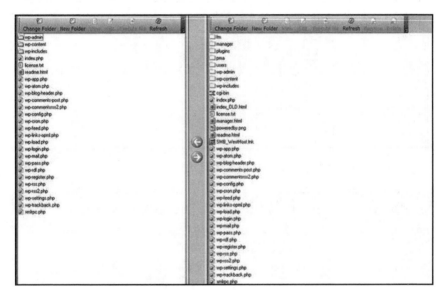

# Installing WordPress

Once all preliminary tasks are complete, the actual installation of WordPress takes around five minutes—see the WordPress famous 5-minute install.[4] To install WordPress, access the WordPress installation script by visiting a specific Web address using a Web browser. Open Firefox or Internet Explorer and visit http://www.YourSite.com/ wp-admin/install.php, where "YourSite.com" is your domain name.

---

[4] http://codex.wordpress.org/Installing_WordPress#Famous_5-Minute_Install.

Follow the instructions to input a blog name, user name, password, and email address, then click "Install WordPress" (see Figure A.13). As long as there are no database errors on the next screen, you will be finished.

## Figure A.13. Installing WordPress

If you do get database errors, check that all of the information in the wp-config.php file is correct, i.e. the database name, the username, the password. If not, correct the config file, re-upload the file using your FTP browser, and try the previous step again. If you continue to get errors, visit the WordPress forums for help.[5]

Once WordPress is installed, you will receive an email message with your admin password, and a link to the login area of WordPress so you can get into the back end and start building your site.

You can get more information from the WordPress codex[6] or from the WordPress forums.[7]

---

[5]http://wordpress.org/support/
[6]http://codex.wordpress.org/Installing_WordPress
[7]http://wordpress.org/support/

# Appendix B: Creating Your Own RSS Feed

To create your own RSS feed, follow these general steps:

- Create an XML file that is formatted specifically for RSS readers
- Populate the file with your articles or "items"
- Save the file and upload it to a folder on the Internet
- The link to the feed (or the feed URL) will then be something like:
  › http://www.yoursite.com/yourRSSfolder/nameoffile.xml

An RSS feed is a way to present information so feed aggregators can read it, the same way HTML is read by Web browsers. This is accomplished using XML.

## XML

XML stands for Extended Markup Language. The language is based on the use of tags. Content is presented inside specific tags that are then interpreted by applications written specifically to decipher the content within the tags. For instance, this is a tagged element:

<title>This is the title.</title>

The beginning of the element is the opening tag "<title>," the content is the sentence "This is the title.," and the end of the element is the closing tag "</title>." An application that is written to do so, will know how to pull the content from between the opening title tag and the closing title tag.

XML is different from HTML. HTML is a markup language that *displays* data, where XML is a language designed to store and transport data across many platforms. XML does not have predefined tags like HTML. HTML tags follow a standard that can be read by all Web browsers. XML tags, on the other hand, do not follow any predefined standard; they are created and defined by the author of the XML document. Of course, without an application to make sense of the data, an XML document does the author little good.

Writing an application or "language" to read XML documents is surprisingly easy. That is why XML is becoming a standard in Web data storage and exchange. One such language is RSS. RSS is a language that is written to read and interpret XML data within specific tags. As long as we know what those tags are, we can write an XML file that can be read by a RSS feed aggregator.

In its simplest form, a RSS feed document consists of a declaration line, a <rss> tag, one <channel> tag, and one <item> tag. Below is a stripped-down version of the RSS feed for Social Media Power:[1]

```
<?xml version="1.0" encoding="UTF-8"?>
<rss version="2.0">
<channel>
   <title>Social Media Power</title>
   <link>http://www.socialmediapower.com</link>
   <description>Discover the Tools of Web 2.0!</description>
   <item>
      <title>We want to make you Plumb Social!</title>
      <link>http://www.socialmediapower.com/2008/10/28/we-want-to-make-
         you-plumb-social/</link>
      <description><Introducing www.PlumbSocial.com, our new service for
         streamlining your presence on the Social Web!></description>
   </item>
</channel>
</rss>
```

---

[1] http://www.socialmediapower.com

The first line is the XML declaration. This line defines the XML version and the character encoding. The one used here is pretty standard. For a more in depth explanation of versions and character encoding go to the World Wide Web Consortium (W3C).[2]

The next line is the RSS declaration. It defines the XML document as a RSS document. Some tags or elements have what are called "attributes" that can contain different values. Attributes are used to further define a tag, and are always contained in quotes. The "version" in this line is an example of an attribute. It declares the RSS version as "2.0."

The two main elements of an RSS feed are the <channel> element and the <item> element. The actual RSS feed is defined with the <channel> element. Each individual article or story is defined within an <item> element.

Nested in the <channel> element are its sub-elements: <title>, <link>, and <description>. Sub-elements are used to further expand an RSS tag. Some sub-elements are required, while others are optional. The <item> element has sub-elements as well: <title>, <link>, and <description> in our example.

In XML, every element must have a closing tag, so the last two lines in our example are the closing tags for the <channel> and <rss> elements.

# The Elements of an RSS Feed

The information in this section is an *unadulterated* reproduction from the Berkman Center for Internet & Society at Harvard Law School's Website[3] under the terms of an Attribution/Share Alike Creative Commons license. Dave Winer is the author of the *unedited* document.

---

[2] http://www.w3.org/International/O-charset
[3] http://cyber.law.harvard.edu/rss/rss.html

# Required <channel> Elements:

| Element | Description | Example |
|---------|-------------|---------|
| title | The name of the channel. It's how people refer to your service. If you have an HTML website that contains the same information as your RSS file, the title of your channel should be the same as the title of your website. | GoUpstate.com News Headlines |
| link | The URL to the HTML website corresponding to the channel. | http://www.goupstate.com/ |
| description | Phrase or sentence describing the channel. | The latest news from GoUpstate. com, a Spartanburg Herald-Journal Web site. |

# Optional <channel> Elements:

| Element | Description | Example |
|---------|-------------|---------|
| language | The language the channel is written in. This allows aggregators to group all Italian language sites, for example, on a single page. For more information go to the W3C (http://www.w3.org/TR/REC-html40/struct/dirlang.html#langcodes). | en-us |
| copyright | Copyright notice for content in the channel. | Copyright 2002, Spartanburg Herald-Journal |
| managing Editor | Email address for person responsible for editorial content. | geo@herald.com (George Matesky) |
| webMaster | Email address for person responsible for technical issues relating to channel. | betty@herald.com (Betty Guernsey) |

| pubDate | The publication date for the content in the channel. For example, the New York Times publishes on a daily basis, the publication date flips once every 24 hours. That's when the pubDate of the channel changes. All date-times in RSS conform to the Date and Time Specification of RFC 822 (http://asg.web.cmu.edu/rfc/rfc822.html), with the exception that the year may be expressed with two characters or four characters (four preferred). | Sat, 07 Sep 2002 00:00:01 GMT |
|---|---|---|
| lastBuildDate | The last time the content of the channel changed. | Sat, 07 Sep 2002 09:42:31 GMT |
| category | Specify one or more categories that the channel belongs to. Follows the same rules as the <item>-level category element. For more information (http://cyber.law.harvard.edu/rss/rss.html#syndic8). | <category>Newspapers</category> |
| generator | A string indicating the program used to generate the channel. | MightyInHouse Content System v2.3 |
| docs | A URL that points to the documentation for the format used in the RSS file. It's probably a pointer to this page. It's for people who might stumble across an RSS file on a Web server 25 years from now and wonder what it is. | http://blogs.law.harvard.edu/tech/rss |
| cloud | Allows processes to register with a cloud to be notified of updates to the channel, implementing a lightweight publish-subscribe protocol for RSS feeds. See below for more information. | <cloud domain="rpc.sys.com" port="80" path="/RPC2" registerProcedure="pingMe" protocol="soap"/> |

| ttl | ttl stands for time to live. It's a number of minutes that indicates how long a channel can be cached before refreshing from the source. See below for more information. | `<ttl>60</ttl>` |
|---|---|---|
| image | Specifies a GIF, JPEG or PNG image that can be displayed with the channel. See below for more information. | |
| rating | The PICS (http://www.w3.org/PICS/) rating for the channel. | |
| textInput | Specifies a text input box that can be displayed with the channel. See below for more information. | |
| skipHours | A hint for aggregators telling them which hours they can skip. For more information (http://cyber.law.harvard.edu/rss/skipHoursDays.html#skiphours) | |
| skipDays | A hint for aggregators telling them which days they can skip. For more information (http://cyber.law.harvard.edu/rss/skipHoursDays.html#skipdays) | |

## \<image\> sub-element of \<channel\>

\<image\> is an optional sub-element of \<channel\>, which contains three required and three optional sub-elements.

\<url\> is the URL of a GIF, JPEG or PNG image that represents the channel.

<title> describes the image, it's used in the ALT attribute of the HTML <img> tag when the channel is rendered in HTML.

<link> is the URL of the site, when the channel is rendered, the image is a link to the site. (Note, in practice the image <title> and <link> should have the same value as the channel's <title> and <link>.

Optional elements include <width> and <height>, numbers, indicating the width and height of the image in pixels. <description> contains text that is included in the TITLE attribute of the link formed around the image in the HTML rendering. Maximum value for width is 144, default value is 88. Maximum value for height is 400, default value is 31.

### <cloud> sub-element of <channel>

<cloud> is an optional sub-element of <channel>.

It specifies a web service that supports the rssCloud interface which can be implemented in HTTP-POST, XML-RPC or SOAP 1.1.

Its purpose is to allow processes to register with a cloud to be notified of updates to the channel, implementing a lightweight publish-subscribe protocol for RSS feeds.

```
<cloud domain="rpc.sys.com" port="80" path="/RPC2" register
Procedure="myCloud.rssPleaseNotify" protocol="xml-rpc" />
```

In this example, to request notification on the channel it appears in, you would send an XML-RPC message to rpc.sys.com on port 80, with a path of /RPC2. The procedure to call is myCloud.rssPleaseNotify.

A full explanation of this element and the rssCloud interface is here.[4]

### <ttl> sub-element of <channel>

<ttl> is an optional sub-element of <channel>.

ttl stands for time to live. It's a number of minutes that indicates how long a channel can be cached before refreshing from the source. This makes it possible for RSS sources to be managed by a file-sharing network such as Gnutella (http://www.gnutellanews.com/).

Example: <ttl>60</ttl>

---

[4] http://cyber.law.harvard.edu/rss/soapMeetsRss.html#rsscloudInterface

### <textInput> sub-element of <channel>

A channel may optionally contain a <textInput> sub-element, which contains four required sub-elements.

<title> -- The label of the Submit button in the text input area. <description> -- Explains the text input area.

<name> -- The name of the text object in the text input area.

<link> -- The URL of the CGI script that processes text input requests.

The purpose of the <textInput> element is something of a mystery. You can use it to specify a search engine box. Or to allow a reader to provide feedback. Most aggregators ignore it.

# <item> Elements:

A channel may contain any number of <item>s. An item may represent a "story"—much like a story in a newspaper or magazine; if so, its description is a synopsis of the story, and the link points to the full story. An item may also be complete in itself, if so, the description contains the text, and the link and title may be omitted. All elements of an item are optional, however at least one of title or description must be present.

| Element | Description | Example |
|---|---|---|
| title | The title of the item. | Venice Film Festival Tries to Quit Sinking |
| link | The URL of the item. | http://nytimes.com/2004/12/07FEST.html |
| description | The item synopsis. | Some of the most heated chatter at the Venice Film Festival this week was about the way that the arrival of the stars at the Palazzo del Cinema was being staged. |
| author | authorEmail address of the author of the item. See below for more information. | oprah\@oxygen.net |

| category | Includes the item in one or more categories. See below for more information. | |
|---|---|---|
| comments | URL of a page for comments relating to the item. See below for more information. | http://www.myblog.org/cgi-local/ mt/mt-comments.cgi?entry_id=290 |
| enclosure | Describes a media object that is attached to the item. See below for more information. | |
| guid | A string that uniquely identifies the item. See below for more information. | http://inessential.com/2002/09/01. php#a2 |
| pubDate | Indicates when the item was published. See below for more information. | Sun, 19 May 2002 15:21:36 GMT |
| source | The RSS channel that the item came from. See below for more information. | |

### <source> sub-element of <item>

<source> is an optional sub-element of <item>.

Its value is the name of the RSS channel that the item came from, derived from its <title>. It has one required attribute, url, which links to the XMLization of the source.

```
<source url="http://www.tomalak.org/links2.xml">Tomalak's
Realm</source>
```

The purpose of this element is to propagate credit for links, to publicize the sources of news items. It can be used in the Post command of an aggregator. It should be generated automatically when forwarding an item from an aggregator to a weblog authoring tool.

### <enclosure> sub-element of <item>

<enclosure> is an optional sub-element of <item>.

It has three required attributes. url says where the enclosure is located, length says how big it is in bytes, and type says what its type is, a standard MIME type.

The url must be an http url.

```
<enclosure url="http://www.scripting.com/mp3s/
weatherReportSuite.mp3" length="12216320" type="audio/mpeg"
/>
```

A use-case narrative for this element is here.[5]

### <category> sub-element of <item>

<category> is an optional sub-element of <item>.

It has one optional attribute, domain, a string that identifies a categorization taxonomy.

The value of the element is a forward-slash-separated string that identifies a hierarchic location in the indicated taxonomy. Processors may establish conventions for the interpretation of categories. Two examples are provided below:

```
<category>Grateful Dead</category>
<category domain="http://www.fool.
com/cusips">MSFT</category>
```

You may include as many category elements as you need to, for different domains, and to have an item cross-referenced in different parts of the same domain.

### <pubDate> sub-element of <item>

<pubDate> is an optional sub-element of <item>.

Its value is a date, indicating when the item was published. If it's a date in the future, aggregators may choose to not display the item until that date.

```
<pubDate>Sun, 19 May 2002 15:21:36 GMT</pubDate>
```

### <guid> sub-element of <item>

<guid> is an optional sub-element of <item>.

guid stands for globally unique identifier. It's a string that uniquely identifies the item. When present, an aggregator may choose to use this string to determine if an item is new.

---

[5] http://www.thetwowayweb.com/payloadsforrss

```
<guid>http://some.server.com/weblogItem3207</guid>
```

There are no rules for the syntax of a guid. Aggregators must view them as a string. It's up to the source of the feed to establish the uniqueness of the string.

If the guid element has an attribute named "isPermaLink" with a value of true, the reader may assume that it is a permalink to the item, that is, a url that can be opened in a Web browser, that points to the full item described by the <item> element. An example:

```
<guid isPermaLink="true">http://inessential.com/2002/09/01.
php#a2</guid>
```

isPermaLink is optional, its default value is true. If its value is false, the guid may not be assumed to be a url, or a url to anything in particular.

### <comments> sub-element of <item>

<comments> is an optional sub-element of <item>.

If present, it is the url of the comments page for the item.

```
<comments>http://ekzemplo.
com/entry/4403/comments</comments>
```

### <author> sub-element of <item>

<author> is an optional sub-element of <item>

It's the email address of the author of the item. For newspapers and magazines syndicating via RSS, the author is the person who wrote the article that the <item> describes. For collaborative weblogs, the author of the item might be different from the managing editor or webmaster. For a weblog authored by a single individual it would make sense to omit the <author> element.

```
<author>lawyer@boyer.net (Lawyer Boyer)</author>
```

## Another Example

The RSS feed below is the further expanded feed for Social Media Power.[6] You will see many of the sub-elements discussed above in this expanded feed.

```
<?xml version="1.0" encoding="UTF-8"?>
<rss version="2.0">
  <channel>
    <title>Social Media Power</title>
    <link>http://www.socialmediapower.com</link>
    <description>Discover the Tools of Web 2.0!</description>
    <pubDate>Tue, 09 Dec 2008 12:18:38 +0000</pubDate>
    <generator>http://wordpress.org/?v=abc</generator>
    <language>en</language>
    <item>
      <title>A shout for our social media e-book.</title>
      <link>http://www.socialmediapower.com/2008/09/05/a-shout-for-our-social-
      media-e-book/</link>
      <pubDate>Fri, 05 Sep 2008 13:05:14 +0000</pubDate>
      <category>Social Media</category>
      <category>Social Media Books</category>
      <category>Social Media Marketing</category>
      <category>Social Media Tools</category>
      <category>Web 2.0</category>
      <category>WordPress</category>
      <category>social media e-book</category>
      <guid isPermaLink="false">http://www.socialmediapower.com/?p=105</guid>
      <description><JD at Social Media gave our e-book a shout, saying it
      was&#8230;worth the price for anyone looking for a grounding in the nuts and
      bolts of social media. And, that it&#8230;will give you the underpinnings
      for the elements you need to address in your organization&#8217;s social
      media strategy.Thank you, JD!></description>
      <comments>http://www.socialmediapower.com/2008/09/05/a-shout-for-our-social-
      media-e-book/#comments/</comments>
    </item>
    <item>
      <title>The 30 Minute Facebook Application</title>
      <link>http://www.socialmediapower.com/2008/08/28/the-30-minute facebook-
      application/</link>
      <pubDate>Thu, 28 Aug 2008 21:05:25 +0000</pubDate>
      <category>Facebook</category>
      <category>Social Media</category>
      <category>Social Media Marketing</category>
      <category>Social Media Optimization</category>
      <category>Social Media Tools</category>
      <category>Bebo</category>
      <category>blog</category>
      <category>facebook applications</category>
      <category>facebook page</category>
      <category>RSS feed</category>
      <category>social networking</category>
      <category>widgetbox</category>
      <guid isPermaLink="false">http://www.socialmediapower.com/?p=67</guid>
      <description><Continuing our series on tapping the power of Facebook, we
      will demonstrate a way for anyone with an RSS feed to painlessly build a
      Facebook application in only 30 minutes. First, what is a Facebook
      application. If you are familiar with Facebook, you probably have an
      application or two on your page or profile already. If not,
      [...]></description>
      <comments>http://www.socialmediapower.com/2008/08/28/the-30-minute-facebook-
      application/#comments</comments>
    </item>
  </channel>
</rss>
```

[6] http://www.socialmediapower.com/feed

## Comments in RSS

The format for a comment is:

<!-- This is a comment. -->

## Adding More Stories

The example above shows two separate items or stories. To add additional stories to your feed, insert additional items using the <item> tag and sub-elements accordingly, then save and replace the XML file.

# Extending RSS

The core functionality of RSS is limited to the elements discussed in the previous sections. Developers extend the functionality of RSS, however, by writing modules or extensions that are defined and accessed using what are called "namespaces." These extensions work just like add-ons to RSS, but are defined in a way that still allow older versions of RSS to work properly.

In the RSS feed example below, there are several namespaces defined within the <rss> element. The namespace is an attribute called "xmlns," and its value is assigned as follows:

xmlns:namespace name="URL of where to find the namespace extensions."

So, in our example, the statement:

```
xmlns:atom="http://www.w3.org/2005/Atom"
```

is telling the RSS reader to go to the URL "http://www.w3.org/2005/ Atom" and include the extensions contained there as part of this RSS document, and that each time it encounters the namespace "atom" to go to this URL for more information.

Looking further down the example code will help clarify. The first line that should look unfamiliar is:

```
<atom:link href="http://www.socialmediapower.com/feed"
rel="self" type="application/rss+xml" />
```

This is not a core element, but we are telling the reader that it can find its definition by going to the defined URL in the namespace "atom" that is defined in the <rss> element.

Similarly, you will see many references in this example to elements that are not core elements (<dc:creator> and <wfw:commentRss> for

```
<?xml version="1.0" encoding="UTF-8"?>
<?xml version="1.0" encoding="UTF-8"?>

<!-- Here are the defined namespaces, within the rss element -->

<rss version="2.0"
  xmlns:content="http://purl.org/rss/1.0/modules/content/"
  xmlns:wfw="http://wellformedweb.org/CommentAPI/"
  xmlns:dc="http://purl.org/dc/elements/1.1/"
  xmlns:atom="http://www.w3.org/2005/Atom">
  <channel>
      <title>Social Media Power</title>
      <atom:link href="http://www.socialmediapower.com/feed" rel="self"
      type="application/rss+xml" />
      <link>http://www.socialmediapower.com</link>
      <description>Discover the Tools of Web 2.0!</description>
      <pubDate>Tue, 09 Dec 2008 12:18:38 +0000</pubDate>
      <generator>http://wordpress.org/?v=abc</generator>
      <language>en</language>
      <item>
          <title>Social Media Tip of the Day: Build a Solid Social Media
          Strategy</title>
          <link>http://www.socialmediapower.com/2008/08/25/social-media-tip-of-the-
          day-build-a-solid-social-media-strategy/</link>
          <comments>http://www.socialmediapower.com/2008/08/25/social-media-tip-of-
          the-day-build-a-solid-social-media-strategy/#comments</comments>
          <pubDate>Mon, 25 Aug 2008 20:01:01 +0000</pubDate>
          <dc:creator>smpadmin</dc:creator>
          <category><![CDATA[Social Media]]></category>
          <category><![CDATA[Web 2.0]]></category>
          <category><![CDATA[social media strategy]]></category>
          <category><![CDATA[Social Media Tools]]></category>
          <guid isPermaLink="false">http://www.socialmediapower.com/?p=103</guid>
          <description><![CDATA[All of the social media tools and technologies that
          are out there can be overwhelming, no doubt. But, if you focus on the sites
          and tools that truly make sense for your business, you will find that the
          choices narrow down substantially. Take the time to build a solid social
          media strategy before you begin [...]]]></description>
          <content:encoded><![CDATA[<p>All of the social media tools and technologies
          that are out there can be overwhelming, no doubt. But, if you focus on the
          sites and tools that truly make sense for your business, you will find that
          the choices narrow down substantially. Take the time to build a solid
          social media strategy before you begin that includes:</p>
          <ul>
          <li>Gathering and preparing your best content, media, and key terms</li>
          <li>Web 2.0 tools to add to your existing Web site</li>
          <li>How you will enter the blogosphere - if at all</li>
          <li>One or two social networking sites that are good fits for your message
          or business</li>
          <li>Several social bookmarking and crowd-sourcing sites whose content tends
          toward your message</li>
          <li>Media communities to share images, events, video, etc. based on media
          you already have</li>
          <li>Badges, widgets, and feeds to pull all of these tools together</li>
          </ul>
          <p>Thank you for your support!</p>
          <p>The Social Media Power team</p>]]></content:encoded>
          <wfw:commentRss>http://www.socialmediapower.com/2008/08/25/social-media-
          tip-of-the-day-build-a-solid-social-media-strategy/feed/</wfw:commentRss>
      </item>
  </channel></rss>
```

instance). They will, however, be preceded by a namespace name that will define where to find the extensions. You can go directly to any of these URLs to learn more about the extensions they contribute to RSS.

# CDATA Sections

One other thing that may look unfamiliar about the RSS feed above is the use of CDATA. A "CDATA section" is a section of content that is marked so that the feed reader interprets the content as character data, not markup data. CDATA is used to ensure that none of the content data is misinterpreted as XML. This is especially useful for tech feeds that may contain coding examples.

# Podcasting

A podcast, like a blog, is an RSS feed. When a feed reader is told that a feed is a podcast, it will look for a file within each item that will become the podcast episode. Use the enclosure element to define podcast episode files within each item of a podcast feed.

Here is the syntax of the enclosure element repeated from its definition above:

```
<enclosure url="http://www.scripting.com/mp3s/
weatherReportSuite.mp3" length="12216320" type="audio/mpeg"
/>
```

So, the "url" will be the location of the audio or video file that makes up your podcast episode, the "length" is the size of the file, and the "type" is the type of file.

Here is a stripped down example taken from the XML of the Social Media Power podcast example used in Chapter 5, "Podcasting, Vidcasting, & Webcasting."

```
<item>
    <title>SMP Podcast Episode 1: Social Media and Web 2.0 Basics for
    Business</title>
    <link>http://www.socialmediapower.com/2009/01/06/smp-podcast-episode-1/</link>
    ...
    <enclosure
    url="http://www.socialmediapower.com/podcasts/SocialMediaPowerEpisode1.mp3"
    length="7107653" type="audio/mpeg" />
    ...
</item>
```

You want to optimize a podcast feed specifically for iTunes and Yahoo! Media as well. To do this, add these namespaces:

```
xmlns:media="http://search.yahoo.com/mrss/"
xmlns:itunes="http://www.itunescom/dtds/podcast-1.0.dtd"
```

You can read more about the elements and syntax of the iTunes namespace at FeedForAll.[7] They also discuss the Yahoo! Media namespace[8].

# Resources and Further Reading

You can find more RSS modules by Googling "RSS Modules" or "RSS Extensions." But make certain that you include modules only from trusted sources.

The W3C specifies the use and development of namespaces here.[9] Another good source of RSS extensions is RSS-Extensions.[10]

See the resource CD for a fillable XML file you can use as a starting point for creating your own RSS feed.

---

[7] http://www.feedforall.com/itunes.htm

[8] http://www.feedforall.com/mediarss.htm

[9] http://www.w3.org/TR/REC-xml-names/

[10] http://rss-extensions.org

# Appendix C: Building Your Own Widget

In Chapter 9: "Widgets & Badges," we talked about creating viral widgets, and even showed you how to create a simple feed widget using your RSS feed or blog on Widgetbox.com. In this appendix we demonstrate a more sophisticated way for you to create a widget, even if you do not have coding experience.

Recall that a widget is a snippet of code that you can place on your Website or blog that pulls information from another source. Widgets are typically written using HTML, JavaScript, Flash, or a combination of these. You can create a widget that displays a dynamic Web page, you can write a JavaScript routine that performs a specific task like pulling and displaying content from a data file, or you can create a Flash application that incorporates animation. Regardless of how you create your widget, the basic premise is that you create the code and make it available for others to copy and place on their own site or blog.

The advent of the "open" Web makes creating online applications of any kind much more accessible for novice developers. We demonstrate this concept here by showing you how to use the Google Gadget Editor to create your own widget by copying existing code and altering it to your own specifications.

## Setting Up the Scenario

A client is writing a book about cootie catchers (origami fortune tellers) and wants a simple yet entertaining widget to help promote the book.

Figure C.1 shows how a typical cootie catcher operates (the dots are colored red, blue, green, and yellow). One person "operates" the device while another chooses numbers, colors, or combinations of other items that determine how many iterations of the device the operator makes to get to the next level. Once the final level is reached, the participant is read her fortune from the corresponding tab her series of choices determined.

### Figure C.1. Origami Fortune Teller (Cootie Catcher)

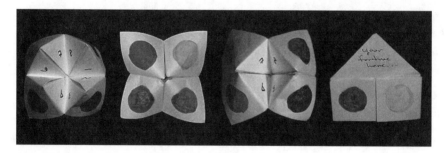

Our goal is to create a simple representation of this process with a little added humor to make it more appealing thus increasing the chances it will go viral. Figure C.2 is the result. This widget pulls in a sock monkey character to present users with a daily origami fortune. The title, "Bootee Catcher," is a play on the "sock monkey cootie catcher" theme of the widget (bootee as in "stocking").

- What the widget should do:
  › Display one of 32 monkey images.
  › Place a fortune on the monkey image.
  › Select the image and fortune randomly.
- How the widget will do this:
  › Extract the data from an XML file and store it in a list that is indexed from 0 to 31.
  › Generate a random number between 0 and 31.

## Figure C.2. Bootee Catcher Widget

> › Pull data from an XML file based on the random number.
> › Display the resulting monkey image and fortune pulled from the XML file.
- The plan of attack:
  > › Create and upload the monkey image files.
  > › Design and upload an XML file that accommodates the fortune data and monkey image file names.
  > › Use the Google Gadget Editor to create a bootee catcher widget that pulls its content from the XML file.
  > › Make the widget available for others to post to an iGoogle page or to a Website.
  > › Add the widget to the Widgetbox.com and other widget galleries.

## Creating and Uploading the Monkey Images

We create 32 images that represent each possible permutation of our cootie catcher. We save the images with the following names:

monkeyred1.jpg
monkeyred2.jpg
...
monkeyred8.jpg
monkeyblue1.jpg
...

monkeyblue8.jpg

monkeygreen1.jpg

...

monkeygreen8.jpg

monkeyyellow1.jpg

...

monkeyyellow8.jpg

We then upload the images to a folder on SocialMediaPower.com from where the XML file and widget code can access them.

## Creating and Uploading the XML File

Please refer back to Appendix B: "Creating Your Own RSS Feed," to learn about XML files, if you do not already know what they are. In a nutshell, XML is a method by which you can define and populate your own data file very easily. You then need to produce code to access the data once it is defined, which is what we demonstrate later.

We define our XML file in the following way. Recall that each "<tag>" and "</end-tag>" is one item or sub-item, and represents a specific portion of the data you are representing, similar to a field in a database, or a column in a spreadsheet. Creating and pulling data from a file like this means that whenever you need to change or add any content used in your widget, you will only need alter and save this file to do so.

```
<bootee> (this defines the main element)
   <catcher> (this tag distinguishes each permutation)
      <fortune>(the fortune of this permutation goes)</fortune>
      <monkey>(the image file name of the monkey image)</monkey>
   </catcher>
</bootee>
```

The actual file looks like the one below, except with 28 additional entries (since we have 32 total permutations to include).

```
<?xml version="1.0" encoding="UTF-8" ?>
<bootee title="BOOTEE CATCHER">
   <catcher>
      <fortune><![CDATA[<div style="color:black;">If you lose your
      mate today, look in the          dryer.</div>]]></fortune>
      <monkey>monkeyred1.jpg</monkey>
   </catcher>
   <catcher>
      <fortune><![CDATA[<div style="color:black;">May your day be
      as fresh as clean socks.</div>]]></fortune>
```

```
        <monkey>monkeyred2.jpg</monkey>
    </catcher>
    <catcher>
        <fortune><![CDATA[<div style="color:black;">True love is
        like a pair of socks: you gotta have two and they've gotta
        match.</div>]]></fortune>
        <monkey>monkeyred3.jpg</monkey>
    </catcher>
    <catcher>
        <fortune><![CDATA[<div style="color:black;">Never run in the
        rain with your socks on.</div>]]></fortune>
        <monkey>monkeyred4.jpg</monkey>
    </catcher>
</bootee>
```

Before continuing, refer back to the scenario we established and to the images depicted in Figure C.1 on page 362 and make sure you understand how the structure of this file represents the bootee catcher content.

An XML file can be created using a text file with no formatting, or with an XML editor like Dreamweaver. We create our XML file using Dreamweaver and call it bootee-data.xml. We then save it and upload it to SocialMediaPower.com so that the widget code can access it—just as we did the image files.

## Creating the Widget Using the Google Gadget Editor

Figure C.3 shows the Google Gadget Editor[1] (GGE). This platform allows you to create, test, and publish your widget (we use the term "gadget" and "widget" interchangeably in this section) all in one place. Even better, Google provides many examples of common uses of widgets that you are welcome to copy and edit for your own use.

Google gadgets are created as XML files containing JavaScript and HTML. In the following example, JavaScript is used to extract the bootee data from our XML file and to create the HTML that stylizes and displays the bootee catcher content.

*Note: Gadgets were formerly called modules, which is why the word "Module" appears throughout the GGE.*

Here is the process we use to create our widget using the GGE:

---

[1] http://code.google.com/apis/gadgets/docs/legacy/gs.html#GGE

## Figure C.3. Google Gadget Editor

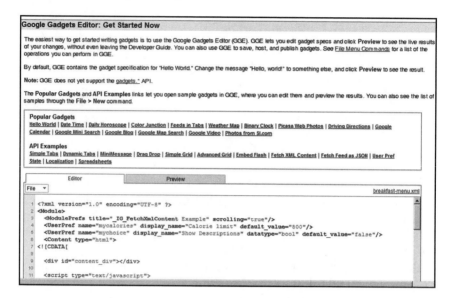

- Select a sample gadget that is similar to what we want
- Save the sample file with another name
- Alter the code of the file to our specifications
- Tweak and test

## Figure C.4. GGE Sample Widget Code View

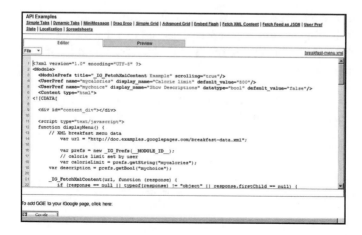

We choose the "Fetch XML Content" sample gadget as the basis for our bootee widget since it already has the infrastructure in place for fetching content from an XML file and displaying it in a widget. Figure C.4 shows the code view for the widget in the GGE, and Figure C.5 shows a preview of how the content is displayed as a widget.

## Figure C.5. GGE Sample Widget Preview

Figure C.17 on page 434 (at the end of this Appendix) shows the sample widget code in its entirety. The widget displays menu choices based on user-entered calorie restrictions.

We now save the file as "bootee-widget.xml" (see Figures C.6 and C.7).

## Figure C.6. GGE Options

## Figure C.7. GGE Saving a File

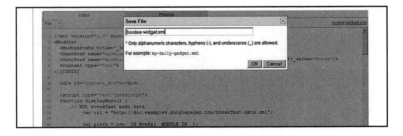

Now we alter the sample code to create our bootee widget code. Generally, here is what the code does:

- Extracts the 32 "catcher" items from the bootee-data.xml file we created using Dreamweaver
- Stores the data in a list that indexes the catcher items from 0 to 31
- Generates a random number between 0 and 31
- Extracts the corresponding catcher from the list
- Extracts the corresponding sub-items for our chosen catcher from the XML file (the fortune (<fortune> and monkey image <monkey>)
- Stylizes and displays the corresponding fortune and monkey image

The following is the code to create our widget with explanations of the code indicated by //. See Figure C.18 on page 436 for the unadulterated code. Refer back to the XML file on page 422 as you review this code.

```
// This first line is to establish the file as an XML file.
<?xml version="1.0" encoding="UTF-8" ?>
<Module>
<ModulePrefs title="Bootee Catcher"
   scrolling="false"
   width="200"
   height="350"
   author="Deltina Hay"
   author_affiliation="Social Media Power"
   author_email="quotes+booteewidget@socialmediapower.com"
   thumbnail="http://www.socialmediapower.com/widgets/booteethumb.
   jpg"
   screenshot="http://www.socialmediapower.com/widgets/
   booteescreenshot.jpg"
   render_inline="optional"
   description="Daily origami fortune from a sock monkey's
   perspective.">
</ModulePrefs>
// The content type (html or URL) tells the GGE where the content
resides: either embedded as HTML or on a remote site, respectively
<Content type="html">
// This is the CDATA section, which means it is not part of the
xml portion of the code
// (see APENDIX#,"Creating Your Own RSS Feed").
<![CDATA[
<div id="content_div"></div>
// Here is where the JavaScript begins that pulls the bootee data:
<script type="text/javascript">
function displaybootee() {
// Here is where the XML data file is defined that we uploaded:
var url = "http://socialmediapower.com/widgets/bootee-data.xml";
// This is a function from the Google Gadget library that fetches
data from the XML file:
```

```
    _IG_FetchXmlContent(url, function (response) {
    if (response == null || typeof(response) != "object" ||
    response.firstChild == null) {
    _gel("content_div").innerHTML = "<i>Invalid data.</i>";
    return;
    }
// Generate a random number between 0 and 31, and store it in the
variable "bootday"
    var bootday= Math.floor(Math.random()*31);
// Get a list of the <catcher> element nodes in the file (see the
XML file)
    var itemList = response.getElementsByTagName("catcher");
// Loop through the <catcher> items that we want to grab - for
this widget we only want one, the one indexed under the random
number we generated, so we only loop from the variable bootday to
one plus bootday
    for (var i = bootday; i < (bootday +1) ; i++) {
// For each <catcher> node, get child nodes.
    var nodeList = itemList.item(i).childNodes;
// Loop through child nodes. Extract data from the text nodes that
are the children of the associated fortune and monkey element
nodes.
    for (var j = 0; j < nodeList.length ; j++) {
        var node = nodeList.item(j);
        if (node.nodeName == "fortune") {
        var fortune = node.firstChild.nodeValue;
        }
        if (node.nodeName == "monkey") {
        var monkey = node.firstChild.nodeValue;
        }
    }
// Store the URL of the extracted monkey image in the variable bg
and make it the current background image
    var bg = "http://socialmediapower.com/widgets/" + monkey;
    document.body.style.backgroundImage = "url("+bg+")";
// Here is the beginning of the HTML string, defined as a variable
called "html"
// we include all of the stylizing in here, too, just as if we
were creating an HTML page.
    var html = "<div style='padding-top: 160px; margin-left:
    45px; margin-right: 30px; font-family:Verdana, Arial,
    Helvetica, sans-serif;text-align:center;text-style:
    strong;font-size:90%';>";
// Append extracted fortune data to the HTML string
    html += fortune;
    html += "<br></div>";
    html += "<div style='padding-top: 75px; font-family:Verdana,
    Arial, Helvetica, sans-serif;text-align:center;text-style:
    strong;font-size:90%';>";
// Add a link to where they can learn more about Bootee:
    html += "<a href='http://www.facebook.com/pages/Bootee-
    Catcher/123441381008880' target='_blank'>Bootee on
    Facebook</a>";
    }
    html += "</div>";
```

```
// Parse the HTML string using a Google Gadget function:
  _gel('content_div').innerHTML = html;
  });
  }
// A Google Gadget Load Handler function:
  _IG_RegisterOnloadHandler(displaybootee);
  </script>
]]>
</Content>
</Module>
```

Figure C.8 shows the preview of our gadget after tweaking the existing code to our specifications.

## Figure C.8. Bootee Gadget Preview

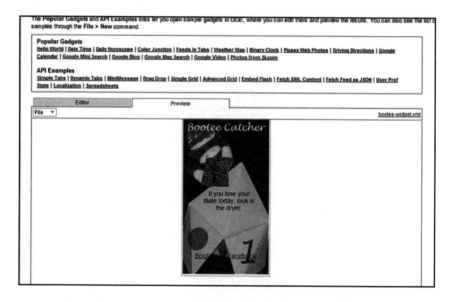

Figure C.17 on page 434 shows the sample widget code that we altered to create our widget. References to the libraries and most of the structure of the code was already in place in this sample code, so all we needed to do was change the item names to match our own XML file, change the formatting within the <div> tags to our liking, and remove some of the code we did not need.

We did not need any custom user preferences for our widget, so we removed all references to them. User preferences are settings that users can make, beyond the default size and color settings, when they prepare a widget's code to place on their site.

In addition, the original sample code loops through all of the items in their XML file adding them to the list of content that is displayed, but we only require one item (specifically the one corresponding to the random number we generate). Therefore, we needed to find a JavaScript function that would generate a random number for us to store in our "bootday" variable. We found such a function easily with a quick Google search using the term "generate a random number in javascript."

It is our hope that this demonstration will encourage you to go to the GGE and try your hand at creating your own widget using some of their existing code as a guide. To learn more about Google Gadgets, go to the gadget development page.[2]

## Publishing the Widget

Figure C.9 shows the publish menu in the GGE. From here you can add the gadget to your iGoogle page, publish it to a Website, or publish it to the iGoogle directory.

### Figure C.9. GGE Publishing Options

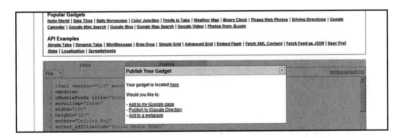

Figure C.10 shows the screen for adding the gadget to an iGoogle page, and Figure C.11 shows what the gadget looks like on an iGoogle page.

### Figure C.10. Add Gadget to iGoogle Page

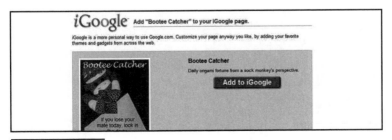

[2] http://www.google.com/webmasters/gadgets/

## Figure C.11. Bootee Gadget On iGoogle Page

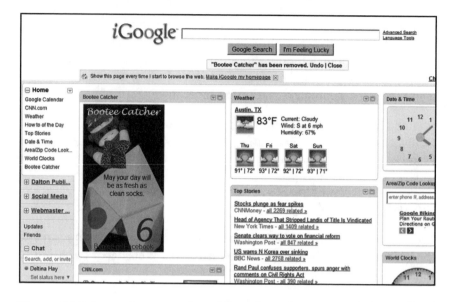

Figure C.12 shows the screen for adding the gadget to a Website. As with any widget, copy the code and place it on your site where you want it to

## Figure C.12. Customizing a Gadget For a Webpage

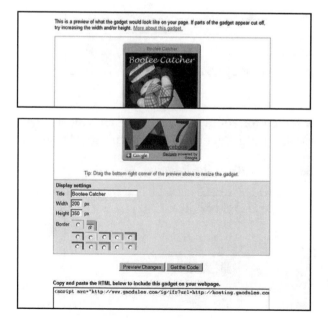

appear. Figure C.13 shows how the gadget looks once placed on a Web page.

## Figure C.13. Bootee Gadget On Webpage

We place this gadget code onto a Web page of its own that we use as a basis for creating a widget in widget galleries such as Widgetbox discussed later.

Figure C.14 shows the HTML code for that Web page which is depicted in Figure C.13.

## Figure C.14. HTML Code For Widget Web Page

Figure C.15 shows the screen for publishing the gadget to the iGoogle directory. The highlighted portion shows the URL of the gadget for reference. We make a note of this so we can promote it to our mailing lists and import it into widget galleries to improve the reach of the widget.

## Figure C.15. Publishing to iGoogle Directory

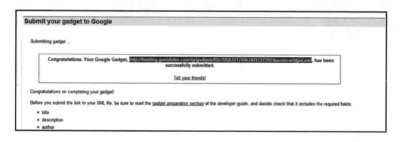

## Improving The Reach Of Our Widget

To summarize, we now have three possible variations of our widget that we can promote:

1. A widget published to a Web page with a URL of "http://www.socialmediapower.com/widgets/booteewidget.html." See Figure C.13.

2. An iGoogle Gadget with the URL"http://hosting.gmodules.com/ig/gadgets/file/105632178967401737291/bootee-widget.xml." See Figure C.15.

3. The following Google Gadget code that can be placed in other Websites or social sites like any other widget (See Figure C.14):

```
<script src="http://www.gmodules.com/ig/ifr?url=http://
hosting.gmodules.com/ig/gadgets/file/105632178967401737291/
bootee-widget.xml&amp;synd=open&amp;w=200&amp;h=350&amp;t
itle=Bootee+Catcher&amp;border=http%3A%2F%2Fwww.gmodules.
com%2Fig%2Fimages%2F&amp;output=js"></script>
```

With these variations of the same widget at our disposal, we can increase the reach of the widget by adding it to widget galleries like Widgetbox.com, placing it on Web pages and blogs, placing it in our profiles or pages of other social sites, promote it by offering the code on our Website, etc. The same way we did many of the widgets highlighted in Chapter 9.

For instance, Figure C.16 shows the Widgetbox screen for adding a widget to their directory. Notice that there are two options we could easily use: We could choose to add our Google Gadget to the directory, or link to our existing Webpage using their "Remote" option.

## Figure C.16. Creating a Widget at Widgetbox.com

## Many Roads To The Same Widget

It is important to understand that the method we used to create and distribute this widget is just one of many ways you can do it. Probably the best way is to create a Flash widget, since most sites allow users to place Flash over JavaScript or HTML.

We encourage you to explore the Widgetbox platform for creating widgets as well. They have a user-friendly platform, good tech support, and a nice widget analytics feature.

## Figure C.17. Sample Widget Code (continued on next page)

```
<?xml version="1.0" encoding="UTF-8" ?>
<Module>
  <ModulePrefs title="_IG_FetchXmlContent Example" scrolling="true"/>
  <UserPref name="mycalories" display_name="Calorie limit" default_value="800"/>
  <UserPref name="mychoice" display_name="Show Descriptions" datatype="bool" default_value="false"/>
  <Content type="html">
<![CDATA[

  <div id="content_div"></div>

  <script type="text/javascript">
  function displayMenu() {
      // XML breakfast menu data
          var url = "http://doc.examples.googlepages.com/breakfast-data.xml";

          var prefs = new _IG_Prefs(__MODULE_ID__);
          // calorie limit set by user
          var calorieLimit = prefs.getString("mycalories");
      var description = prefs.getBool("mychoice");

      _IG_FetchXmlContent(url, function (response) {
          if (response == null || typeof(response) != "object" || response.firstChild == null) {
          _gel("content_div").innerHTML = "<i>Invalid data.</i>";
          return;
      }

              // Start building HTML string that will be displayed in <div>.
      // Set the style for the <div>.
              var html = "<div style='padding: 5px;background-color: #ccf;font-family:Arial,
Helvetica;" +
                  "text-align:left;font-size:90%'>";

      // Set style for title.
      html +="<div style='text-align:center; font-size: 120%; color: yellow; " +
              "font-weight: 700;'>";

      // Display menu title. Use getElementsByTagName() to retrieve the <menu> element.
      // Since there is only one menu element in the file,
      // you can get to it by accessing the item at index "0".
      // You can then use getAttribute to get the text associated with the
      // menu "title" attribute.
      var title = response.getElementsByTagName("menu").item(0).getAttribute("title");

      // Alternatively, you could retrieve the title by getting the menu element node
      // and calling the "attributes" function on it. This returns an array
      // of the element node's attributes. In this case, there is only one
      // attribute (title), so you can display the value for the attribute at
      // index 0. For example:
      //
      // var title = response.getElementsByTagName("menu").item(0).attributes.item(0).nodeValue;

              // Append the title to the HTML string.
              //html += title + "</font></h3>";

      // Append the title to the HTML string.
      html += title + "</div><br>";

      // Get a list of the <food> element nodes in the file
      var itemList = response.getElementsByTagName("food");
      // Loop through all <food> nodes
      for (var i = 0; i < itemList.length ; i++) {
              // For each <food> node, get child nodes.
              var nodeList = itemList.item(i).childNodes;
              // Loop through child nodes. Extract data from the text nodes that are
              // the children of the associated name, price, and calories element nodes.
          for (var j = 0; j < nodeList.length ; j++) {
          var node = nodeList.item(j);
                      if (node.nodeName == "name") {
                  var name  = node.firstChild.nodeValue;
                      }
              if (node.nodeName == "price") {
                  var price  = node.firstChild.nodeValue;
                      }
                  if (node.nodeName == "calories")  {
```

```
                            var calories = node.firstChild.nodeValue;
                        }
                // If the user chose to display descriptions and
                // the nodeName is "#cdata-section", grab the
                // contents of the description CDATA for display.
                if (node.nodeName == "description" && description==true)
                {
                    if (node.firstChild.nodeName == "#cdata-section")
                        var data = node.firstChild.nodeValue;
                }
                    }

            // Append extracted data to the HTML string.
                    html += "<i><b>";
                    html += name;
                    html += "</b></i><br>";
            html += " ";
            html += price;
            html += " - ";
                    // If "calories" is greater than the user-specified calorie limit,
                    // display it in red.
                    if(calories > calorieLimit) {
                html += "<font color=#ff0000>";
                        html += calories + " calories";
                        html += " </font>";
                    }
                    else
                        html += calories + " calories";
            html += "<br>";

            // If user has chosen to display descriptions
            if (description==true)
            {
                html += "<i>" + data + "</i><br>";
            }

        }
        html += "</div>";

            // Display HTML string in <div>
            _gel('content_div').innerHTML = html;
        });
}

_IG_RegisterOnloadHandler(displayMenu);
</script>

]]>
</Content>
</Module>
```

## Figure C.18. Unadulterated Bootee Code

```
<?xml version="1.0" encoding="UTF-8" ?>
<Module>
<ModulePrefs title="Bootee Catcher"
    scrolling="false"
    width="200"
    height="350"
    author="Deltina Hay"
    author_affiliation="Social Media Power"
    author_email="quotes+booteewidget@socialmediapower.com"
    thumbnail="http://www.socialmediapower.com/widgets/booteethumb.jpg"
    screenshot="http://www.socialmediapower.com/widgets/booteescreenshot.
jpg"
    render_inline="optional"
    description="Daily origami fortune from a sock monkey's perspective.">
</ModulePrefs>
<Content type="html">
<![CDATA[
<div id="content_div"></div>
<script type="text/javascript">
function displaybootee() {
var url = "http://socialmediapower.com/widgets/bootee-data.xml";
_IG_FetchXmlContent(url, function (response) {
if (response == null || typeof(response) != "object" || response.firstChild
== null) {
_gel("content_div").innerHTML = "<i>Invalid data.</i>";
return;
}
var bootday= Math.floor(Math.random()*31);
var itemList = response.getElementsByTagName("catcher");
for (var i = bootday; i < (bootday +1) ; i++) {
    var nodeList = itemList.item(i).childNodes;
    for (var j = 0; j < nodeList.length ; j++) {
        var node = nodeList.item(j);
        if (node.nodeName == "fortune") {
        var fortune = node.firstChild.nodeValue;
        }
        if (node.nodeName == "monkey") {
        var monkey = node.firstChild.nodeValue;
        }
}
var bg = "http://socialmediapower.com/widgets/" + monkey;
document.body.style.backgroundImage = "url("+bg+")";
var html = "<div style='padding-top: 160px; margin-left: 45px; margin-
right: 30px; font-family:Verdana, Arial, Helvetica, sans-serif;text-align:
center;text-style:strong;font-size:90%';>";
html += fortune;
html += "<br></div>";
html += "<div style='padding-top: 75px; font-family:Verdana, Arial,
Helvetica, sans-serif;text-align:center;text-style:strong;font-size:90%';>";
html += "<a href='http://www.facebook.com/pages/Bootee-
Catcher/123441381008880' target='_blank'>Bootee on Facebook</a>";
}
html += "</div>";
_gel('content_div').innerHTML = html;
});
}
_IG_RegisterOnloadHandler(displaybootee);
</script>
]]>
</Content>
</Module>
```

# Appendix D: Preparing Your Content for the Semantic Web

In Chapter 13: "Looking to the Future," we discuss how the Semantic Web relies upon markup languages that tag Web content so it is easier for machines to interpret. This is accomplished through one of two methods, structured data or linked data. This appendix provides an introduction to the markup languages used by these two methods.

## Microformats and RDFa for Structured Data

Microformats and RDFa are the standard markup formats used to create structured data. Like any markup language, they consist of tags and attributes that are used to "mark up" your Web content so that a search engine can recognize the content as structured data.

Return to Chapter 13 and read the "Structured Data" section before continuing. We continue, then, with the Google Rich Snippets example from that section. Again, from the Google site:

*To display Rich Snippets, Google looks for markup formats (microformats and RDFa) that you can easily add to your own web pages. In most cases, it's as quick as wrapping the existing data on your web pages with some additional tags. For example, here are a few relevant lines of the HTML from Yelp's review page for "Drooling Dog BarBQ" before adding markup data:*

```
<h1>Drooling Dog Bar B Q</h1>
. . .
<img class="stars_4" scr="stars_map.png" alt="4 star
rating" />
<em>based on 15 reviews<em/>
. . .
<strong>Price Range:</strong> $$
```

and now with microformats markup:

```
<div class="hreview-aggregate">
  <div class="item vcard">
    <h1 class="fn org">Drooling Dog Bar B Q</h1>
    . . .
    <img class="stars_4 rating average" src="stars_
    map.png" alt="4 star rating" />
    <em> based on <spcan class="count">15</span>
    reviews</em>
    . . .
    <strong>Price range:</strong> <span
    class="pricerange">$$</span>
  </div>
</div>
```

*or alternatively, use RDFa markup (not listed here). Either format works.*

*By incorporating standard annotations in your pages, you not only make your structured data available for Google's search results, but also for any service or tool that supports the same standard. As structured data becomes more widespread on the web, we expect to find many new applications for it, and we're excited about the possibilities.*

What Google demonstrates here is how to "tag" your data as structured data using microformats or RDFa markup so that it can be properly read and subsequently displayed as such by search engines and other tools that support structured data.

To transform your data into structured data using one of these formats, you will simply add some additional classes and tags to your existing HTML, adhering to the appropriate markup standard.

Using the microformats standard, let's look at some ways that you can start marking up your data now so that when Google and other search engines are regularly using structured data in their search results, you will be ready.

There are a few essential microformats standards:

**hCard:** Use this format for marking up information about people, companies, organizations, and places.

Here is an example:

```
<div id="hcard-Deltina-Hay" class="vcard">
  <a class="url fn" href="http://www.
  daltonpublishing.com">Deltina Hay</a>
  <div class="org">Dalton Publishing</div>
  <a class="email" href="mailto:deltina@deltina.
  com">deltina@deltina.com</a>
  <div class="adr">
  <div class="street-address">1234 Manchaca
  Road</div>
    <span class="locality">Austin</span>
    <span class="region">Texas</span>
    <span class="postal-code">78767</span>
    <span class="country-name">USA</span>
  </div>
  <div class="tel">512-555-9999</div>
</div>
```

This is how it will appear on your Website:

Deltina Hay
Dalton Publishing
deltina@deltina.com
1234 Manchaca Road
Austin , Texas 78767 USA
512-555-9999

To the naked eye, there is nothing special about this content. It is nothing more than your contact information with links. Search engines and Internet browsers, however, will now be able to interpret the content as structured data (specifically structured contact and location information about you and your company) and display it or use it accordingly. All you need to do is mark up your existing contact information using the microformats standards. Microformats.org[1] even has an hCard creator that you can use to generate the code.

Other formats you may want to use include:

**hCalendar:** For marking up events (microformats.org also has an hCalendar creator).

**hProduct:** For marking up your products and services.

**hReviews:** For marking up reviews.

**rel-tag:** By adding rel="tag" to a hyperlink, a page indicates that the destination of that hyperlink is an author-designated "tag" (or keyword/subject) for the current page.

# An Introduction to RDF for Linked Data

Linked data is published to the Web using a very specific model called the "RDF data model." The interlinking data from different data sources adheres to a special linking structure known as "RDF links." Refer to Chapter 13: "Looking to the Future," for more information on linked data in general.

The following is a very basic explanation of how data is represented using RDF. RDF is typically used to represent large datasets that are to be added to the Linked Open Data cloud. Unless you have a large database to add to the cloud, you won't likely need to know more than what is explained here.

RDF stands for Resource Description Framework. As its name implies, RDF is a way to define resources using a specific framework. That framework is based on the concept of "triples." Each resource is represented by a number of triples.

A triple consists of a subject, a predicate, and an object that mirrors a simple sentence structure like:

[1] http://microformats.org/get-started

| SUBJECT | PREDICATE | OBJECT |
|---------|-----------|--------|
| Deltina | [has the] Web site | http://www.deltina.com |
| Deltina | [is] employed at | http://www.socialmediapower.com |
| Deltina | Knows | John Smith |
| John Smith | [is] also known as | http://DrWho.com |

RDF triples take on the following forms:

1. The subject is a URI (a type of link) identifying the described resource

2. The object can be a literal value like a text value, number, or date; or it can be the URI of another resource that is in some way related to the subject

3. Like a basic sentence structure, the predicate indicates what kind of relationship exists between the subject and the object, such as a name or date of birth (in the case of a literal, i.e., not a link) or an employer or someone the person knows (in the case of another resource represented by a link).

The predicate is also a URI, but predicate URIs come from established *vocabularies*—collections of URIs that can be used to represent information about a broad topic. For example:

- *Friend-of-a-Friend (FOAF)* is a vocabulary for describing people.
- *Music Ontology* provides terms for describing artists, albums and tracks.
- *Review Vocabulary* is a vocabulary for representing reviews.
- *GoodRelations* is a standardized vocabulary for product, price, and company data.

Even if you don't have large sets of data, you still want to get yourself into the Linked Open Data cloud. Luckily, there is an easy way to do that. You can create what is called a "static RDF file" and upload it to your Website server.

The most popular of these static files is the Friend-of-a-Friend file or a FOAF file. The FOAF file uses the FOAF vocabulary to represent information about you: your name, your place of employment or business, your Website, etc. It can also contain information about people you know, links to your profiles on social networking sites, and links to resources that are associated with you, such as your books or other publications. You can create your own FOAF file using a tool like FOAF-a-Matic[2].

Below is *part* of an example FOAF file. Keep in mind that the purpose of the Semantic Web is to make content easier for *machines* to understand. As a result, these files are not necessarily intuitive to us. More and more tools like the FOAF-a-Matic are being developed to help us technologically challenged humans produce our own RDF files to get our content into the Web of Data.

```
<rdf:RDF
...
<foaf:Person rdf:ID="me">
  <foaf:name>Deltina Hay</foaf:name>
  <foaf:givenname>Deltina</foaf:givenname>
  <foaf:family_name>Hay</foaf:family_name>
  <foaf:mbox rdf:resource="mailto:deltina@deltina.
  com"/>
  <foaf:homepage rdf:resource="http://www.deltina.
  com"/>
  <foaf:workplaceHomepage rdf:resource="http://www.
  socialmediapower.com"/>
  <foaf:workInfoHomepage rdf:resource="http://www.
  socialmediapower.com/about"/>
  <foaf:knows>
    <foaf:Person>
      <foaf:name>John Smith</foaf:name>
      <foaf:mbox rdf:resource="mailto:john@example.
      com"/>
      <rdfs:seeAlso rdf:resource="http://www.example.
      com/john/foaf.rdf"/>
    </foaf:Person>
  </foaf:knows>
  <foaf:knows>
    <foaf:Person>
      <foaf:name>Jane Doe</foaf:name>
      <foaf:mbox rdf:resource="mailto:jane@example.
      com"/>
    </foaf:Person>
  </foaf:knows>
</foaf:Person>
</rdf:RDF>
```

[2] http://www.ldodds.com/foaf/foaf-a-matic

What this file indicates is that I am a person with a name, an email address, a Web site, a place of employment, and that I know some people—one of whom has his own RDF file that others can now access to learn more about him.

Once you have your basic FOAF file, save it in the root directory of your Website server as foaf.rdf. This way, semantic Web browsers can find and recognize the file for what it is and display its content accordingly. You can continue to add additional content to your FOAF file such as book information, links to your blogs, links to online communities like Facebook and LinkedIn, and much more. Look on the resource CD for tools that can help you do this.

# A Practical Example: The RDF Book Mashup

The RDF Book Mashup demonstrates how Web 2.0 data sources like Amazon, Google, or Yahoo can be integrated into the Semantic Web. The RDF Book Mashup makes information about books, their authors, reviews, and online bookstores available on the Semantic Web. RDF tools can use this information and you can link to it from your own Semantic Web data (i.e., your FOAF file).

To add information about you *as an author* to your FOAF file, go to the RDF Book Mashup[3] site and follow the instructions. First, search the Book Mashup using your name to be certain all of your books are listed. Figure D.1 shows the result from mine.

## Figure D.1. Book Mashup Search Results

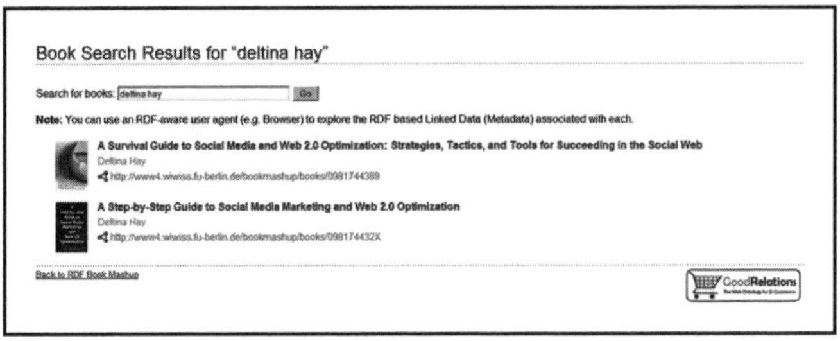

Book Search Results for "deltina hay"

Search for books: deltina hay    Go

Note: You can use an RDF-aware user agent (e.g. Browser) to explore the RDF based Linked Data (Metadata) associated with each.

A Survival Guide to Social Media and Web 2.0 Optimization: Strategies, Tactics, and Tools for Succeeding in the Social Web
Deltina Hay
http://www4.wiwiss.fu-berlin.de/bookmashup/books/0981744389

A Step-by-Step Guide to Social Media Marketing and Web 2.0 Optimization
Deltina Hay
http://www4.wiwiss.fu-berlin.de/bookmashup/books/098174432X

Back to RDF Book Mashup                                    GoodRelations

---

[3] http://www4.wiwiss.fu-berlin.de/bizer/bookmashup/

Next, add this line to your FOAF file (using your own name, of course):

```
<owl:sameAs rdf:resource ="http://www4.wiwiss.fu-
berlin.de/bookmashup/persons/Deltina+Hay" />
```

Now, not only are you "in the Web" as a person who knows some other people and has a Website and an email address, but you are interlinked with other sources in the Web of Data as an author of specific books. When others find your FOAF file, they can link to information on your book(s) as well. They also will be able to find information on you if they happen upon your book in the Book Mashup.

Though much of this information may seem overwhelming, it is important to understand the general principles. Once you have a general understanding of Linked Data and what the Linked Open Data cloud is, you can start to understand how to position yourself for what is quickly becoming the next generation of Internet search.

# Index

## Symbols

30 boxes 313

## A

Aaron Uhrmacher 369
AddThis 265
AddtoAny 247
  bookmark plugin 281
  feed widget 58, 92, 264
  sharing widget 93, 267, 280
Akismet 120
All in One SEO Pack 80, 119, 121
Amazon Author Central 188
Amazon Web Services 361
Amazon widgets 276
analytics services 384
analytics tools 377
Apache 108
API 325

Audacity 132
Audio Acrobat 131
Austin Chronicle 58

## B

badges 248. *See also* widgets
  Flickr 218
Bebo 187
Berkman Center for Internet & Society
  405
Bing 370
blidget. *See* widgets
blip.tv 143
blog 69–78
  decisions for starting 45
  definition 69
  optimizing 78–95
  options for starting 72
  planning 76
  types of 71
blog directories 78, 88–96
  submission software 91
  submitting to 89
blog post
  elements of 72–75
  embedding images 222
  preparing content 51
BlogPulse 380
blog search engines 374
blogTV 143
Book Share Books 163
bootee catcher widget 420
Brightkite 274, 314
BuddyPress 189
building a widget 419–431
  bootee catcher example 420
  creating the code 426
  Google Gadget Editor 423
  JavaScript and 423
  preparation 421

## C

category
  crowd-sourcing 205
  in blog post 74
  social media newsrooms and 291
  WordPress 291
  YouTube 224
Chicklet Chooser. *See* FeedBurner
cloud computing 360
  infrastructure-as-a-service 361
  platform-as-a-service 361
  software-as-a-service 362
cloud tools 320
CMS 23, 58, 60, 98, 358
  and WordPress 97
  definition 23
collaborative technologies 320
  asynchronous 320
  synchronous 321
comment

and crowd-sourcing  203
  in Flickr  214
  on blogs  77
conferencing tools  321
content management system. *See* CMS
creating an RSS feed  403–416
  adding new stories  415
  and podcasting  417
  CDATA sections  417
  elements of an RSS feed  405
  namespaces  415
  RSS declaration  405
  RSS feed document  404
crowd-sourced news sites  202
  Digg  201
  Mixx  207
  reddit  207
  searching  203
  social media newsroom and  292
  submission guidelines  204
  using  204
crowd-sourcing  201–208
  definition  201
  in action  201
  preparation  207
  strategy  206
  tracking  207
  widgets  267
CSS  117
CuteFTP  109

**D**

Dave Winer  405
Dbpedia  358
Delicious  194–198, 292
  and social networking  186
  integrating into other sites  339
  purpose-built pages  199
  widget  269
Diaspora  190
Digg  201–207
  widget  269
Dimdim  321

DISQUS  78
distributed social networking  272, 326
document sharing sites  232–239
  and Facebook  234
  and Twitter  234
  categories  236
  copyright settings  236
  in action  232
  preparation  239
  searching  244
  setting up  234
  sharing on social sites  233
  tags  239
  uploading documents  236
  using  234
document sharing strategy  239
domain account  108
Dreamweaver  126
Dropbox  362
Drupal  98, 189

**E**

Eventbrite  313
Event Tools  311

**F**

Facebook  146–167
  analytics  165
  badge  166
  fan box  257
  feed  146
  Google search results and  155
  groups  154
  home page  148
  Insights  377
  integrating  342, 347
  integrating images  338
  integrating RSS feeds and blogs  336
  integrating video  338
  like box  165
  marketplace  147
  people search  147
  plugins  272

profile 150–152
  promoting 165
  settings 151
  social plugins 272
  status updates 153
  Twitter and 250
Facebook applications 160, 283, 339
  Book Share Books 163
  My Flickr 163
  RSS-Connect 164
  ShopTab 164
  Social RSS 164
Facebook Connect 272, 327
Facebook page 155–166
  creating 156
  settings 160
Facebook privacy 166, 272
feed aggregator. See RSS feed
FeedBurner 82–87
  and podcasts 138
  Browser Friendly 84
  BuzzBoost 84
  Chicklet Chooser 86, 141
  Email Subscriptions 85
  Event Feed 84
  FeedFlare 84
  FeedMedic 94
  Link Splicer 84
  multiple feeds in 87
  PingShot 86, 89, 140
  Smart Feed 84
  social media newsroom and 297
  Troubleshootize 94
  widget 247
FeedForAll 63–65, 131
  and namespaces 418
  and podcasts 137
feed reader. See RSS feed
FeedShot 91
feed URL 83
feed widget. See widgets
file names 51
  conventions of 295
Filezilla 109

FireFTP 109
Flash 122, 419
Flickr 212–221
  as a social network 186
  badge 106, 218–221, 258
  gallery 221
  in blog posts 222
  integrating 338, 342
  integrating with plugins 324
  optimizing 217
  optimizing images 214
  search results 240
  set 212
  tags 213
  uploading images 214
  Uploadr 217
  widget 247
Flickr Tag 221
Flickr Viewer 222
FOAF-a-Matic 442
folksonomy 196
Force.com 362
Foursquare 314
Friend-of-a-Friend 441
FriendFeed 188, 315, 332
  integrating with widget 324
FTP 109, 391, 398

G

gadget 248
gallery
  image 221
  video 228
geo tagging 188, 313
  widgets 274
GoodReads 187
GoodRelations 441
Google 370
  Ads 277
  AJAX API 61
  Alerts 379
  Analytics 377
  Trends 380

video search  243
  YouTube and  243
Google AdSense  277
Google App Engine  362
Google Apps  362
Google Blog Search  78, 374
Google Book Search  359
Google Buzz  187
  integrating  346, 349
Google Chrome OS  363
Google Docs  320
Google Feed Control Wizard  61–62
Google Feed Reader  54, 59, 92
  and podcasts  142
Google Friend Connect  326
Google Gadget directory
  282
Google Gadget Editor
  and creating widgets  423
Google Gadgets  265, 283
Google Me  190
Google Rich Snippets  357, 437
Google Wave  320
GoToMeeting  321
Gowalla  314
Grapple Mobile  364

**H**

Hakia  372
HipCast  131
HootSuite  185, 330, 346, 377
hosting account  108
  and installing WordPress  399
HTML  24, 122, 126, 356, 438
  and widgets  419
  compared to XML  404
  widgets and  249
Hubpages  320
hybrid social tools  314

**I**

iGoogle  92, 429
image sharing  211–224

optimizing  217, 223
SEO and  224
strategy  223
using  214
installing WordPress  391–400
  configuration file  397
  creating database  395
  preliminary tasks  391
  troubleshooting  401
instant messaging services  298
  social media newsrooms and  292
integrating
  adding new tools  341
  events  339
  images  338
  integration plan  336
  methods  323
  other tools  339
  RSS feeds or blogs  336
  video  338
  with applications  325
  with embedded code  325
  with internal settings  324
  with plugins  324
integration plan
  adding new tools  349
  distributing images  344, 348
  distributing presentations  349
  distributing rss feeds  343, 347
  distributing video  344, 349
  example  342, 346
  mapping  342
  testing  350
  updating status updates  343, 348
  updating Twitter  343, 348
integration tools  317, 326
  FriendFeed  332
  HootSuite  330
  Ping.fm  329
  Posterous  333
IntenseDebate  78, 119

**J**

JavaScript 122
    and widgets 419
    bootee widget and 429
JitterJam 384
Joomla 98, 189

**K**

key terms
    crowd-sourcing and 205
    definition 25
    image sharing and 223
    in document sharing sites 236
    in Facebook 158
    in RSS feeds 67
    podcasts and 132, 138
    preparing 47
    social bookmarking and 199
    social networking and 191
    THE FINAL WORD ON 389
    YouTube and 224, 228
keywords 81
    definition 25
Kickapps 362
Klout 185, 381

**L**

landing page 137
    definition 25
    podcast 135, 138
LibraryThing 186
lifestreaming 315, 353
Lijit 270
    integrating into other sites 339
link 79
    external 82
    text 79
link baiting 82
linked data 358, 440
    example 443
    with RDF 440
LinkedIn 168-171
    groups 170
    integrating 342, 347

integration 339
profile 168
widgets 253
LinkedIn applications 171, 339
    Blog Link 171
    SlideShare 171
Linked Open Data cloud 190, 358, 441
location tools 313

**M**

Mashable 187, 365, 369, 386
measuring social media efforts 377
media communities 211–236
    definition 211
    widgets and 258
MediaWiki 320
metadata 25, 80, 354
    and podcasts 134, 138
    definition 25
meta description 25
meta keywords 25
meta title 25
micro-blogging 171-184
    widgets 274
microformats 358, 437
    hCalendar 440
    hCard 439
    hProduct 440
    hReviews 440
    rel-tag 440
Mixx 207
Mobify.me 364
mobile analytics 364
mobile applications 364
mobile directories 364
mobile plugins 364
mobile Web 363
    optimizing for 364
    preparing for 363
mobile Websites 364
mod_rewrite 108
MP3 134
Mpexo 365

multimedia
  preparation 51
  social media news release and 301
  social media newsroom and 292, 296
Music Ontology 441
MyMSN 92
MySpace 187, 247
MySQL 108
  WordPress and 391
MyYahoo 92

**N**

name servers 109
Netiquette 387
Netvibes 92, 265
netvibes ecosystem 282
niche social networking sites 186
Ning 189
  integrating images 338
  integrating RSS feeds and blogs 336

**O**

OneRiot 372
open source 98

**P**

PageFlakes 92
PercentMobile 364
permalink 72, 81
Peter Kim 368
PHP 98, 108, 127, 290
  WordPress and 391
phpMyAdmin 391
Ping-O-Matic 88, 91
Ping.fm 329, 346
pinging 88
placing code 24
Plixi 176
Plugins 98
PLUMB Web Solutions 285
podcast 129–144
  definition 129

optimizing 138–142
plugin 130, 137
publishing options 130
recording 132
script 131
services 131
podcast directories 142
podcatchers 141
Posterous 187, 317, 333
PostRank 382
preparing content for semantic Web 437
Pretty Links 376
publishing a widget 429
  to iGoogle page 429
purpose-built Delicious page 199
  social media newsroom and 297

**R**

RackSpace 361
Radian6 384
RDF 358
  for linked data 440
  triples 441
  vocabularies 441
RDFa 358, 437
RDF Book Mashup 360, 443
ReadWriteWeb 365, 386
Ready.mobi 364
real-time search engines 372
reddit 207
resource CD 27
Review Vocabulary 441
RSS 404
RSS-Extensions 418
RSS feed 23, 45, 53–69
  content for 68
  creating. See creating an RSS feed
  integrating 342
  multiple 66, 87
  on a Website 60
  optimizing 78–95
  planning 66–69
  social media newsrooms and 292

validation 94
XML and 63
RSS feed directories. *See* blog directories
RSS feed reader 54
RSS icon 56
RSS Submit 91

## S

Scribd 232
  collections 232
  embedding links 234
  settings 236
  widget 237
search engine optimization. *See* SEO
Searchles 201
search optimization 370
  accuracy 375
  diversity 375
  for all engines 374
  frequency 375
  landing pages 376
  meaning 375
  relevancy 375
  tracking tactics 376
search optimization tactics 375
SecondLife 321
semantic search engines 372
Semantic Web 356
semantic Web browser 359
SEO 25, 369
  and image sharing 224
  and media communities 240
  for blogs and RSS feeds 80
ShareThis 267
  social media news release and 302
Shelfari 187, 247
  widget 255, 280
SHIFT Communications 288, 304
ShopTab 164
signature 80
Simple Viewer 222
Skype 321
Slashdot 187

SlideShare 237
  and Yahoo! 245
  integrating 339, 346, 349
  searching 244
  slidecasts 237
  widget 237
social bookmarking 193–201
  and blogs 93
  as social networks 186
  guidelines 198
  in action 194
  preparation 207
  searching 196
  social media news release and 302
  social media newsroom and 288, 292
  strategy 198
  tags 197, 199
  using 197
  widgets 267
social calendars 311–313
  preparation 50
SocialMedia.biz 365, 386
social media consultants 31
social media news release 299–303
  creating 299
  definition 299
  example 300, 309
  multimedia 301
  sections 301
  social bookmarking and 302
  Technorati tags and 302
  WordPress and 303
social media newsroom 287-299
  building 290–299
  definition 287
  examples 304
  FeedBurner and 297
  gathering content 295
  multimedia and 296
  optimizing 299
  populating 293–299
  preparing items for 293
  purpose-built Delicious pages and 297
  scrollable content boxes 291

social bookmarking and  288
social networking and  295
Technorati and  298
theme  290
widgets and  292, 295
WordPress and  290
social media ROI  367
   qualitative framework  368
   quantitative framework  369
social media strategies  37–50
SocialMediaToday  386
social networking  145–170
   creating your own  188–193
   definition  145
   future of  190
   media communities and  186
   promoting  191
   similar tools  187
   social bookmarking sites and  186
social networking strategies  186
social pages  318
Social RSS  164
social search engines  372
Squidoo  318
   integrating RSS feeds and blogs  336
   integrating social bookmarks  339
   integrating widgets  339
streamlining tools  329
structured data  357, 437
   with microformats  439
StumbleUpon  186, 198, 200, 292
Surchur  372

**T**

tags
   and social bookmarking  194
   definition  25
   Flickr  213
   in blog posts  74
Technorati  78, 90, 198, 200, 292, 380
   social media newsroom and  298
Technorati tags
   social media news release ad  302

social media newsroom and  292
Timothy Berners-Lee  354
tools for measuring ROI  377
trackback  75
Tumblr  188, 318
Tweetmeme  185
Twitpic  176
Twitter  171-184
   @replies  177
   background  174
   external tools  185
   Facebook and  250
   find people  174
   hashtags  179
   integrating  342, 346
   lists  180
   location  177
   new platform  182
   posting images  176
   posting tweets  175
   posting video  176
   promoting  184
   retweeting  176
   setting up  173
   timeline  171
   widgets  250, 274, 278
Twittercounter  185
TwitterFeed  185
Twitter Search  185, 382
Twitter tools  185
   HootSuite  185
   Klout  185
   Tweetmeme  185
   Twittercounter  185
   TwitterFeed  185
   TwitterSearch  185

**U**

Upcoming  311
   badge  312
   integrating with other sites  339
   widget  247
URL shortening  175, 376

**V**

vidcast. *See* podcast
video feed. *See* podcast
video sharing 224–231
    optimizing 224, 231
    strategy 231
Vimeo 176
virtual worlds 321
vlog. *See* podcast

**W**

Wapple 364
WaveMaker 362
Web 2.0 354
Web 3.0 353
    defined 355
Webcast 143
Webcast2000 143
Webcasting.com 143
Website
    optimization plan 334
Westhost 108
Widgetbox 92, 122, 261, 271, 283, 364
    and bootee widget 433
    blidget 259
    mobile sites 364
    mobile Web app 364
    publishing widgets and 432
widget communities 282
widget directories 282
widget integration plan 284
widgets 106, 247–285
    adding to WordPress 278–283
    AddtoAny
        feed widget 264
        sharing widget 267, 280
    Amazon 276
    blidget
        creating 259–264
    Brightkite 314
    creating 282. *See* building a widget
    crowd-sourcing and 267
    definition 23, 248

Delicious 269
Digg 269
Eventbrite 313
feed 92, 259–266
Flickr and 258
FriendFeed 316
Google Ads 277
installation 249
interactive 268
Lijit 270
LinkedIn 253
media communities and 258
placing on Websites 255, 281
searching for 259
security and 284
ShareThis 267
Shelfari 255, 280
social bookmarking and 267
social media news release and 302
social media newsroom and 292, 295
social networking and 250
strategy 284
Twitter 250, 278
WordPress 106, 114, 122, 278
WordPress pages and 280
WordPress posts and 280
WordPress sidebars and 278
WordPress text widgets 278
YouTube and 258
WikiDot 320
Wikipedia 358
wikis 320
WikiSpaces 320
WordPress 97–128
    and podcasts 130, 135
    as a CMS 97
    blog post. *See* blog post
    configuration file 397
    custom menus 120
    dashboard 110
    footer 105
    header 104
    hosting accounts 108
    installing 108. *See also* installing Word-

Press
navigation menu  104
permalinks  111
plugins  113, 118–121, 120, 281, 324
scrollable content boxes  291
security settings  111
sidebars  105, 122
sidebar widgets  105, 221, 278
social media news release and  303
social media newsroom and  290
static home page  112
text widgets  278
themes  99, 114
widgets  278. *See also* widgets
widgets in pages  280
widgets in posts  280
widgets in sidebars  278
WordPress codex  401
WordPress Exploit Scanner  121
WordPress forums  97, 401
WordPress pages  106
building  124–126
template  127
WordPress plugins  118, 120
security  111, 120
SEO  120
spam blocker  120
stats  120
WordPress Stats  120
World Wide Web Consortium (W3C)  405
Feed Validation Service  94
WP-Security Scan  111, 121
WP Email Capture  376
WS_FTP  109

**X**

Xinu  384
XML  55
and RSS feeds  403
declaration  405
defined  403
for creating a widget  422

**Y**

Yahoo!  245, 370
Flickr and  242
image search  242
Yahoo! Media namespace  418
YouTube  224–230
and Twitter  176
as a social network  186
channel  226
channel settings  226
embed video  228
favorites  227
galleries  228
handbook  230
integrating  325, 342
Playlists  227
queues  227
search results  242
uploading to  224
Webcasting and  143
widgets and  258

# About the Author

Deltina Hay is a veteran Web developer, publisher, and a pioneer of social media and Web 2.0, especially as it applies to small business and the publishing industry. She is an avid writer, presenter, educator, and blogger.

Hay's deep working knowledge of social media concepts, as well as how to apply them in the real world, make her writings and presentations some of the most exciting and accessible in the industry today. As the facilitator of Drury University's social media certificate graduate course online, she educates businesses and students on the strategies, technologies, and tools for creating a sustainable and optimized presence in the Social Web.

As a publisher and small business owner, Hay knows firsthand the amount of traffic that social media optimization and marketing can drive to a Website, as well as the millions of potential customers and readers it can reach and influence. Her writings are filled with practical training in social media due to her in-depth knowledge of the tools. She intuitively knows how to apply social media technologies because she can actually develop and adapt those applications for business purposes.

A long-time advocate of open source technologies, Hay has been programming and/or developing for the Web for over 25 years. Her graduate education includes computer science, applied mathematics, numerical analysis, fluid dynamics, nonlinear dynamics, and psychology. Hay joined the International Marketing Standards Board's Global Board of Advisors in 2010.

Though a native Alaskan, Ms. Hay lives in Austin, Texas, with her two cats, Wolfgang and Ludwig. When she is not in a wireless cafe contemplating the future of the Internet, she is hiking in a Texas State Park, contemplating silence.

More information can be found at http://www.deltina.com.